KEYGUIDE TO INFORMATION SOURCES IN
Archaeology

KEYGUIDE TO INFORMATION SOURCES IN

Archaeology

Peter Woodhead

MANSELL PUBLISHING LIMITED
London and New York

First published 1985 by Mansell Publishing Limited
(A subsidiary of The H. W. Wilson Company)
6 All Saints Street, London N1 9RL, England
950 University Avenue, Bronx, New York 10452, U.S.A.

British Library Cataloguing in Publication Data

Woodhead, Peter
  Keyguide to information sources in archaeology.
  —(Keyguide to information series)
  1. Archaeology—Information services
  2. Archaeology—Bibliography
  I. Title II. Series
  930.1'07   CC82

  ISBN 0–7201–1745–3

Library of Congress Cataloging in Publication Data

Woodhead, Peter.
  Keyguide to information sources in archaeology.

  Includes index.
  1. Archaeology—Information services. 2. Archaeology—
Bibliography. 3. Archaeology—Societies, etc.—Directories.
4. Reference books—Archaeology. I. Title.
CC120.W66 1985   016.9301   84–20112
ISBN 0–7201–1745–3

Filmset by Latimer Trend & Company Ltd, Plymouth, England
Printed in Great Britain by Whitstable Litho Ltd., Whitstable, Kent

To my mother and father, with memories of days
at Old Trafford, some rewarding, some frustrating.

Contents

Part III   List of selected organizations

Introduction

Data retrieval poses as great a problem to present-day British archaeology as it does to every branch of academic study. The broad spectrum of subject matter and time-scale covered, coupled with the very indiscipline of a discipline which embraces every shade from the amateur – in the strict sense – to the total professional, have resulted in a crisis of preservation and presentation of knowledge no less severe than that involved in the preservation and presentation of the ancient monuments and artefacts themselves.

The above remarks, part of Professor J. V. S. Megaw's Foreword to the Report of the seminar *Problems of information handling in archaeology* (British Library Research and Development Report No. 5329, 1977) indicate some of the information problems in modern archaeology. More and more archaeological research produces more and more information in the form of literature, which proliferates at an alarming rate. Monographs appear regularly on every conceivable topic; new journals and newsletters spring up to cater for some aspect of archaeology only partially covered previously. Yet it is often difficult to find out what is available. Bibliographical control over archaeological literature is less complete than in most other disciplines, the problem often being financial, as exemplified by the current uncertainty over the future status of *British Archaeological Abstracts* [245].

Contents and arrangement

This *Keyguide* is very much a first source of information. It aims to provide an integrated guide to the documentation, reference aids and key organizational sources of information in archaeology worldwide.

Part I is a narrative account of the major forms of archaeological literature, together with a brief historical introduction to the subject and a discussion of the scope of modern archaeology and its relationship with other subjects, the various bodies in the field, education and careers, and the origins and utilization of archaeological information. Part I discusses relationships between the various reference aids available and covers a high proportion of the works listed in Part II; numbers within square brackets refer the user to the full bibliographical details given in Part II. Part I also discusses some publications not included in Part II; these are works that are too general to be included in Part II or that are mentioned to illustrate particular points. Documentation studies are listed at the end of chapters, and Chapters 1 and 2 include reference sources as well as documentation studies.

Part II is an annotated bibliography of reference sources. The basic arrangement is regional, thereby reflecting one of the main ways in which the subject is studied, and largely follows the arrangement used by the *Anthropological Index to Current Periodicals in the Museum of Mankind Library* [21]. There are numerous important sources of an international or multi-regional nature, as shown by the large General Archaeology section, and the increasingly significant sub-discipline of Archaeological Science needs a section of its own. Main sections are subdivided by form of material, e.g. general bibliographical guides; abstracting, indexing, current awareness services, etc. Almost all the publications listed have been personally inspected. The choice of entries has necessarily been selective, although it is hoped that most major sources have been included. At a regional level I have included sources known to be useful to researchers and recommended by experts in the archaeology of particular parts of the world. The selective approach applies particularly to monograph material; all the monographs included received good reviews at the time of publication, but archaeology is such a fast-moving subject that a more up-to-date account of any given area or aspect of archaeology will almost certainly appear in the near future. More emphasis has been placed on periodicals, which, of course, give more up-to-date information. Some of the periodicals listed under particular regional sections sometimes cover other parts of the world too; they have been allocated to those areas with which they are principally concerned. The languages in which periodical articles appear are given in abbreviated form as part of the bibliographical information supplied; explanations for these are listed on p. xv. For publications other than periodicals, the language in which they appear can be assumed to be that of the title. Translations of titles in 'difficult' languages appear in brackets after the original.

Part III is a list of selected archaeological organizations which can serve as useful contact points for information. This list is explained more fully at the start of Part III.

Acknowledgements

I should like to record my thanks to all those who have helped with the compilation of this work. It is impossible to name all who have provided information so generously but some must be thanked for the particular help given.

Special mention must go to four people who gave particularly detailed assistance and read the manuscript: Heather Bell and her colleagues at the Library of the Institute of Archaeology, University of London; Brian Burch, Librarian, University of Leicester; Cherry Lavell, Council for British Archaeology; and Myra Shackley, Department of Archaeology, University of Leicester, who all devoted a great deal of time to the work and made many valuable suggestions.

The following people helped with the archaeology of particular areas of the world: Warwick Bray, Ian Glover, John Nandris, Peter Parr (all at the Institute of Archaeology, University of London); Ann Dornier, Vincent Megaw, David Parsons, Derek Simpson, John Wacher (all academic colleagues at the University of Leicester); Anna Healey, Librarian of the Institute of Classical Studies, University of London; Jonathan King, Museum of Mankind, London; David Phillipson, University Museum of Archaeology and Anthropology, Cambridge; David Ridgway, University of Edinburgh; Carole Travis, Librarian of the Institute of Latin American Studies, University of London.

Charles d'Orban, School of Oriental and African Studies, University of London, helped with some Chinese titles, and John Hopkins, Librarian of the Society of Antiquaries of London, assisted with various references. Henry Cleere, Director of the Council for British Archaeology, and Geoffrey Lewis, Director of the Department of Museum Studies, University of Leicester, gave much help with Part III and various other references.

I am also grateful to library colleagues at the University of Leicester – especially Pamela Dixon for her valiant and expert typing of a difficult manuscript, Michael Grose, and my long-suffering colleagues in the Reference and Information Department – to Tony Harvey, Head of the Department of Library Services, British Museum (Natural History) for his help and advice, and to the University of Leicester Establishment Board for granting me a term's leave of absence to work on this book. I should also like to thank my wife, Sylvia, for her encouragement, and Vanessa and Jonathan for moving my files so often.

This work has been aided by grants from the University of Leicester Research Board and the Marc Fitch Fund, and I am grateful to both of these bodies for their financial help.

List of abbreviations used for languages

Al	Albanian		It	Italian
Ar	Arabic		Ja	Japanese
Bu	Bulgarian		Ko	Korean
Ch	Chinese		La	Latin
Cz	Czech		Nd	Dutch
Da	Danish		No	Norwegian
De	German		Np	Nepali
En	English		Pl	Polish
Es	Spanish		Pt	Portuguese
Fi	Finnish		Rm	Romanian
Fr	French		Ru	Russian
Gr	Greek		Sl	Slovak
Hu	Hungarian		Sw	Swedish
Ic	Icelandic		Th	Thai
In	Indonesian		Vi	Vietnamese
Ir	Irish		We	Welsh

PART I

Overview of archaeology and its literature

1   The History and Scope of Archaeology

Historical Introduction

The word 'archaeology' derives from the Greek 'archaia' (ancient things) and 'logos' (theory, knowledge or science). There have always, of course, been people interested in 'ancient things' – for example, Greeks such as Herodotus made valuable anthropological and ethnographical observations, as noted by Phillips (1964) but such discoveries that were made were accidental and not made in deliberate search for knowledge of former ages.

From the 15th century onwards, antiquaries studied the visible remains of the past in their own countries. In Britain, for example, William Camden (1551–1623) travelled extensively, in 1586 producing his *Britannia*, the first general guide to the antiquities of Britain. The birth of serious field studies is exemplified by John Aubrey (1626–97) who wrote in detail on Stonehenge and Avebury and in 1662 was one of the founder members of the Royal Society of London. This encouraged interest in the past by holding meetings and publishing accounts of antiquities and from the 1680s onwards, archaeological articles (Hunter, 1971).

As part of the reviving interest in ancient Greece and Rome, travelling noblemen (dilettanti) in 15th- and 16th-century Europe began collecting and studying antiquities such as statues and vessels, an activity more akin to art collecting. However, from the late 18th century onwards, with the excavations of the Roman cities of Pompeii and Herculaneum, archaeology began to take on its modern meaning, namely the study of the material remains of man's past.

The development of archaeology into a scientific study in the 19th century was due to three factors: a geological revolution, an antiquarian revolution and the doctrine of evolution. Charles Lyell (1797–1875), in his work *Principles of geology*

(1830–33) propagated the principle of uniformitarian stratigraphy, which determines the age of fossil remains by the stratum they occupy. The locating of man's early stone tools, first identified as such in the late 18th century, in certain strata, showed that man had lived long before 4004 BC, the date calculated earlier from biblical chronology. Discoveries of artefacts in the Somme Valley, France, by de Perthes, and in Devon, England, by MacEnery, Pengelly and others, demonstrated the great antiquity of man about the same time as the publication of Darwin's *Origin of species* (1859). The idea that man evolved from some animal species at some remote time in the past implied a vast extension in the range of human history.

Earlier, Scandinavian archaeologists, through their work in museums and in excavation, postulated the idea of successive technologies in man's past – the three Ages of Stone, Bronze and Iron – which has been described as the cornerstone of modern archaeology. Christian Thomsen (1788–1865) arranged the material in the National Museum in Copenhagen in 1819 on the basis of the Three-Age system, which was developed further by Thomsen's pupil and successor Jens Worsaae (1821–85). In his *Danmarks Oldtid oplyst ved Oldsager og Gravhoje* (translated into English as *The primeval antiquities of Denmark*) (1843), Worsaae gave for the first time a clear exposition of the principles of excavation, an awareness of the comparative method, and of the need to interest the public in archaeology, contributions which made him the real father of modern archaeology (Daniel, 1967).

The theory of a succession of technological stages was confirmed by excavation of prehistoric Swiss lake dwellings in the 1850s. John Lubbock (1834–1913) divided the Stone Age by introducing the terms Palaeolithic and Neolithic in his *Prehistoric times as illustrated by ancient remains and the manners and customs of modern savages* (1865). Mesolithic was soon added, creating a Five-Age system. Oscar Montelius (1843–1921) later distinguished five or six subdivisions of the Bronze Age and four in the Neolithic.

The middle years of the 19th century saw the birth of archaeology as a science. A significant year was 1866 when the first international congress 'pour les études préhistoriques' met at Neuchâtel. This was the first ever international gathering devoted to archaeology. It soon became the Congrès International d'Anthropologie et d'Archéologie Préhistoriques and met regularly up till the First World War. In 1932, a new congress, the Union Internationale des Sciences Préhistoriques et Protohistoriques (UISPP) was founded and met in London, followed by other sessions later.

Classical archaeology was enhanced in the late 19th century by the work of Heinrich Schliemann (1822–90) at Troy, Mycenae, Tiryns and Orchomenos, of Biliotti at Rhodes, of the German Archaeological Institute at Olympia, and of Conze at Samothrace. Conze's account of the excavation, with photographs, was the first modern report of its kind. The Minoan civilization, ancestor of classical Greece, was discovered by Arthur Evans (1851–1941) in the early 20th century.

Napoleon's invasion of Egypt enabled scholars to record archaeological remains, and in 1822 Jean Champollion (1790–1832) deciphered ancient Egyptian hieroglyphics using the Rosetta stone. Flinders Petrie (1853–1942) made great discoveries in Egypt and in Palestine, developing a systematic method of excavation which he described himself in *Methods and aims in archaeology* (1904). The most spectacular discovery in Egyptian archaeology, the tomb of Tutankhamun, was made in 1922 by Howard Carter (1873–1939) and Lord Carnarvon (1866–1923).

In Mesopotamia, Botta at Nineveh and Khorsabad and Layard at Nimrud and other sites carried out important excavations, with Layard's book *Nineveh and its remains* (1849) becoming the earliest archaeological best-seller. In 1846, Henry Rawlinson (1810–95) deciphered the Mesopotamian cuneiform writing. A previously unknown people, the Sumerians, were revealed, and Leonard Woolley (1880–1960) excavated the Royal Tombs at Ur in 1926. Many other excavations, particularly in Iran, Anatolia, Palestine and Syria, have provided a very detailed picture of the great early urban civilizations of the Near East.

In the late 19th century, Upper Palaeolithic sculpture and cave paintings were discovered by de Sautuola, Breuil and others at Altamira and various other sites in France and Spain. Other finds were made in the 20th century, the most famous being at Lascaux, France, in 1940.

The foundations of modern scientific archaeological field technique including photography were laid by Pitt-Rivers (1827–1900) with his excavations of prehistoric and Roman sites at Cranborne Chase, Dorset, England. These methods were developed and improved by Mortimer Wheeler (1890–1976) and later described by him in *Archaeology from the earth* (1954).

Twentieth-century archaeology has expanded beyond the Near East, Mediterranean and Europe to other parts of the world. In the 1920s, the prehistoric Indus civilization was revealed through excavations at Mohenjodaro and Harappā (in present-day Pakistan). Palaeolithic and Neolithic cultures were discovered in China. Louis Leakey (1903–72) in his excavations at Olduvai Gorge in Tanzania found human skeletal remains and stone tools over two million years old. The rediscovery of the ancient American civilizations began about 1840 with Stephens's visit to abandoned Mayan cities and continued with Maudslay's excavations (1881–94).

North American archaeology developed simultaneously with much closer links with anthropology and ethnology than in the Old World; the lifestyle of many of the present Indians was, until recently, very similar to that of their prehistoric ancestors. Here, and in the Americas as a whole, archaeology has always been regarded as a sub-discipline of anthropology.

The Five-Age system was the basis of the framework of prehistory in the later 19th and early 20th centuries, and these Ages began to be divided into smaller compartments. They were, however, gradually being given different connotations, such as cultural, chronological, racial, diffusionist, functional, economic, instead of being the simple technological stages propounded by Thomsen and Worsaae. Another problem was that excavation in different parts of the world led to a need for different successions of ages and, disturbingly, it was discovered that some of the epochs into which prehistoric time had been divided were in fact contemporary with each other; they were really different patterns of material culture.

The idea of 'a culture' in prehistory derived from anthropology which developed as a science alongside archaeology in the 19th century. Gordon Childe (1892–1957), a great experimenter with ideas, wrote his *Prehistoric communities of the British Isles* (1940) using not the divisions of the Five-Age system but an arrangement of periods defined by the cultural sequence. What archaeology so clearly needed was an absolute chronology which could be used to speak in terms of years. So far, it had relied for dating on cross-dating, i.e. dating a site by means of datable objects from another culture found at it, and relative dating, i.e. relating the date of objects found to the date of other things found in the immediate neighbourhood. Man-made chronology goes back only to about 3000 BC in Egypt and the Near East. The first geochronological techniques to be developed were clay-varve counting (counting the thin layers of clay left behind by the melting glaciers) and dendrochronology (dating by tree ring counts). The greatest revolution in dating and one of the most important events in archaeology occurred in 1947 with the discovery by Willard Libby of the existence of radioactive carbon (carbon 14) in organic matter and the realization that this radioactive isotope, decaying at a fixed rate, could be used to date archaeological material. Many other techniques of absolute dating have been developed since, well described by Fleming [195]. The extent to which these new dating techniques have revolutionized archaeology was explained by Renfrew (1973 (1)), who showed how the previously accepted dating framework (as given by, for example, Burkitt and Childe (1932)) had been completely disrupted.

The modern archaeologist has at his disposal various sophisticated techniques to trace remains without actually excavating. Deep probes using various electromagnetic devices have been developed. Lerici invented the periscope method of investigating underground chambers. Cousteau's invention of the aqualung in 1943 made possible underwater archaeology. Aerial photography began early in the 20th century and expanded rapidly after the First World War when the results of air reconnaissance could be shared. Since then, it has resulted in the discovery of thousands of new sites that could not be seen on the ground.

Histories of archaeology

There are several works covering the history and development of archaeology worldwide. G. Daniel's *A short history of archaeology* (London: Thames and Hudson, 1981. 232 pp.) – the one hundredth volume in the series *Ancient Peoples and Places* – summarizes the main developments and themes. The same author's *A hundred and fifty years of archaeology*,(2nd ed. London: Duckworth, 1975. 410 pp.), a more detailed work, includes a chronological table of main events in the history of archaeology 1820–1970, and a long, comprehensive bibliography on the subject, covering also biographies and autobiographies of archaeologists, geologists and anthropologists. The same author's *The origins and growth of archaeology* (Harmondsworth: Penguin, 1967. 302 pp.) is an anthology of key writings of archaeologists with a bibliography listing further anthologies; these include R. F. Heizer (ed.) *Man's discovery of his past: a sourcebook of original articles* (Tunbridge Wells (England): Costello Educational, 1980. 301 pp.), which acts both as a reader for the general public and as a sourcebook for the specialist, and J. Hawkes's *The world of the past* (New York: Knopf, 1963. 2 vols.), a large reference work of extracts, with a long introductory essay providing an excellent summary.

Many histories of the archaeology of particular areas of the world are listed in the bibliography of Daniel's *A hundred and fifty years of archaeology*, mentioned above. Examples are (for German archaeology) H. J. Egger's *Einführung in die Vorgeschichte* (Munich: Piper, 1959. 317 pp.) and (for American archaeology) G. R. Willey and J. A. Sabloff's *A history of American archaeology* (2nd ed. San Francisco: Freeman, 1980. 326 pp.). The volume *Towards a history of archaeology* (papers read at the first Conference on the History of Archaeology, Aarhus, 1978), edited by G. Daniel (London: Thames and Hudson, 1981. 192 pp.) covers a number of areas, as does K. Sklenár's *Archaeology in Central Europe: the first 500 years* (Leicester: Leicester University Press, 1983. 190 pp.). I. Bernal's *A history of Mexican archaeology: the vanished civilizations of Middle America* (London: Thames and Hudson, 1980. 208 pp. (The World of Archaeology)) relates the development of Mexican archaeology to the political, social and ideological struggles within that country, emphasizing the fact that there are some very important differences in the way the subject has developed in various parts of the world. L. Deuel's *Flights into yesterday: the story of aerial archaeology* (London: Macdonald and Co., 1971. 320 pp.) well describes the development of air photography.

Briefer accounts of the history of archaeology can be found in some textbooks, e.g. Sharer and Ashmore [85] and in some archaeological atlases, e.g. Branigan [127]. New publications on the subject can be traced through appropriate bibliographies, abstracts and indexes (see Chapters 4 and 5).

Modern Archaeology

Modern archaeology can be defined as the systematic and scientific collection, preservation and study of the material remains of man's past without restriction of time or place. Alcock (1975) has noted that the absence of a temporal restriction asserts positively that the past began yesterday and consequently that archaeology is not concerned solely with the prehistoric past – the period before written records first appeared. This, of course, occurred in different parts of the world at different times, but the term 'prehistory' is sometimes used (especially by the French) as if it applied simultaneously throughout the world, prehistory ending with the first Mesopotamian clay tablets about five thousand years ago.

Prehistoric archaeology is the main source of information for over ninety-nine per cent of the human past, going back to the first hominids in East Africa, now dated to over two and a half million years ago; other sources include physical anthropology and deductions from language. Historic archaeology deals with the material remains of societies that are documented through written records. In the early part of this period, known as protohistory, the material remains are at least as important as the written sources. In the later periods of man's development, as written sources become more plentiful and important, the archaeologist works alongside the historian.

In spite of the increasing interest in the subject, there is still some confusion in the public mind over exactly what archaeology is and what an archaeologist does. Evans (1975) attributes this state of affairs partly to the relatively recent growth and rather patchy development of the subject and partly to the fact that certain aspects of archaeology, often the more sensational discoveries, have always been considered newsworthy and so have attracted an unfair share of attention.

To the general public, excavation may seem the main and certainly the most exciting aspect of archaeology. This, however, represents only part of the archaeologist's work. An essential preliminary to excavation is fieldwork – the discovery and recording of archaeological sites by methods other than the use of the spade and the trowel. Sites may be discovered by field walking, by aerial photography, by a study of old records or place-names, or by examining the distribution of artefacts. Once discovered, sites must be recorded on maps, and skilful techniques have been developed both for marking sites on ordinary topographical maps and for producing special period and artefact distribution maps.

Excavation can be regarded as the surgical aspect of archaeology. Most important excavations are planned in the sense that their aim is to find evidence about a particular site or group of sites. Some are done from necessity: in heavily populated parts of the world emergency excavations are carried out to rescue information from known sites threatened by construction projects before remains are obliterated for ever. Partial destruction of cities by bombing in World War II allowed rescue excavation to take place before rebuilding (a temple of Mithras – and much else – in London and a 6th-century BC Greek settlement at Marseilles were discovered in this way). Discoveries are sometimes made by chance and can lead to major excavations: farmers unearth remains while ploughing; the painted cave at Lascaux was discovered by schoolboys retrieving their dog; the first of the Dead Sea scrolls was found in 1947 by a Bedouin searching for a stray animal.

The many types of archaeological sites make it impossible to apply a single set of rules to excavation as a whole. Some sites, such as ancient cities, palaces, forts, temples, roads, industrial remains, are frequently visible on the ground: examples are the great man-made mounds (tells) of the Near East, such as those at Troy and Ur, created by the accumulation of the remains from centuries of human habitation. Another type consists of closed sites: barrows (burial mounds), pyramids, chambered tombs and sealed caves. Other sites, with no traces visible on the surface, can be revealed only by aerial or electromagnetic methods.

Another type is cliffs and gravel beds, where many Palaeolithic finds have been made.

In the excavation itself, the context in which evidence is found is most important. An artefact is much more valuable when its associations and stratigraphical position are recorded. Since the stratigraphical evidence is actually destroyed as excavation proceeds, it survives only in so far as it was correctly observed and recorded during the excavation. It follows from this that all the evidence must be published and this aspect is discussed in Chapter 2. Sometimes evidence is lost through the destructive activities of 'treasure hunters', often using metal detectors; this problem is well discussed by Baker [247]. It cannot be emphasized too strongly that people who remove objects from their archaeological context in this way are enriching themselves at the expense of human knowledge and heritage.

Some archaeologists do not excavate at all: they concentrate on interpreting the facts established by excavation or by study of museum objects. This leads to the other part of the archaeologist's work: placing knowledge gained in a total environmental, historical and cultural context. He must describe, classify and analyse his artefacts, if necessary relying on colleagues specializing in sciences such as geology, petrology and metallurgy. For information on environmental conditions he may need to turn to colleagues in zoology and botany. If his material is not self-dating or cannot be dated through written records, he has to find some means of dating it on the lines discussed earlier.

Finally, he makes a historical judgement on the remains he has studied. Dymond (1967) has stressed two very important characteristics of archaeological evidence: first, it is at its safest and strongest when used to reconstruct the technological side of human life, but in details of social and political organization it can give only indirect help; secondly, the archaeological record of any site cannot represent the full material equipment of the original inhabitants since the perishable materials like wood, hides and basketry do not usually survive.

In spite of these difficulties, many modern scholars concentrate on social archaeology, that is, the reconstruction of past social systems and relations (Renfrew, 1973(2)). The ethnoarchaeologist, for example, compares the patterns recognized in the material culture from archaeological contexts with patterns established through the study of living societies (for example, Hodder [77]). Renfrew (1982) has argued that it is possible to go further and establish cognitive archaeology: the archaeology of peoples' modes of thought and belief structures.

An excellent summary of the development of modern archaeology in its various aspects appears in Part 1 of the *Cambridge encyclopedia of archaeology* [143]. This discussed its origins and growth; the revolution in archaeological thinking in the late 1960s and 1970s involving studies of processes in economic and social change; advances in field archaeology; the application of new analytical techniques such as systems theory; economic archaeology involving, for example, the relationships between early populations and their resources, historical archaeology involving documentary evidence; recent advances and current trends – for example, in dating, in trace element analysis, and in sampling procedures in field archaeology. Covering similar ground, but at a more introductory level, Greene's *Archaeology: an introduction* [73] discussed the history, principles and methods of modern archaeology.

Some of the main trends of modern research in archaeology and prehistory were identified and discussed by De Laet (1978). The section on archaeology made brief observations on, for example, archaeological reconnaissance, excavation, description and classification of material, dating, and problems of conservation and restoration. The prehistory section included notes on prehistory and its subdivisions, classification of the sources of prehistoric archaeology, problems of interpretation in prehistoric archaeology, ideological currents and schools in prehistoric archaeology, along with some additional observations on the interdisciplinary aspects of research in archaeology and prehistory.

Relationship with Other Subjects

It will be clear from what has been said already that archaeology's closest links are with history. Dymond (1974) noted that archaeologists are in reality historians using special methods and sources including documentary sources, but the influence of other subjects too is apparent (see Fig. 1). Classical archaeology can be regarded as a branch of classics. Prehistoric archaeology was much helped by the development of anthropology. The relationship between archaeology and art history is discussed by Daniel (1970). Geology provided a rough chronology for early human development in the glacial and post-glacial periods. Palaeozoology revealed the animals hunted by man; animals changed from cold-loving to tropical species and back again, thereby implying climatic changes proved also by palaeobotany which threw light on the kinds of plants eaten by man and the extent of his forest environment.

From an early stage, archaeology was aided by various scientific disciplines and this trend has accelerated in recent years with the development of archaeological science. One aspect of this is environmental archaeology, emphasizing that the study of man cannot be divorced from the study of his environment (Shackley [196]). Physics and chemistry have provided a whole range of techniques to help the archaeologist analyse the age of material, its place of origin and methods of manufacture – techniques well summarized in the introductory chapter of Brothwell and Higgs [194]. Various statistical techniques have been borrowed from mathematics and geography, as Hodder and Orton [78] show. The point is perhaps best illustrated by the several archaeological science journals such as *Journal of Archaeological Science* [201] and *Science and Archaeology* [209] that have appeared in recent years.

This multi-disciplinary character was well illustrated by a survey carried out by the Centre for Research on User Studies, University of Sheffield (Corkill, 1981) on the information needs and behaviour of a small group of eleven

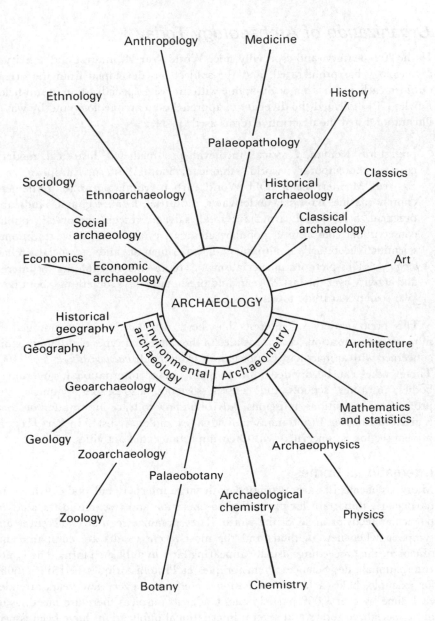

Figure 1. Relationship of archaeology with other major subjects and sub-disciplines.

humanities postgraduate research students, including three studying prehistory and archaeology, who began research at that university in 1976. Overlap with other disciplines in the range of material required was most marked for the prehistory and archaeology students.

Organization of Archaeology Today

In the 20th century, and especially since World War II, interest and activity in archaeology has proliferated, and the subject has developed from the origins outlined earlier into a major discipline with intensive specialization in sub-fields. Fowler [70] indicated the diversity of approaches to archaeology and by way of illustration listed the descriptive terms used (p. 14):

> prehistoric, Roman, Classical, medieval, post-medieval, historical, modern, current, contemporary; world, American, South Western, European, Near Eastern, Mediterranean, Old World; urban, rural, agrarian, settlement, church, marine, nautical, underwater, industrial; local, regional, landscape, practical, field, aerial; armchair; total; salvage, rescue, motorway, public, conservation, community, popular; amateur, professional; new, traditional, scientific, theoretical, environmental, experimental; and ... social archaeology ... This plethora of specialisms ... represents an explosion of interest and activity over the last 25 years and presumably says something about post-War society's attitude towards its past.

This great variety of interests has been developed and encouraged by numerous organizations, and some idea of the range and types of different bodies concerned with archaeology can be gained from the *Archaeologists' year book* [160]. These bodies can be divided into six main classes: international; government bodies; institutes, schools and centres; societies, associations, councils, etc.; professional institutions; museums. Advice on how to trace information on them is given in Chapter 3 (and many individual examples are listed in Part III); the present section is concerned with their importance and activities.

International bodies

Many archaeologists are associated with large international bodies which are particularly important for promoting co-operation and research in the study of particular fields or areas of the world. They organize regular conferences and symposia when new methods and the most recent results are compared and discussed, the proceedings usually appearing later in published form. The Union Internationale des Sciences Préhistoriques et Protohistoriques (UISPP) [608], for example, holds a large international conference every few years attended each time by over 1,000 participants. Under its auspices there are meetings on more specialized topics and several international publications have been issued. It has affiliated to it several international organizations more limited either in geographical coverage or in aims: for example, the Pan African Congress on Prehistory and Quaternary Studies, the Far Eastern Prehistoric Association, the International Quaternary Association (INQUA), and the International Union of Slavic Archaeology. UISPP is a member of the International Council for Philosophy and Humanistic Studies which has affiliated to it other bodies with archaeological interests such as the International Federation of the Societies of Classical Studies and the International Union of Anthropological and Ethnological Sciences (IUAES) [603].

UNESCO has long shown a concern for cultural heritage and has over the years made various recommendations concerning the world's heritage in general and excavation in particular. These culminated in the *Convention concerning the Protection of the World Cultural and Natural Heritage* (commonly known as the *World Heritage Convention*), adopted by the UNESCO General Conference in 1972 and brought into force in 1975. By October 1982, sixty-seven states had ratified the Convention, which, along with UNESCO's other work in promoting international co-operation in the preservation and presentation of the world's cultural heritage, is described in the information bulletin *World Cultural Heritage* (Paris: UNESCO, 1973–. Irreg.).

Government bodies

Many countries, realizing the threat to their heritage, have passed legislation establishing governmental bodies to control various aspects of their national antiquities. Often known as the National Board of Antiquities (or similar wording) and sometimes under the country's Ministry of Education, the role of such a body usually includes some or all of the following: co-ordination of all archaeological activity in the country; preservation and protection of the country's heritage, including archaeological sites; control of all excavation carried out in the country; control of the movement and export of archaeological objects; research work, including excavation; dissemination of the results of research; maintenance of the country's national museum and any other museum under its supervision; educational work. Examples include Belize [621], Brazil [627], Finland [652], India [670], Ireland [674], Malawi [693], Sweden [736], Syria [738], and Zambia [758].

Institutes, schools, centres

Since archaeological studies of a particular area frequently involve knowledge of culture, language, art form, etc., many of the numerous worldwide archaeological institutes, schools and centres study other subjects besides archaeology. Not surprisingly, they figure prominently in places of special archaeological interest: for example, in Athens, there are schools of archaeology run by six foreign nations. Schools of archaeology overseas are a particular feature, and a valuable national asset in the countries where they operate. Britain, for example, currently has ten research institutes overseas with archaeological research one of their prime functions; these are sponsored by the British Academy, whose *Handbook* (British Academy, 1977) gives details, as does the periodical *Archaeology Abroad* [104].

Societies, associations, councils

Many parts of the world have long had national archaeological societies and associations, and also numerous local ones, usefully supplementing work done at national level. Increasing interest in archaeology has produced societies covering every aspect of the subject: for example, the Council for Nautical Archaeology, the Society for Post-Medieval Archaeology. Typical objectives are to promote and conduct research in a particular area (national or local) or aspect of archaeology, and disseminate information through meetings and conferences and through publications, some of these being leading journals in their fields. In Britain, local archaeological bodies formed the framework of archaeological activity from the 1840s onwards (Piggott, 1974). An organization unique to Britain is the Council for British Archaeology [748], a representative Council of all the bodies concerned with British archaeology (such as societies, museums and universities), which represents and co-ordinates British archaeological opinion.

Professional institutions

Our archaeological heritage is an irreplaceable resource which should be made available to everyone. Archaeologists both corporately and individually have a responsibility to help conserve it, to use it economically in their work, to conduct their studies in such a way that reliable information may be acquired, and to disseminate the results of their studies. It was with these points in mind that two professional institutions have been established. In Britain, the Institute of Field Archaeologists (c/o The Museum of London, London Wall, London EC2Y 5HN) exists to advance the practice of field archaeology and allied disciplines, to define and maintain proper standards and ethics in training and education in field archaeology, in the execution and supervision of work, and in the conservation of the archaeological heritage; and to disseminate information about field archaeologists and their areas of interest. In the USA, the Society of Professional Archaeologists (Secretary, Federal Building, Room 474, 100 Centennial Mall North, Lincoln, Nebraska 68508) has similar aims.

Museums

The primary record of an excavation is composed of the material remains extracted from the soil and the site archive (i.e. the site records, such as photographs, computer listings, diaries, etc., and documents deriving from the preliminary sorting, such as card indexes, context sheets listing and quantifying cultural or environmental data, etc.). The primary record must be preserved, and detailed recommendations have been made (Longworth, 1982) on museums' role in curating material remains.

The archaeological importance of museums – and in particular, national museums – frequently extends beyond the curating role. In many countries, a museum (often the national one) has been given some or all of the following responsibilities: control of the national archaeological collections; provision of information services on the national collections; dissemination of information, including publication, about the national collections and the national heritage in general; examination of sites and monuments; research work, including excavation; issuing of excavation permits. Examples include Botswana [626], Canada [633], Madagascar [692], Malaysia [694], Papua New Guinea [715], Philippines [718], and Tanzania [740].

Education and careers

The development of archaeology as an academic discipline was marked by events such as the election of Champollion to the first European chair of Egyptology at the Collège de France in 1831 and the establishment of a professorship of classical archaeology at Oxford University in the 1880s. In the United States, the Smithsonian Institution was founded in 1846 and the Peabody Museum of Archaeology and Ethnology at Harvard University in 1866; the latter was one of the first United States institutions to employ full-time archaeologists. Formal archaeological education and training is now well developed worldwide; the list in the *Archaeologists' year book* [160] of universities, colleges and institutes with departments of archaeology, anthropology or related subjects comprised 345 entries. There are shifts of emphasis: for example, in the United States, archaeology is usually taught as part of anthropology, while in the Soviet Union it is the science of human social development viewed in terms of Marxist theory.

Details of education in British archaeology are given in the Council for British Archaeology's *Archaeological resources handbook for teachers* [246] which gives guidelines for the teaching of archaeology in schools, information on resources available, details of examinations at various levels (CSE, A/O level, A level), and post-school education and training including the CBA Diploma in Archaeological Practice. The CBA has also published (Council for British Archaeology, 1982) a series of booklets specially prepared for teachers by its Schools Committee. At university level, Roe and May's handbook (Roe and May, 1983) brings together all the information needed by those who wish to study archaeology at university. Evans (1975) discussed archaeology as a subject in education, the way it is taught and the training of professional archaeologists in Britain. More recently, Baker [247] briefly considered education and training at all levels in aspects of the British historic environment.

The CBA's *Archaeological resources handbook for teachers* [246] also includes a section on careers in archaeology, which in Britain can be found mainly in Trusts and Research Units, Local Authorities, Museums, and Government Departments. The section has been published separately (Council for British Archaeology, 1981) and expanded to include brief descriptions of specific working environments – for example, in the field, in an urban unit, the work of a County

Archaeological Officer, working as an Inspector of Ancient Monuments, and archaeological conservation. For careers in museums, the Museums Association (1977) has produced an information sheet; much more information is given by Wenborn (1983). For North America, Rowe (1979) explained the requirements and rewards of a career in archaeology.

References

Alcock, L. 1975. The discipline of archaeology. Reprinted from *College Courant, Journal of Glasgow University Graduates Association.* 7 pp.

British Academy. 1977. *A handbook to the British schools and institutes abroad.* London: British Academy. 46 pp.

Burkitt, M. and Childe, V. G. 1932. A chronological table of prehistory. *Antiquity*, 6:22, 185–205.

Corkill, C., Mann, M. and Stone, S. 1981. *Doctoral students in humanities: a small-scale panel study of information needs and users 1976–79.* Sheffield: University of Sheffield, Centre for Research on User Studies. (CRUS Occasional Paper, 5.) (BLR and DD Report, 5637.) 70 pp.

Council for British Archaeology. 1981. *A job in archaeology: information for young people, teachers and careers advisers.* London: Council for British Archaeology. 8 pp.

Council for British Archaeology. 1982. *Archaeology for schools (series of booklets).* London: Council for British Archaeology.

Daniel, G. 1967. *The origins and growth of archaeology.* Harmondsworth (England): Penguin. 302 pp.

Daniel, G. 1970. *Archaeology and the history of art.* Hull (England): University of Hull. (Inaugural lecture.) 19 pp.

De Laet, S. J. 1978. Archaeology and prehistory. In J. Havet (ed.), *Main trends of research in the social and human sciences. Part 2, vol. 1: Anthropological and historical sciences; aesthetics and the sciences of art*, pp. 177–226. Paris: UNESCO.

Dymond, D. P. 1967. *Archaeology for the historian.* London: Historical Association. (Helps for Students of History, 7.) 28 pp.

Dymond, D. P. 1974. *Archaeology and history: a plea for reconciliation.* London: Thames and Hudson. 192 pp.

Evans, J. D. 1975. *Archaeology as education and profession.* London: University of London, Institute of Archaeology. (Inaugural lecture.) 12 pp.

Hunter, M. C. W. 1971. The Royal Society and the origins of British archaeology. *Antiquity*, 65; Part I: no. 178, 113–21; Part II: no. 179, 187–92.

Longworth, I. H. and others. 1982. *Selection and retention of environmental and artefactual material from excavations: a Report by a Working Party of the British Museum.* London: British Museum. 15 pp.

Museums Association. 1977. *Careers in museums.* 5th ed. London: Museums Association. (Museums Association Information Sheet.)

Phillips, E. D. 1964. The Greek vision of prehistory. *Antiquity*, 38: 151, 171–8.

Piggott, S. 1974. The origins of the English county societies. *Transactions of the Birmingham and Warwickshire Archaeological Society*, 86, 1–15.

Renfrew, C. 1973(1). *Before civilization: the radiocarbon revolution and prehistoric Europe*. London: Cape. 292 pp.

Renfrew, C. 1973(2). *Social archaeology*. Southampton: University of Southampton. (Inaugural lecture.) 20 pp.

Renfrew, C. 1982. *Towards an archaeology of mind*. Cambridge (England): Cambridge University Press. (Inaugural lecture.) 34 pp.

Roe, F. and May, J. 1983. *Guide to undergraduate university courses in archaeology*. 2nd ed. London: Council for British Archaeology. 58 pp.

Rowe, J. H. 1979. *Archaeology as a career*. Rev. ed. New York: Archaeological Institute of America.

Wenborn, N. 1983. *Careers in museums and art galleries*. London: Kogan Page. 93 pp.

2 Archaeological Information: Its Origins and Utilization

Channels of Communication

Archaeological information is transmitted by means of very diverse channels which vary throughout the world in their relative importance. Lavell (1981) described in detail communication channels in British archaeology, while Zubrow (1981) commented on shifts in American patterns of archaeological publishing. Peters (1981) discussed the development of various forms of archaeological publications, using mainly British examples.

One of the most important channels for communicating research in archaeology, as in most other fields, is the journal or periodical. (Throughout this book these terms are used interchangeably to indicate a publication issued at regular or irregular intervals, each issue normally numbered consecutively, with no pre-arranged termination date.) They include such publications as, for example, the memoirs, bulletins, proceedings, transactions, etc. of societies. Since the *Philosophical Transactions of the Royal Society of London* began publishing archaeological articles in the 1680s (Hunter, 1971), the journal has been a well-established medium for reporting, for example, important discoveries, excavation at a particular site (which will probably have been recorded originally in notebook form), a reinterpretation or a new technique. An informal version of the journal, the newsletter, is sometimes used to give, for example, progress reports on excavations – reports which may be published later in journals or monographs in a more permanent and scholarly form. A high proportion of these journals and newsletters are published by national and local archaeological societies throughout the world. This is particularly true of Britain, which has always had a strong tradition of journal publication by local societies (Piggott, 1974), some of which are now having financial problems with their journals (Lavell, 1981).

Research is also submitted for a degree in the form of a thesis, or published as a conference paper. The results of these methods of communication – journal, thesis, conference paper – are normally vetted by experts in the field before acceptance, with the result that there is some control over standards.

The monograph has always played an important role, especially in reporting the results from excavations and in surveying the archaeological record of a particular area. In Britain, the real start of the monograph tradition is represented by Pitt Rivers's four great volumes on his Cranborne Chase excavations (1887–98), with their extremely detailed descriptions and beautiful illustrations (Lavell, 1981). With rising production costs, it is no longer possible to afford such standards of elegance and full publication.

Problems of expense and speed have encouraged the rise of the typewriter-set, offset-litho printed volume with paper covers, the leading British example being the *British Archaeological Reports* series [43]. In Britain, other monographs are published by, in the main, societies, museums, HMSO, the Council for British Archaeology, university presses and departments, and a few commercial publishers. On the European Continent, many more commercial and government publishers produce scholarly monographs. In the United States, monographs of national importance are being published by fewer publishers, resulting in a centralization of archaeological publishing for significant major works. On the other hand, many more local publishers of site reports and primary data have appeared, producing a vast diversity of archaeological information from universities, museums, government agencies, contracting corporations and from subdivisions of each of these organizations (Zubrow, 1981). Yet, a grave problem in modern US archaeology is that much work done under CRM (Cultural Resource Management) is not published at all: since developers on some sites have to pay for 'mitigation', i.e. archaeological rescue work performed under contract in advance of development (see the periodical *American Archeology* [440]), they also pay for the subsequent reports and sometimes do not see the need to publish them properly (Renfrew, 1983).

Some monographs take the form of textbook material, in which case they are usually syntheses of material previously published. A similar kind of process takes place to produce various kinds of reference works such as indexes and abstracts, dictionaries and encyclopaedias, etc. (see later chapters).

A most important non-publication channel of communication between archaeologists themselves is the 'invisible college'. This is the process (operating in all disciplines) whereby researchers in a particular field of archaeology become aware over a period of time through, for example, meetings and informal newsletters, who their fellow workers are and who are the acknowledged experts in the field. This system of direct communication between relatively small groups of people may speed up the transfer of information but can also lead to lack of awareness of the existence and relevance of important bibliographical tools. It may involve sending round so-called 'preprints' – preliminary, tentative reports, later modified in the light of comment and criticism – which by their very nature cannot be subject to any form of bibliographical control.

Archaeologists have a duty to communicate their results to the public who are their paymasters, as well as to themselves. Wheeler was one of the first to see the value of explaining to the general public what the archaeologist was trying to do (Wheeler, 1954), and others follow this kind of approach today. Various non-commercial publishers make archaeological information available to the general public: in Britain, this is done by HMSO for the Department of Environment (e.g. guides to archaeological sites), by archaeological trusts and units, by the Council for British Archaeology, by museums and by local authorities (Lavell, 1981). Archaeological communication must start in schools, but for libraries in British schools at least, enough funds have not been made available to replace the many old, hopelessly outdated books which give a misleading and inaccurate picture of modern archaeology.

Television and radio, when used well, can be powerful media for communicating to the general public. The main problem is that archaeology, like many scientific subjects, cannot be treated properly at a simplistic level: too many British television programmes have stressed the 'buried treasure' aspect, although recent years have seen a great improvement. Even that immensely popular programme 'Animal, Vegetable, Mineral?' in the 1950s was best noted for the witty remarks of the archaeologists concerned. Radio, at least in Britain, has a good record, and the reporting of archaeology by the national press is now much improved.

Archaeological Data

The vast amount of archaeological research now undertaken worldwide results in the production of a huge quantity of data, particularly since in modern excavations *all* material tends to be retained. The full product of a dig from start to finish – everything from letters about ownership of finds, the artefacts, scientific samples, the plans and sections, to the complete documentary side – can be regarded as the excavation archive. Aims and objectives for such an archive have been discussed by Rhodes (1980). All or part of this archive may be deposited in a museum (documentation practices in museums worldwide have been surveyed in detail by Roberts and Light (1980)), or elsewhere. To prevent this material being forgotten or even lost, some countries are establishing a central index or databank of all excavation reports and records. The English National Monuments Record, for example, has records relating to about a quarter of a million archaeological sites, has over half a million air photographs of archaeological sites, and is building up a collection of copies of excavators' site records (Lavell, 1981).

Some governments strongly support the creation of national databanks. Many important European programmes of this kind are described by Verhaeghe [239]:

for example, the planned computerization of the inventory of monuments and art objects in France (programme MISTRAL). Verhaeghe [239] concluded that the major problems with databanks were the financial side and the difficulty of agreement amongst archaeologists on the necessary thesaurus. The incompatibility of different computer systems is a further difficulty. Databanks are being developed also at regional level – Britain has its County Sites and Monuments Records (Lavell, 1981) – and special subject level: for example, the British Museum Research Laboratory's databank on radiocarbon dates.

Other databanks relevant to archaeology are being developed at international level and may be part of a documentation centre. A specialized databank on the protection of the heritage (ICOMMOS) has been created at the UNESCO–ICOMOS Documentation Centre [601]. The latter, along with the ICCROM Documentation Centre [598], is of obvious archaeological importance, while the ICOM one [600] can supply information on archaeological museums or collections. The descriptors (subject headings) used at all three centres are currently being used to compile a thesaurus, an organized list of subject headings, covering all aspects of the protection of the cultural heritage.

Computers are being increasingly used in archaeology, and the way in which they are used is changing. Whereas in 1970 the work was largely statistical, now in the 1980s about ninety per cent of computer usage is for data storage and retrieval. They are being used in basically two ways: for various kinds of databanks, as mentioned above, and for research purposes, such as statistical analyses of archaeological assemblages or types of artefacts. Computer analysis has greatly enriched many excavations. Gaines [72] discussed successful applications of computers for managing archaeological data in North America, Britain and France as well as general considerations for archaeologists contemplating the computerization of almost any type of data. Gaines and Gaines (1980) summarized technical trends and examined future trends in data base processing. This is obviously a rapidly changing field and current information must be obtained from current issues of periodicals included in the 'Archaeological science' section of Part II. Some archaeological references can be found in the abstracting publication (see Chapter 4) *Computer and control abstracts* (London: Institution of Electrical Engineers, 1966–. Monthly).

For details of current research in information work in archaeology, *Current Research in Library and Information Science* [165] became international in scope from 1983. Prior to this, coverage was limited to the United Kingdom and included such projects as the work done at the Research Centre for Computer Archaeology, North Staffordshire Polytechnic, a body concerned with the promotion of computer applications in archaeology, and the KRAS (Keyword References on Archaeological Science) project for establishing a keyword-accessed index for the literature of archaeological science at the University of Leicester.

Writing and Publication

An important archaeological maxim is that excavation reports must be well written and carefully laid out. Good practical advice on the presentation of reports is given in Grinsell, Rahtz and Williams [74] – generally regarded as the most helpful guide of its kind – which cites examples of good excavation reports. Maney [82] gives advice on the preparation of archaeological illustration for reproduction. At the editorial stage, the CBA's booklet *Signposts for archaeological publication* [67] contains invaluable guidelines on the production and dissemination of archaeological material, paying particular attention to the problem of high publication costs. Although aimed principally at editors, it is helpful for anyone involved in writing or publishing in archaeology.

Until recently, it had generally been considered that excavators had a duty to publish their findings in full, possibly exhaustive, detail. In Britain, this principle derived from the work of Pitt-Rivers (1887–98) mentioned earlier. It has for some time, however, been too expensive to continue the 'Cranborne Chase' tradition – exhaustive publication by conventional letterpress.

Lavell (1981) discussed the problems resulting from this dilemma as they affected British archaeology. A government-sponsored Working Party (Frere, 1975) provided a new framework for publication of excavation results, recognizing that it was no longer possible to publish the full data from an excavation (Level III) and recommending instead that the information be published at one further remove (Level IV). The excavator would write his full report at Level III, deposit it in a suitable archive where microform or xerox copies would be available on request to interested parties, and then prepare a shortened version for conventional publication at Level IV.

Alcock (1977–78) argued that the purpose of publication was primarily to convey information (rather than to enable the reader to reconstruct the site on paper or to re-interpret it from the published evidence or to judge the quality of the excavation) and that the needs of the reader should be paramount. He advocated a comprehensive primary report, to be deposited in an archive, probably in microform, and made available on payment, and an illustrated summary account to be published in the conventional way, in book or journal form. Most readers will be satisfied with the summary account; only a few specialists will have the time or need to consult the primary report.

One solution to the financial problems of publication favoured by many British archaeologists is the 'text-fiche' (Brown, 1980) in which the Level IV report is accompanied at the time of publication by a set of microfiches containing all the Level III data (such as bone data, flint statistics, common pottery catalogues, etc.) photographed from typescript. Lavell (1981) discussed the merits of text-fiche and indicated further literature.

Publication on the lines recommended by the Frere Report (Frere, 1975) has led to a significantly increased commitment to post-excavation work, together with an increase in the amount of material presented in synthesis for final publication. In 1981, the CBA and the Department of the Environment set up a joint Working Party to re-examine existing practices and to suggest a new approach to the processing and publication of data resulting from excavations. The report of the Working Party (Cunliffe, 1983) recommended, amongst other things, that greater emphasis must be placed on selectivity in excavation and post-excavation work; that a site archive and a research archive, both to be actively curated, must be prepared for each excavation; and that a published report will normally contain two elements: a report digest (volume printed) and a fiche print.

Libraries

Most archaeological information is sooner or later published in some form or other, and the resulting literature is collected and organized in libraries, which provide the usual means of access to it. The vast extent of archaeological literature and the wide popular appeal of the subject mean that archaeology is well represented in large numbers of different kinds of libraries, each library varying in the size and strength of its stock particularly with respect to the regional aspects. Libraries worldwide are usually divided into four main groups: national, academic, public and special.

National libraries

Most countries maintain national libraries. There is information on these (and on bibliographical activities generally in each country) in the UNESCO handbook *Bibliographical services throughout the world* published at regular intervals by UNESCO [2]. There is usually a law of copyright which ensures that at least one copy of everything published within the country is deposited in a national collection. These libraries also make selective purchase of foreign works, and over a period of time large research collections develop which can normally be used for reference purposes though not for borrowing. Examples of such national libraries are the British Library Reference Division (London), the Library of Congress (Washington), the Bibliothèque Nationale (Paris), and the Lenin Library (Moscow).

Academic libraries

Academic libraries are the libraries of universities, polytechnics, colleges and similar establishments. Archaeology is taught and studied in many of these institutions, which means that supporting library collections must be maintained. Since these libraries basically serve their own readership, some will not lend to outsiders but most will allow other students and researchers to use their facilities for reference purposes.

Public libraries

Public libraries are available to all, and most contain at least some archaeological material. Such material may well include a local archaeological collection of great value. The librarian in charge of such a collection can be a helpful source of information and contacts.

Special libraries

Special libraries are the libraries of societies and associations (e.g. the Yorkshire Archaeological Society), institutes (e.g. the British Institute in Eastern Africa), research organizations and government bodies. The libraries of museums also fall into this category. Many of these libraries cover only certain aspects of archaeology (for example, certain parts of the world), often in great depth. Archaeology may also be represented in other libraries principally devoted to other subjects, for example classical studies.

Directories of libraries

Information about these various types of libraries – their address, number of volumes, etc. – can be found in directories. On an international scale, the *World guide to libraries* [176] is the most comprehensive, the sixth edition listing over 42,000 libraries. The comprehensive directory *World of learning* [179] covers the libraries of a whole range of educational institutions, including details of special collections. Also relevant are some of the directories discussed in Chapter 3 listing archaeological organizations, many of which maintain specialized libraries in addition to their other roles.

On a continental scale, Lewanski [238] includes over 100 major European archaeological libraries. Ash [447] plays a similar role for North America, complemented by the *Directory of special libraries and information centers* [449], listing over sixty in archaeology. Some other directories of libraries can be traced in Walford [17] and Sheehy [15], some extending to regional level. For Britain, for example, the series *Library resources in* . . . , published by the Library Association Reference, Special and Information Section, indicates which libraries in a particular region have archaeological collections.

No library can be completely self-sufficient, even when limited to archaeological material only. Consequently, schemes have been established for interlibrary lending, and these vary from country to country. A useful summary of them is given in the UNESCO handbook *Bibliographical services throughout the world* [2].

Classification

There are many different classification schemes in use in libraries, some of them specially designed to deal with archaeological literature in libraries whose subject content is entirely or mainly archaeological. It is, however, the classification of archaeology in *general* libraries that tends to cause most problems. Given archaeology's close relationship with so many disciplines (as shown in Fig. 1), scatter of material is inevitable.

A detailed study of library classification in archaeology was made by Cook

(1974) in a thesis which critically examined the six major general classification schemes – Dewey Decimal (DC), Universal Decimal Classification (UDC), Library of Congress Classification (LC), Ranganathan's Colon Classification, Brown's Subject Classification and Bliss's Bibliographic Classification – and considered what sort and range of provision was made for archaeology and related topics; it must be remembered that some of the schemes have since been revised to a greater or lesser extent.

Dewey Decimal (DC)

The DC scheme, at present in its nineteenth edition (1979), is the one most widely employed (often in modified form) and is therefore most familiar to the average library user including the local archaeologist. The scheme divides knowledge into ten main classes, as follows:

000   Generalities
100   Philosophy and related disciplines
200   Religion
300   Social sciences
400   Language
500   Pure sciences
600   Technology (applied sciences)
700   The arts
800   Literature
900   General geography and history

These ten main classes can each be subdivided: for example, 900, of particular interest to the archaeologist, is subdivided as follows:

910   General geography; travel
920   General biography and genealogy
930   General history of the ancient world
940   General history of Europe
950   General history of Asia
960   General history of Africa
970   General history of North America
980   General history of South America
990   General history of other areas

Each of these classes can in turn be subdivided: 930, where the archaeology of the ancient world is placed, is subdivided as follows:

930   General history of the ancient world to *c.* AD 499
931   China to AD 420

932   Egypt to AD 640
933   Palestine to AD 70
934   India to AD 647
935   Mesopotamia and Iranian Plateau to AD 637
936   Europe north and west of Italian peninsula to c. AD 499
937   Italian peninsula and adjacent territories to AD 476
938   Greece to AD 323
939   Other parts of the ancient world to c. AD 640

Archaeology in general is classed at 930.1 (a decimal point is placed after the first three digits) with subdivisions as follows:

930.1	Archaeology (study of past civilizations through discovery, collection, interpretation of material remains) [Prehistoric archaeology is classed here]
930.102	Miscellany
930.1028	Techniques, procedures, apparatus, equipment, materials
930.102804	Underwater archaeology
930.10282	Discovery of remains
930.10283	Excavation of remains
930.10285	Interpretation of remains (including dating techniques, use of data processing)

Specific archaeological ages are classed at 930.11–930.16 as follows:

930.11   Eolithic Age
930.12   Paleolithic (Old Stone) Age
930.13   Mesolithic Age
930.14   Neolithic (New Stone) Age
930.15   Copper and Bronze Age
930.16   Iron Age

General history of the ancient world is classed at 930.2–930.5 as follows:

930.2   to 4000 BC
930.3   3999–1000 BC
930.4   999–1 BC
930.5   AD 1–499

Archaeology of the modern world is classed at 940–990 (General history of the modern world). To these base numbers are added 'area numbers', listed in a separate table in DC, so that, for example, England is 942, Guatemala 972.81, New Zealand 993.1. It is useful for the archaeologist to learn to recognize these area numbers for parts of the world in which he has an interest. DC includes other special tables – for example, one for racial, ethnic and national groups, and one for languages – which are sometimes used in conjunction with base numbers. These tables, along with the schedules themselves and a relative index and an editor's introduction comprise the three volumes which fully describe DC.

It can be seen from the above outline that in its shelf position, archaeology is usefully linked to ancient and modern history. There are other sections of DC likely to contain archaeology-related material and the main ones can be summarized as follows:

Various numbers in the 220s represent aspects of Biblical archaeology: e.g. 220.93 Archaeology (material remains) [of Bible lands in Bible times]

560	Paleontology. Paleozoology
561	Paleobotany
569.9	Hominidae (Humankind and forebears)
573	Physical anthropology
573.3	Prehistoric man, e.g. Pithecanthropus (Java man), Cro-Magnon, Neanderthal, Rhodesian, Peking man
709.01	Arts of nonliterate peoples and ancient times
722	Ancient and Oriental architecture
732	Nonliterate, ancient, Oriental sculpture
733	Greek, Etruscan, Roman sculpture
737	Numismatics and sigillography
738	Ceramic arts
739	Art metalwork
759.01	Painting and paintings of nonliterate peoples and ancient times to AD 499

Cook (1974) noted that archaeology in DC is still regarded as an auxiliary of other subjects, and especially history, rather than as a subject in its own right; even where national chronologies have been expanded backwards in time, the purpose has been to enlarge the scope of national history rather than accommodate archaeological data. The few numbers that are provided for archaeological techniques are too long. It must be said that DC is not really a suitable classification for archaeology, although its popularity and the expense of reclassification probably guarantee its dominant position in libraries worldwide.

Universal Decimal Classification (UDC)

The UDC scheme preserves the ten main classes of Dewey but introduces greater flexibility and more complex notation in order to represent more precisely the subject content of a publication. The DC method of always having three figures before the decimal point is abandoned in favour of a contracted form, e.g. 39 Ethnology. Ethnography. The two most important numbers for archaeology are:

902   Archaeology. Methods and techniques for the study of past civilizations and cultures based on discovery and interpretation of material remains or relics.

903   Prehistory, Prehistoric remains, Artifacts, Antiquities. Interpretation and synthesis of the material relics of ancient man, his culture forms and civilizations.

The many subdivisions of these two numbers show a real attempt to treat archaeology as a subject in its own right and to reflect recent scientific developments: e.g. 902.6 (dating techniques in archaeology) can be subdivided twenty-six times. It is also possible to use compound numbers consisting of main numbers combined with other main numbers and, where necessary, with signs and numbers from the auxiliary tables provided, e.g.:

902.56   Palaeontological archaeology
902(611):937   Archaeology of Tunisia as an aid in the study of Ancient Roman history
903(44–14)   Prehistory of South West France

Other related main numbers include:

56   Palaeontology
57.072   Fossil remains
572   Anthropology
931/939   Ancient history

Full details of UDC are given in the schedules themselves which are published in many languages. English versions are published by the British Standards Institution (BSI) as British Standard 1000. Details of revisions of particular subjects are given in the serial *Extensions and corrections to the UDC* published by the International Federation for Documentation, which is cumulated from time to time, e.g. *Cumulated UDC supplement 1965–1975*.

Library of Congress Classification (LC)

With the LC scheme, archaeological material is scattered throughout the schedules to a considerable degree, making it difficult for archaeologists to use. It is, however, a popular scheme with academic libraries. Like DC and UDC, it has sometimes been adapted to suit the particular needs of individual libraries: for example, the University of London Institute of Archaeology library.

The other three major general classification schemes – Ranganathan's Colon Classification, Brown's Subject Classification, and Bliss's Bibliographic Classification – are used in fewer libraries.

Cook (1974) concluded that Bliss's Bibliographic Classification was probably the best of the general schemes on the grounds of its basic order (most archaeological material is classified in Main Classes K and L), the wide range of possible alternatives and the brevity of its notation. In fact, most major archaeological libraries in England have not used one of the available general schemes but have devised their own schemes, often under the direction of a scholar in a particular field rather than a librarian.

Library catalogues

However helpfully they arrange publications on library shelves, classification schemes cannot serve as primary finding tools. This role is filled by library catalogues, use of which is essential to determine whether a library has a particular work in stock and to locate it on the shelves. Recent years have seen a shift towards brevity in the amount of information given in catalogues; fuller details of specific works can be found in publications such as national bibliographies.

The card catalogue is the dominant form, especially in archaeological libraries. Alternatives are printed books (the published catalogues of national libraries, discussed in Chapter 5, often appear in this form), loose-leaf folders with entries on individual slips of paper (also known as a guardbook or ledger catalogue), and the increasingly popular microfiche, usually a product of COM (computer output microfilm).

The entry in a catalogue is under the name of the author or editor (followed by forenames or initials), or the name of the corporate body responsible for the work, sometimes with additional entries under title. Conferences and symposia are usually entered under title; government publications under the name of the country followed by department or ministry.

In addition, it is usually possible to discover what a library has on a particular subject by means of a separate catalogue. There are basically two ways of doing this. The first is to arrange cards alphabetically by subject descriptors which are added to each entry as headings, e.g.

ARCHAEOLOGY – LAW AND LEGISLATION
PROTT, Lyndel V.
Law and the cultural heritage, by Lyndel V. Prott and P. J. O'Keefe . . .

Often, these subject entries are interfiled with author entries giving a *dictionary catalogue* (favoured particularly by US libraries). The second way is to have a *classified catalogue*, in which cards are arranged in classified, i.e. shelf order, often supported by a *subject index* (favoured particularly by British libraries).

Another useful type of catalogue sometimes found in special archaeology libraries is a *site index*, listing references to individual archaeological sites in monographs and sometimes also periodicals.

The scattering of archaeological literature in most general libraries makes it particularly important to learn to use these catalogues efficiently when tracing material.

References

Alcock, L. 1977–8. Excavation and publication: some comments. *Proceedings of the Society of Antiquaries of Scotland*, 109, 1–6.

Brown, A. E. 1980. Having one's cake and eating it? *Northamptonshire Newsletter and Calendar*, Autumn, 11–13.

Cook, B. M. 1974. *Library classification in archaeology*. M.Sc.Thesis, University of Strathclyde (Scotland). 179 pp.

Cunliffe, B. W. and others. 1983. *The publication of archaeological excavations: the Report of a Joint Working Party of the Council for British Archaeology and the Department of the Environment*. London: Department of the Environment. 10 pp.

Frere, S. S. and others. 1975. *Principles of publication in rescue archaeology*. London: Ancient Monuments Board for England, Committee for Rescue Archaeology. 18 pp.

Gaines, S. W. and Gaines, W. M. 1980. Future trends in computer applications. *American Antiquity*, 45:3, 462–71.

Hunter, M. C. W. 1971. The Royal Society and the origins of British archaeology. *Antiquity*, 65; Part I: no. 178, 113–21; Part II: no. 179, 187–92.

Lavell, C. 1981. Publication: an obligation: archaeological documentation in Britain today. *Bulletin of the Institute of Archaeology, University of London*, 18, 91–125.

Peters, E. 1981. Archaeology and publishing. In J. D. Evans, B. Cunliffe, and C. Renfrew (eds.), *Antiquity and man: essays in honour of Glyn Daniel*, pp. 195–202. London: Thames and Hudson.

Piggott, S. 1974. The origins of the English county societies. *Transactions of the Birmingham and Warwickshire Archaeological Society*, 86, 1–15.

Pitt-Rivers, A. L. F. 1887–98. *Excavations in Cranborne Chase*, vols. i–iv [privately printed].

Renfrew, A. C. 1983. Divided we stand: aspects of archaeology and information. *American Antiquity*, 48:1, 3–16.

Rhodes, M. 1980. Some thoughts concerning the definition of aims and objectives in the development of excavation archives. *Museum Archaeologist*, 5, 28–35.

Roberts, D. A. and Light, R. B. 1980. Progress in documentation: museum documentation. *Journal of Documentation*, 36:1, 42–84.

Wheeler, R. E. M. 1954. *Archaeology from the earth*. Oxford: Clarendon Press. 234 pp.

Zubrow, E. 1981. The centralization and cost of archaeological information. *American Antiquity*, 46, 443–6.

3 Who, what, where?

Organizations

Part III of this Keyguide comprises a list of organizations willing to act as contact points for their respective countries or aspects of archaeology. Some of these bodies issue leaflets explaining how archaeology is organized in their countries; these leaflets can conveniently summarize arrangements which are often complex. These organizations are, of course, only a selected few of the thousands worldwide that are connected with archaeology in some way, as a glance at the *Archaeologists' year book* [160] shows. This work, when published for 1973 and 1977, went some way towards acting as an international archaeological directory. It gave basic information on a great number of archaeological and archaeology-related organizations of all kinds, in separate British and inter-national (i.e. non-British) sections, with an index of individuals' names but no organizations index (which can make finding an organization somewhat time-consuming). Unfortunately, in spite of its title, no further editions are planned. A good deal of the information is therefore now out of date, particularly the references to individuals, but the work can still be helpful, if used with care.

Names and addresses found in the *Archaeologists' year book* should be checked in *World of learning* [179], a major international guide to educational, scientific and cultural institutions of all kinds, including many archaeological bodies. It has the great advantage of being an annual publication and therefore up to date. With its index of over 24,000 institutions, it sometimes usefully confirms (or otherwise) an organization originally traced in the *Archaeologists' year book*. The *World guide to scientific associations and learned societies* [177] gives brief entries for a selection of archaeological bodies worldwide, but with a great bias towards the UK.

Detailed accounts of organizations of all kinds in British and American archaeology, including their schools overseas, appear in Day's *Archaeology: a reference handbook* [5] but the lack of a subject approach limits the user to known names. Day is particularly useful for the history and developmental aspects. Baker [247] discusses the many organizations, official and private, concerned with the historic environment in Britain.

For Europe, the two CBD Research publications are helpful standard works: Part 2 of the *Directory of European associations* (excluding Britain) [237] is useful for national and important regional archaeological associations (the 1979 edition included well over 100); the 1980 edition of its companion work *Directory of British associations* [270] included well over 100 such bodies. More detailed than these is *Zusammenstellung* [240] which lists prehistoric and protohistoric institutes, along with other information such as forthcoming courses, seminars, etc., for Germany, Austria, Switzerland, Luxemburg, Belgium and the Netherlands. Covering the field of natural science in archaeology in Western Europe (except for Yugoslavia and Portugal), Verhaeghe's survey [239] is an excellent detailed inventory of existing facilities, which also considers topics such as training, documentation, databanks, archives, publication and conservation.

For the USA, the *Encyclopedia of associations* [450] includes nearly fifty national archaeological organizations, with helpful summaries of aims and work done, etc. At local level, the *Directory of historical societies and agencies in the United States and Canada* [448] listed nearly 6,000 organizations in all branches of history, but the special interest index listed only forty-eight under 'Archaeology'.

Of directories of museums, the most comprehensive is Hudson and Nicholls' *The directory of museums* [168]. The second edition covered about 30,000 museums worldwide, included summaries of the national situation in each country, and (in the select bibliography) a list of museum directories for individual countries. The third edition of *Museums of the world* [173] listed nearly 18,000 worldwide, included a list of national and international museum associations, and had detailed indexes. Publications on archaeological collections within individual museums can be traced in ICOM's *International Museological Bibliography* (Prague: Ústřední muzeologický kabinet, 1967–. Annual. Delay: about three years). For details on the permanent collections of museums and their publications and audio-visual materials, *World museum publications* [185] is useful. For addresses and other information on all aspects of art and museums in general, the *International directory of arts* [171] covers groups and topics such as antiquarian and art booksellers, numismatics, art and antique dealers, etc.

Various reference works exist to help archaeologists trace sources of funding. Section L of the *Archaeologists' year book* [160] listed thirty-three grant-making institutions giving a brief note on awards, with emphasis on the United Kingdom. On an international scale, the *Grants register* [167] is up to date, well signposted, and the bibliography lists further sources. For Britain, the eighth edition of *Directory of grant-making trusts* [271] included thirty-eight trusts under 'Archaeology'.

Individuals and Current Research

Names of staff in academic institutions worldwide are listed in *World of learning* [179] but only down to Reader level. The *International handbook of universities and other institutions of higher education* [172] gives more detail on the institutions themselves, but again, only senior officers are listed. For staff names, the best source is the *World guide to universities* [178], or, for Commonwealth countries, the *Commonwealth universities yearbook* [164], both of which have name indexes. Calendars of individual institutions naturally give more detail. For North American academics, the *National faculty directory* [452] is a single alphabetical listing of names with addresses; the American Anthropological Association publish a *Guide to departments of anthropology* [446] (the twenty-first edition in 1982–83 included 5,394 names); for Canada, staff in university departments of archaeology and in museums are listed in Herman and Carstens' *Guide* . . . [451].

Biographical information can be found in some periodicals, sometimes at the start of articles. There may be lists of archaeologists working in particular fields: for example, the *Journal of Field Archaeology* [118] includes lists of archaeometrists. Some societies issue membership lists which provide names and addresses (e.g. the Society for Medieval Archaeology), and sometimes also individual areas of specialization (e.g. the International Institute for Conservation of Historic and Artistic Works [602]).

Well-known current archaeologists may appear in national biographical works such as *Who's who, Who's who in France*, etc. There have been few 'Who's who' type volumes specifically in archaeology: two examples are P. Åstrom's *Who's who in Cypriote archaeology* [388] and the wide-ranging *Who was who in Egyptology* [412]. Former archaeologists and antiquarians can be found in retrospective works such as (for Britain) the *Dictionary of national biography*. An extremely valuable and extensive international index to biographies pre-1950 is Hyamson's *Dictionary of universal biography of all ages and of all peoples* [169]. Well-known archaeologists may have obituaries in *The Times* [174], and obituaries appear in some journals, e.g. *Antiquaries Journal* [226], *American Antiquity* [427].

For current research, the most up-to-date and detailed information appears in the appropriate periodical(s). Some have a section devoted to summaries of current research, e.g. *American Antiquity* [427], *Azania* [417]. This may take the form of 'excavation roundups' – summaries of excavation work done during the previous year: examples are *Archéologie Médiévale* [304], *Anatolian Studies* [509], *Mainzer Zeitschrift* [316] and *Iran* [516]. *Archaeological Reports* [101] is entirely devoted to summaries of recent excavations in the Mediterranean area. For Britain, each of the period journals *Proceedings of the Prehistoric Society of London* [265], *Britannia* [254], *Medieval Archaeology* [263] and *Post-Medieval Archaeology* [264] includes summaries of the previous year's work. From 1978 the *Annual Reports of the Ancient Monuments Board for England* contain lists of publications of Department of the Environment-sponsored excavations which formerly appeared in *Archaeological Excavations: a brief summary of prehistoric, Roman and medieval sites throughout the country excavated in advance of destruction* (London: HMSO, 1968–76), which in turn replaced the former Ministry of Works' *Excavations Annual Report* (1961–67). Much Department of the Environment work is currently reported in *Archaeology in Britain* [253].

Some countries maintain a national register of current research for all or some subjects. For Britain, *Research in British universities, polytechnics and colleges* [272] includes a good deal of archaeology in volumes 2 and 3 (with overlap), giving details of individual research interests at particular institutions. Specifically archaeological is the *Répertoire de la recherche archéologique française* [323], regularly updated. For the USA and Canada, *Research Centers Directory* [175] gives good coverage for archaeology. Its companion volume *International Research Centers Directory* [175] should prove useful when fully established. Also international but limited to medievalists is the *Répertoire international des médiévistes/International directory of medievalists* [162], covering forty-three countries and including the particularly useful feature of a list of each individual's published and planned work. An example of a directory covering archaeologists (and others) working in a particular part of the world is *Latinoamericanistas en Europa* [432], and one of resources in a particular field is Wiseman's *European research resources: Assyriology* [530] which needs updating but is still useful.

Other more general directories, some for individual countries, can be traced in Sheehy [15] and Walford [17]. It should be remembered that many such directories depend on replies by individuals to questionnaires, and can therefore be only as good as their response rate.

4 Keeping up to date with Current Publications, Developments and Events

Major Indexes, Abstracts, Current Bibliographies

The vast extent of archaeological literature has long made it impossible to keep up successfully with current work simply by scanning individual publications, important though this is. For this reason, and also to enable retrospective searching to be done, various indexing and abstracting tools and current bibliographies have been developed. These are guides to the contents of published literature, and especially periodical literature. Hasso (1978), in a bibliometric investigation into the characteristics of archaeological journals and secondary services, found that in a limited sample of indexing and abstracting publications in archaeology, about 92% of the documents covered were journals, about 4.5% were monographs of various kinds, and about 3.5% were other forms of material. However, recent years have seen such a large increase in 'one-off' publications that if a similar survey were to be conducted now, the percentage for monographs would be much higher.

Indexing journals list the authors, titles and other bibliographical details of publications. Abstracting journals give the same information but also include abstracts (i.e. summaries) of publications; the abstract may be in the language of the original or be translated into English or some other language. Some current bibliographies include annotations, others do not. There are wide differences in the time taken for the various services to appear in print. Modern archaeology is such a fast-moving subject that delays of much over a year greatly reduce a publication's value.

Archaeology is not so fully covered by indexes and abstracts as are most other subjects; there is no archaeological equivalent of works such as *Chemical Abstracts* or *Psychological Abstracts*. Hasso (1978) concluded that indexes and abstracts in archaeology were deficient in their coverage of foreign-language material and non-journal material. For a comprehensive search on a topic it is usually necessary to consult more than one publication, although there is a good deal of overlap, and many useful publications cover other subjects as well as archaeology. Archaeological material can be hard to find in these more general listings: indexers may miss important publications through not recognizing concepts such as 'Bronze Age'.

The most extensive coverage worldwide and period-wise is provided by the three sections of *Bulletin Signalétique* [27] [28] [220], all sub-files of the data base FRANCIS and searchable online (see below), most references including brief abstracts. For a quick outline of recent periodical literature worldwide, *Recently Published Articles* [36] is the most comprehensive listing on all aspects of history but its archaeological content is small.

Art and Archaeology Technical Abstracts [191] well covers the technical and conservation side of the literature worldwide; a particular feature are the annotated bibliographies on specific topics published as supplements. For the museum aspects, the Canadian Museums Association's *Bibliography* [29] attempts to be comprehensive. For archaeozoology, *Bibliographie zur Archäo-Zoologie und Geschichte der Haustiere* [192] covers a wide field and in particular the history of domestic animals.

For the anthropology-related aspects of archaeology, the *Anthropological Index* [21] gives comprehensive geographical coverage, has a large number of entries, and appears with minimum delay. *Anthropological Literature* [22] covers similar ground but although it includes journals not covered by *Anthropological Index*, its arrangement, lack of a detailed subject index and longer delay make it less useful. *Abstracts in Anthropology* [18] covers fewer journals and is a slower service, as is *Abstracts in German Anthropology* [19] which covers publications in German on a worldwide basis. The *International Bibliography of Social and Cultural Anthropology* [34] is also useful but slow to appear.

Classical archaeology is particularly well covered. The best listing in terms of coverage and speed of appearance is *Archäologische Bibliographie* [24]. This is usefully supplemented by *L'Année Philologique* [20], a slower service but covering all aspects of Greek and Roman antiquity, with a valuable 'Antiquités' section for archaeology. *Fasti Archaeologici* [30] covers far fewer periodicals and is very slow.

For the art history aspects of archaeology, *Art Index* [25] covers the serial literature with minimum delay, although only about 200 journals are consulted. For abstracts of articles on coins worldwide, *Numismatic Literature* [35] gives good coverage from earliest times to modern. For archaeology (and other subjects) in the Islamic world from the 7th century AD onwards, *Index Islamicus* and its continuation *Quarterly Index Islamicus* [33] cover a wide range of journals and other collective works. For UNESCO publications on archaeology, the *UNESCO List of Documents and Publications* [39] is comprehensive.

There are several other indexes and abstracts basically covering the archaeology (and often other subjects) of a particular part of the world. For medieval Europe, *International Medieval Bibliography* [221] covers a wide range of periodicals, with minimum delay. Within Europe, *British Archaeological Abstracts* [245] covers the most significant material currently published on British archaeology in foreign as well as British publications, with a high percentage of non-journal titles. There is coverage not only of all aspects of British archaeology but also, for example, of new theories emanating from North America or Europe and of other aspects of non-British archaeology (recent examples are the work of the Netherlands State Archaeological Service, an analysis of sectors of French archaeology, and monument protection in Europe). Hasso (1978) found that of services examined, *British Archaeological Abstracts* had the best subject and journal coverage according to the Bradford–Zipf distribution theory.

There are three close imitations of *British Archaeological Abstracts: Polish Archaeological Abstracts* [353], *Nordic Archaeological Abstracts* [277], which includes a high percentage of non-journal titles, and *Résumés d'Archéologie Suisse* [294], each covering their respective areas, although the Swiss publication covers only the Roman period at present. For Sweden, the *Swedish Archaeological Bibliography* [278] includes valuable narrative surveys. For abstracts of Bulgarian articles, there is *Zentralblatt der Bulgarischen Wissenschaftlichen Literatur: Geschichte, Archäologie und Ethnographie* [372].

For Africa, the *International African Bibliography* [391] covers archaeology well. It excludes Egypt, which is covered by the *Annual Egyptological Bibliography* [399] which has lengthy annotations but a delay of several years.

For America as a whole, *Bibliographie Américaniste* [424] covers linguistics, archaeology, prehistory, anthropology, human geography, and ethnohistory; the *Index to Literature on the American Indian* [425] gives useful coverage of the native population. For North America, *America: History and Life* [438] gives good detailed coverage of archaeology. For Latin America, the *Handbook of Latin American Studies* [456] gives excellent archaeological coverage, particularly the social sciences volumes, a useful feature being summaries of research and publication trends in each area. Also to be noted, though less useful, is *Hispanic American Periodicals Index* [457].

The *Bibliography of Asian Studies* [486] includes a good deal of archaeology on the Far East, South and Southeast Asia but the delay is about three years. Even longer delayed in publication is the *Annual Bibliography of Indian Archaeology* [534] giving comprehensive coverage of the Indian subcontinent and areas within its cultural influence. Current Soviet archaeological publications are covered by *Novaya Sovetskaya Literatura po Istorii, Arkheologii i Etnografii* [491]; the highly regarded *Arkheologiya SSSR: Svod Arkheologicheskikh Istochnikov* [490] – a corpus of archaeological sources for the USSR – appears at intervals in the form of separate fascicles. For China, the *Revue Bibliographique de Sinologie* [560] has a section 'Archéologie, art et épigraphie', with annotations in French and English.

For Australasia, the main source is the *Annual Bibliography of the Australian*

Institute of Aboriginal Studies [577]. The *Australian Public Affairs Information Service* [578] includes some archaeology.

For Polar regions, *Recent Polar and Glaciological Literature* [592] includes some archaeology.

Online Services

Many indexing and abstracting services are now produced by computer, and the data bases for these are being made available so that literature searches can be done using a computer terminal for online access. In some cases the printed versions have in fact been discontinued, and the only access is via computer. Many large libraries, especially academic ones, can arrange for such a search to be done. These developments are well advanced in the sciences and social sciences but have had only a small effect so far in archaeology for two main reasons: the large amount of parochial archaeological information held by each country which would be of little interest to outsiders; and the difficulty of selecting items of international significance for inclusion in such a data base (Lavell, 1981). Nevertheless, the data base FRANCIS does produce three archaeological sub-files [27] [28] [220]; currently these have about 100,000 archaeological references back to 1972 and grow at an annual rate of about 20,000 references.

A list of the principal English-language online bibliographic data bases in all subjects can be found in J. L. Hall and M. J. Brown's *Online bibliographic databases: a directory and sourcebook* (3rd ed. London: Aslib, 1983). Online services are a complex and rapidly changing field and expert advice from a librarian or information officer is usually necessary.

Other Indexes and Abstracts

There are several indexing and abstracting publications whose coverage of archaeology is so slight that they cannot be regarded as *major* information sources and have therefore not been included in Part II of this *Keyguide*. Nevertheless, they often contain important references, especially in archaeological science, and many of them can be searched online. *Chemical Abstracts* (Columbus (Ohio): Chemical Abstracts Service 1907–. Weekly. Available online) includes some archaeology, mainly in the section 'History, education and documentation'. So do *Biological Abstracts* (Philadelphia (Pennsylvania): BioSciences Information Service, 1926–. Twice a month. Available online) in the sections 'Physical anthropology: ethnobiology', 'General biology – History and archaeology', 'Paleobiology', 'Paleobotany', 'Paleozoology', and 'Palynology'; *Index Medicus* (Washington: US Dept of Health, Education and Welfare, Public Health Service, 1879–. Monthly. Available online); and *Current Work in the History of Medicine* (London: Wellcome Institute for the History of Medicine, 1954–. Quarterly).

The two parts of *Historical Abstracts* (*A: Modern history abstracts 1450–1914; B: Twentieth century abstracts 1914–present*) (Santa Barbara (California): ABC-Clio, 1955–. Quarterly. Available online) contain a small amount of archaeology but more will be found in national historical bibliographies such as, for example *Bibliographie Annuelle de l'Histoire de France* (Paris: Centre National de la Recherche Scientifique, 1955–. Annual) which includes a section on French medieval archaeology; similar national bibliographies can conveniently be traced in the 'History and area studies' section of Sheehy [15]. For references on the geographical sciences (for example, climate, Quaternary, etc.), *Bibliographie Géographique Internationale* (Paris: Centre National de la Recherche Scientifique, 1891–. Quarterly) and *Geo Abstracts Section D* (Norwich (England): Geo Abstracts Ltd, 1972–. Six times a year) are useful. Other online services which include a small amount of archaeology are *Geo Ref* (American Geological Institute, 1961–) basically covering geological literature and the *NTIS* service (Springfield (Virginia): National Technical Information Service, US Department of Commerce, 1964–) covering US government-sponsored research.

Citation Indexes and Current Contents

A rather different type of indexing tool is the citation index. This works on the principle that if there is one reference known to be relevant for the search in hand, it can be looked up, and the citation index will list details of other publications citing it. These in turn can be looked up, leading to more references. However, the works in question – the *Arts and Humanities Citation Index* (Philadelphia (Pennsylvania): Institute for Scientific Information, 1976–. Three times a year) and the *Social Sciences Citation Index* (Philadelphia (Pennsylvania); Institute for Scientific Information, 1966–. Three times a year. Available online as *Social Scisearch*) – are only marginally relevant for archaeologists since each includes at present only a small number of archaeological journals. They become more useful, however, if a search is extended to include non-archaeological topics.

The same is true of the *Current Contents* series of publications (Philadelphia (Pennsylvania): Institute for Scientific Information, 1961–. Weekly) which reproduce the contents pages of particular journals. The most useful sections for archaeology are *Social and Behavioral Sciences* and *Arts and Humanities*, with a few papers on archaeological science in the *Physical, Chemical and Earth Sciences* and *Life Sciences* sections, but again, only a few archaeological journals are covered.

Current Bibliographies within Journals

Because indexing and abstracting publications are subject to publishing delays (details in Part II show that the time lag between the publications that are indexed and the service itself can vary from only a few months to several years), they cannot include articles from the most recent issues of journals. The researcher has therefore no choice but to examine current issues as they appear, not only to keep up with new publications but also to find various other kinds of information not usually covered by indexes and abstracts.

One convenient way of keeping up with new literature is to consult those journals which themselves include bibliographical listings, although these, too, may of course be subject to delay. One of the most valuable of such current bibliographies appears in the *Antiquaries Journal* [23]; this is a list of accessions to the library of the Society of Antiquaries in London and a listing of the contents of selected British and non-British journals. Some issues of *Ausgrabungen und Funde* [219] include 'Neue Schriften: Bibliographie zur Ur- und Frühgeschichte' – a list of books and articles on prehistory and early history, mainly European, arranged by subject, area and period. The *Bulletin de la Société Préhistorique Française* [26] includes regular bibliographies comprising the Society's library's intake of books and periodicals, sometimes including French theses. Each issue of *Zeitschrift für Archäologie des Mittelalters* [222] includes a bibliography on medieval archaeology (1945–75) for a particular country or region of Germany. Some issues of *Technology and Culture* [38] include a current bibliography on the history of technology. Other examples: *Helinium* [293] has a detailed, classified bibliography for the Netherlands, Belgium and Luxemburg; *Germania* [31] includes a list of additions to the library of the Römisch-Germanische Kommission; *Archeologické Rozhledy* [218] lists the contents of periodicals and new books; *Archaeológiai Értesítö* [352] has lists of current Hungarian archaeological literature; *Historical Metallurgy* [32] includes abstracts of publications in the field; *Sprawozdania Archeologiczne* [37] includes abstracts on the Neolithic of East-Central Europe; *Orientalia* [503] includes 'Keilschriftbibliographie' – detailed listings covering the Middle East.

Book Reviews

Book reviews are a significant feature of most major archaeological journals. They can often be traced through the indexes of appropriate journals. Some book review sections – for example, those in *Antiquity* [98] and *American Antiquity* [427] – are very lengthy, as are the reviews in the *Quarterly Review of Archaeology* [121], which is entirely devoted to book reviews, with emphasis on the Americas. Individual reviews can be useful for summarizing the present state of archaeological knowledge on a given topic, although it is always wise to consult more than one review for the same book, if possible. Some journals often cannot review all the books sent to them for this purpose and may include a separate listing of books received. There may often be a significant delay between the publication of a book and its review.

Another source for reviews of some archaeological books is the *Times Literary Supplement* (London: Times, 1902–. Weekly) which carries book reviews on all subjects; reviews of individual works are traceable through the *Times Index* (Reading, Research Publications Limited, 1790–. Monthly) which covers the *TLS* and other *Times* supplements as well as *The Times*, which, like other 'quality' newspapers, is itself a useful way of tracing archaeological news of general interest.

Forthcoming Books

For books about to be published, some journals carry publishers' advertisements and announcements. Publishers' catalogues and leaflets are also important sources. For British books recently published, the *Bookseller* (London: Whitaker, 1858–. Weekly) comprises an author and title list which cumulates into *Whitaker's Books of the Month and Books to Come*, which also includes a large proportion of the books announced to appear during the following two months. These titles also appear in a classified arrangement in *Whitaker's Classified Monthly Book List* which cumulates quarterly to form *Whitaker's Cumulative Book List*. The Spring and Autumn Export numbers of the *Bookseller* are devoted to new books scheduled to appear over the next few months. Each section (there is one for archaeology) is a selective guide to the 'best books', briefly summarizing their contents. All titles in print subsequently appear in *British Books in Print* (London: Whitaker, 1965–. Monthly (microfiche); Annual (hard copy)).

For the USA, there is *Publishers' Weekly* (New York: Bowker, 1872–) and *Forthcoming Books* (New York: Bowker, 1966–. Every two months) which lists books about to be published by author and by title. Details of similar works for other parts of the world can be found in Sheehy [15].

Notes and News

Some journals include a 'notes and news' section giving up-to-date information on matters such as forthcoming conferences and meetings, professional appointments, resignations, retirements, obituaries, study tours, lectures, scholarships, etc. Some newsletters and bulletins are entirely devoted to news of this type and may also include details of excavations requiring volunteer workers: for example, *CBA Newsletter and Calendar* [256], the American *Archaeological Fieldwork and Opportunities Bulletin* [441], the French *Nouvelles de l'Archéologie* [318], and *Archaeology Abroad* [104].

State-of-the-Art Reviews

A few journals, such as *Archaeometry* [200], sometimes include review articles in addition to original research papers. Two publications entirely devoted to state-of-the-art reviews are *Advances in World Archaeology* [93], which aims to provide syntheses of current archaeological knowledge worldwide, each volume comprising chapters each covering a particular part of the world; and *Advances in Archaeological Method and Theory* [92] which synthesizes recent methodological and theoretical advances. The *Annual Review of Anthropology* [96] includes state-of-the-art articles on archaeology worldwide.

Similar publications in some other subject fields may prove useful. Their titles usually begin with the words *Progress in* ... or *Advances in* ... and they can be traced in *Ulrich* [89]. One example is *Progress in Human Geography: an International Review of Geographical Work in the Social Sciences and Humanities* (London: Arnold, 1977–. Quarterly), which contains review articles on all aspects of human geography including historical.

Guides to Conferences

As noted earlier, current journals are usually the best guide to forthcoming conferences. For published conference proceedings, the most helpful source in terms of coverage and ease of use is the British Library Lending Division's *Index of Conference Proceedings Received* [161]. The 1964–81 microfiche cumulation listed about 250 conference proceedings under 'archaeology' and related headings. For details of individual papers given at conferences, the *Index to Social Sciences and Humanities Proceedings* [170] includes archaeology and anthropology.

For a history of four major international archaeological and anthropological organizations, with descriptions of their meetings and publications, Comas's very detailed work [163] covers the period 1865–1954.

References

Hasso, M. H. 1978. *A bibliometric study of the literature of archaeology*. M.Phil. Thesis, City University (England). 193 pp. + refs.

Lavell, C. 1981. Publication: an obligation: archaeological documentation in Britain today. *Bulletin of the Institute of Archaeology, University of London*, 18, 91–125.

5 Finding out about the Literature of Archaeology

Bibliographies

Many of the indexing and abstracting publications discussed in Chapter 4 will help with retrospective as well as current searching. Many of them, however, are of relatively recent origin and put the emphasis on periodical publications. To obtain a more complete picture of archaeological literature, other bibliographical guides are needed in addition. A bibliography is, strictly speaking, a list of books, but its scope is usually extended to include periodical articles and other publications in addition to books. Good bibliographies can, of course, be found at the end of significant periodical articles and books (for example, the bibliography at the end of Clark's *World prehistory in new perspective* [55] contains over 600 references). Others have been published in book form. Their coverage is obviously restricted to works published before a certain date and they must therefore be updated by the types of works discussed in Chapter 4. In this *Keyguide*, indexes and abstracts which have ceased publication are treated as bibliographies, since they are used for retrospective and not current searching.

A good starting point for tracing pre-1963 archaeological bibliographies on a world scale is Besterman's *A world bibliography of bibliographies* [3]. Some of those produced since 1963 can be found in works that are, in effect, continuations of Besterman: *Toomey* [3], *Bibliographic Index* [3] and *Bibliographische Berichte* [3]. If bibliographies for Europe are required, a better source is Gerlach and Hachmann's massive *Verzeichnis vor- und frühgeschichtliche Bibliographien* [214] which lists 3,103 bibliographies for European countries, excluding Greece and Portugal. Because of this work's comprehensiveness, only a few of the more significant European pre-1970 bibliographies have been included in Part II of this *Keyguide*. This exclusion applies also to older bibliographies for other parts of the world which tend, like all types of older works, to be listed in more recent publications (for example, in the *Handbook of Latin American Studies* [456]).

Library Catalogues

The most comprehensive retrospective bibliographies covering all subjects including archaeology are the catalogues of the world's larger libraries, several of which have been published in book form. Examples are (for the USA) the *National union catalog* (formerly the *Library of Congress catalog*) and (for Britain) the *General catalogue of printed books* of the British Library (formerly the British Museum Library). Details of such catalogues, and also of national bibliographies such as the *British national bibliography*, the *Australian national bibliography*, etc. can be found in Beaudiquez's *Bibliographical services throughout the world* [2].

Some of the world's larger archaeological libraries have published their catalogues. Details of these can be found in Nelson [12] whose subject index includes twenty-nine entries under 'archaeology'. Some of these more significant ones are included in Part II of this *Keyguide*: for example, the *Kataloge der Bibliothek des Deutschen Archäologischen Instituts* [6] and the *Author and subject catalogs of the library of the Peabody Museum of Archaeology and Ethnology, Harvard University* [13].

General Archaeological Bibliographies

The vast scale of archaeological literature has understandably led to few attempts to make comprehensive worldwide listings. One very detailed project, the *COWA surveys and bibliographies* [4], included surveys of work done worldwide (except for the Americas) with extensive bibliographies for each area. One useful single-volume starting point is Heizer's *Archaeology: a bibliographical guide to the basic literature* [9] containing 4,818 unannotated references. The section 'Sources of primary data' included seventy-four bibliographies on various aspects of archaeology worldwide but with strong emphasis on North America; some of the more recent and significant ones appear in Part II of this work.

For British, American, biblical, industrial and nautical archaeology, Day's *Archaeology: a reference handbook* [5] is a guide to the various forms of literature and reference material, including bibliographies, but the alphabetical arrangement limits use to known titles, names and (through the index) authors. For industrial archaeology, easier sources to use are Koch's *Industrial archaeology: a selected bibliography* [10] and the select bibliography in Hudson's *World industrial archaeology* [57]. For nautical archaeology, Muckelroy's *Maritime archaeology* [58] includes a useful bibliography.

In the field of archaeological science, the bibliographies by Bleck [187] and Gaudel [188] together cover topics such as the scientific investigation of artefacts and methods of restoration and conservation. Hester and Heizer [189] cover lithic technology, Armelagos and others [186] palaeopathology, and Polach

[190] radiocarbon dating. Some of the supplements to *Art and Archaeology Technical Abstracts* [191] cover archaeological topics.

Regional Archaeological Bibliographies

As with other types of archaeological publication, the most common form of bibliography is the regional one. For classical archaeology, Coulson's work [213] is a useful starting point. Much more comprehensive is Borroni's '*Il Cicognara*' [212], a detailed listing of the sources of classical archaeology and Italian art. For Europe as a whole and individual countries within Europe (except for Greece and Portugal), Gerlach and Hachmann's comprehensive work [214], mentioned earlier, is essential. For the European Upper Palaeolithic, Schmider [216] has 4,999 entries.

For Britain, the *Archaeological bibliography* and its predecessors [241] provided a comprehensive annual listing. Also indispensable are the three Bonser bibliographies, [242], [243], [244]. The CBA's *Archaeological resources handbook for teachers* [246] gives invaluable lists of publications of all kinds for the use of teachers in schools as well as details of other resources.

For Scandinavia, Lamm [276] gave a complete list of all Nordic archaeological bibliographies up to 1976, continued for Norway by Bakka [274] and for Denmark by Becker [275]. For France, the works by Gandilhon and Samaran [291] and Montandon [292] include a great number of archaeological items. For Hungary, Banner [349] gives good retrospective coverage. Jakabffy and Banner [351] covered the Middle Danubian basin. For Poland, the *Bibliography of Polish prehistorical and mediaeval archaeology for the years 1970–1974* [350] covers material published over a short period. For Bulgaria, Georgieva and Velkov [369] have nearly 10,000 entries and for Albania, Jubani [371] about 700. For Romania, Comşa's volumes [367] [368] cover the Palaeolithic, Mesolithic and Neolithic.

For Africa, the massive *Africa south of the Sahara: index to periodical literature 1900–1970* [389] contains much archaeology. Holm's *Bibliography of South African pre- and proto-historic archaeology* [418] has over 1,000 entries mostly for the Republic of South Africa, and Phillipson and Derricourt [419] listed 220 works for Zambia. For Egypt, Pratt's *Ancient Egypt: sources of information in the New York Public Library* [398], though old, is a good starting point because of its comprehensiveness.

For America as a whole, *Abstracts of New World archaeology* [422] unfortunately ran for only two years. Wolf and Folk's bibliography *Indians of North and South America* [423] covers the native inhabitants of the New World. For North America, in addition to Heizer's work [435], discussed earlier, Murdock and O'Leary's massive *Ethnographic bibliography of North America* [436] includes much archaeology. For the United States Beers's two works [433] are helpful, especially for individual states. For Canada, there is the National Museum of Canada's *Bibliography of Canadian anthropology 1954–62* and earlier listings [437].

For Central America, Bernal's comprehensive *Bibliografía de arqueología y etnografía* [453] has nearly 14,000 items. This can be supplemented by Kendall's *The art and archaeology of pre-Columbian Middle America* [454], restricted to works in English. For South America, O'Leary's comprehensive *Ethnographic bibliography of South America* [469] includes much archaeology.

For the USSR, *Sovetskaya arkheologicheskaya literatura; bibliografiya* [488] is a comprehensive listing. Field's *Bibliography of Soviet archaeology and physical anthropology, 1936–72* [489] is a small selected list of publications translated from Soviet sources.

For the Middle East as a whole, the *Catalogue de la Bibliothèque de l'École biblique et archéologique française* [498] is a major bibliography, especially for biblical archaeology. Vanden Berghe and Mussche's work [502] covers Assyriology and the Near East. For Anatolia, Battersby [497] lists over 5,000 publications. Iran is covered by Pearson [500] and, more comprehensively, by Vanden Berghe [501]. For Iraq, Al-Haik compiled *Key lists of archaeological excavations in Iraq* [496] covering the period 1842–1971, while Ellis's *Bibliography of Mesopotamian archaeological sites* [499] lists the literature on individual sites.

For South Asia, Patterson's large work *South Asian civilizations* [533] includes much archaeology. King produced a comprehensive listing for Pakistan archaeology [531], and Pande and Ramachandran [532] covered the Harappan culture.

For China there is the extensive *Zhongguo Kaoguxue Wenxian Mulu 1949–1966* (*Bibliography of Chinese archaeological literature, 1949–1966*) [554] and the more selective *Wenwu Kaogu Gongzuo Sanshinian 1949–1979* (*Thirty years of cultural relics work and archaeology 1949–1979*) [555]. For English readers there is the *T. L. Yüan bibliography of Western writings on Chinese art and archaeology* [559], the more limited *Chinese archaeological abstracts* [558], and Chen and Stamps's *Index to Chinese archaeological works . . . 1949–1965* [553]. Other major English-language bibliographies on the Far East are Befu and others [552] and Okada and others [557] for Japan, and Knez and Swanson [556] for Korea.

For the Arctic and sub-Arctic regions, Dekin's *Arctic archaeology* [591] is the most comprehensive listing.

Archaeology-related Bibliographies

There are many bibliographies giving archaeology only partial coverage but nevertheless containing important related materials. Arntzen and Rainwater's major *Guide to the literature of art history* [1] limits archaeological coverage to basic reference literature and general works of an art historical nature. D. L. Ehresmann's two works *Applied and decorative arts: a bibliographic guide to basic reference works, histories and handbooks* (Littleton (Colorado): Libraries Unlimited, 1977. 232 pp.) and *Fine arts: a bibliographic guide to basic reference works, histories and handbooks* (2nd ed. Littleton (Colorado): Libraries Unlimited, 1979. 349 pp.) both cover their subjects from earliest times, each with a total of over 1,000 annotated entries. G. S. Duncan and V. Dimbleby's *Bibliography of glass* (London: Dawson, 1960. 552 pp.) has 15,752 entries covering all kinds of publications on glass from earliest times to 1940. W. T. Divale's *Warfare in primitive societies: a bibliography* (Rev. ed. Santa Barbara (California); Oxford (England): ABC-Clio, 1973. 153 pp.) lists 1,655 publications of all kinds. F. Lake and H. Wright's *Bibliography of archery* (Manchester: Simon Archery Foundation, University of Manchester, 1974. 518 pp.) lists 5,000 publications on the use of the bow for hunting, war and recreation from the earliest times to the present. Other relevant bibliographies can be traced through works already mentioned, particularly Besterman and its continuations [3] and national bibliographies.

Guides to the Literature

Another form of bibliographical aid – the guide to the literature – goes further than the bibliography in that it introduces and systematizes the literature of a particular subject area, often also including details of organizations in the field. This *Keyguide* is an example of this type of publication for archaeology. Magee's work [455] is a guide to the literature for Mesoamerican archaeology. A brief but useful guide to a closely related field is Stansfield's *Sources of museological literature* [16].

Guides to the literature of some of the other subjects linked to archaeology (as illustrated in Fig. 1) can be traced in Sheehy [15] and Walford [17]. Examples are J. G. Brewer's *The literature of geography: a guide to its organisation and use* (2nd ed. London: Bingley, 1978. 264 pp.) and J. W. Mackay's *Sources of information for the literature of geology* (2nd ed. Edinburgh: Scottish Academic Press for the Geological Society of London. 1974. 64 pp.).

Guides to Reference Material

The standard guides to reference material in all subjects including archaeology are those two major works already mentioned: Sheehy [15] and Walford [17]. Each work has specific 'Archaeology' sections but the section in Sheehy [15] is very short, works on the archaeology of particular areas and countries being listed within the section 'History and Area studies'. The index in each work is an invaluable starting point not only for archaeology but also for related subjects such as anthropology, epigraphy, etc.

Sheehy and Walford are worldwide in scope; other useful guides limit themselves to a particular area: for example, Duignan's *Guide to research and reference works on sub-Saharan Africa* [390]. Mention should also be made of the periodical *Reference Services Review* (Ann Arbor (Michigan): Pierian Press, 1972–. Quarterly) which occasionally includes articles relevant to archaeology: for example, Haas's article on reference sources for anthropology, updated by Perry and Nelson [8], and the same author's article on reference sources for the study of the North American Indian [434].

6 The Literature of Archaeology

The development of archaeology in all its aspects, discussed earlier in Chapter 1, has, not unexpectedly, produced a vast literature of original contributions which continues to grow. Peters (1981) noted that in the 1950s, Export numbers of the *Bookseller* announced a mere eight to ten archaeological books per issue; the Spring 1980 number carried forty-five titles. Hasso (1978) found a growth rate of 6.45% from 1974 to 1976 for entries in selected indexing and abstracting services covering all forms of archaeological publication.

Not surprisingly, this worldwide literature appears in many languages. Hasso (1978), in an examination of nearly 6,000 citations from seven (mainly English language) indexing and abstracting services covering 1,000 journals, found that English was the original language of publication of 50.4% of the citations, with 13.4% in French and 10.3% in German, indicating a significant amount of non-English language material. The literature consulted for *Bulletin Signalétique subfile 525: Préhistoire et Protohistoire* [27] shows the following breakdown: French 35%; English 23%; German 15%; other Romance languages 12%; Slav languages 12% – the French predominance being due to the detailed coverage of French prehistory.

Periodicals

The importance of periodicals in the archaeological literature, mentioned earlier, is clearly evident from the sheer number of titles. There is space in Part II of this *Keyguide* for only a selection of the more significant titles. No absolutely comprehensive list of archaeological periodicals is available but Hasso (1978) produced a list of 1,649 titles by amalgamating lists from several sources. This list included non-archaeological periodicals which sometimes contain articles of archaeological interest: for example, *Nature*, *New Scientist* and *Scientific American*. Lavell (1981) noted that in order to keep up with British archaeology alone, one should be aware of over 250 titles.

Many periodicals basically cover a particular area, although there is a significant number of international and multi-regional titles. Some of the more recent titles are the result of the development of specialized interests discussed in Chapter 1: for example, the *International Journal of Nautical Archaeology and Underwater Exploration* [116], *Post-Medieval Archaeology* [264] and *Industrial Archaeology Review* [115]. Hasso (1978) produced a list of seventeen 'core journals' (those cited four or more times over a certain period by selected abstracting and indexing services), representing only 1.3% of the total number of titles cited, evidence of the wide spread of journal publication. The most frequently cited journal in her survey was *Antiquity* [98], followed by *American Antiquity* [427].

Lists of archaeological periodicals can be found in most of the indexing and abstracting publications and current bibliographies listed in Part II of this *Keyguide*. Two of the most useful sources are *Bulletin Signalétique 525* [27], *526* [28] and *530* [220] and *Archäologische Bibliographie* [24]. The *Ulrich* periodical directories [89] include full, but by no means comprehensive, listings, as does the *History periodicals directory* [88] which takes 'History' in its widest sense and includes archaeological titles. The latter volumes have a clearer layout than the Ulrich publications and also include brief summaries of subject scope for each title. An increasing number of periodicals appear in microform as well as hard copy; these can be traced in *Serials in microform* (Michigan: University Microfilms International), the 1983 edition of which listed over 13,000 titles in all subjects, including fifty-four under 'Archaeology'.

Periodical abbreviations

A common problem with periodicals is abbreviation of titles. Archaeologists frequently need to know how to abbreviate a particular title when preparing work for publication. The CBA publication *Signposts for archaeological publication* [67] includes a standard list of abbreviated titles of selected current periodicals and series (as at June 1979), which follows the American Standard ASA Z.39–5. 1963 which is virtually the same (for archaeological titles) as the British Standard BS 4148: Pt. 1, 1970 and Pt. 2, 1975. Further official advice on how to abbreviate titles is contained in the (American) National Clearinghouse for Periodical Title Word Abbreviations's *Word-abbreviation list* (American National Standards Institute, 1971) which lists words and their corresponding abbreviations. This is supplemented and updated by the *International list of periodical title word abbreviations* published at regular intervals by the International Center for the Registration of Serials in Paris.

Deciphering such abbreviations can be a problem. Many publications adopt their own system of periodical abbreviations, often explained in the publications themselves. Indexing and abstracting works often include useful lists of abbreviations: such a list appeared in the periodical *Acta Praehistorica et Archaeologica* [91], vol. 9/10 (1978/9). General works such as L. G. Alkire's *Periodical title abbreviations* ... (4th ed. Detroit (Michigan): Gale, 1983. 3 vols.) include many archaeological titles, but the most detailed guide is Wellington's work [90] which collects and explains the abbreviations of journals, serials and standard works used most frequently by classicists; archaeological titles are included.

Theses

Dissertation abstracts international [156] lists and summarizes North American doctoral theses on all subjects and those from selected European universities. The theses listed are available in hardback, paperback or microform from the publisher, University Microfilms, who also produces free subject catalogues of doctoral dissertations on selected subjects (for example, anthropology, classical archaeology). The definitive list of North American doctoral theses is given in *Comprehensive dissertation index* [156].

For Britain, the *Index to theses accepted for higher degrees in the universities of Great Britain and Ireland and the Council for National Academic Awards* [157] is the standard work covering all subjects. For archaeological theses in progress in Britain, *Archaeological theses in progress in British universities* [159] includes theses at all levels from BA to PhD. Guides to theses for other parts of the world can be traced in Sheehy [15] and Walford [17]. For classical archaeology, Thompson's works [158] are useful. Theses are also listed in some periodicals; for example, French archaeological theses appear in some issues of *Bulletin de la Société Préhistorique Française* [307], Swedish ones in *Fornvännen* [285], and North American ones in *American Antiquity* [427].

Series

Series are a major feature of archaeological literature. Some comprise mono-graph volumes reporting original research (e.g. *British Archaeological Reports* [43], *CBA Research Reports* [257]); other volumes synthesize current knowledge on a particular area or aspect of archaeology. One of the most extensive of the latter type is *Ancient Peoples and Places* [41], an excellent starting point for the archaeology of many areas and peoples, although some volumes are now dated. Fagan (1982) gave an overview of this series. Other major international series are *Studies in Archaeology* [51], *Studies in Archaeological Science* [210] (both published by Academic Press whose archaeological publications were reviewed by Cordell (1981)), *New Directions in Archaeology* [48], *New Aspects of Antiquity* [47], *Archaeo-logical Guides* [42], *Ancient Civilisations* [40], *New Studies in Archaeology* [49], *New Approaches in Archaeology* [46], and at a more popular level, *The Making of the Past* [44]. On the theme of the protection and preservation of cultural property and the formation of cultural policies, the three UNESCO series, [45], [50], [52], are important.

The above titles are only a selection of the major English language archaeological series. Details of the individual volumes within these and other series (up to 1978) are given in Day [5], with publishers' catalogues giving the latest information.

Surveys

Examples of archaeological syntheses of particular areas are included throughout Part II under 'Surveys'. On a world scale, key examples are Clark [55], Fagan [56], and the massive *Handbuch der Vorgeschichte* [59]. Industrial and maritime archaeology are covered on a world scale by Hudson [57] and Muckelroy [58] respectively. The pace of modern archaeology means that such syntheses soon need updating; the latest works can be traced through the sources described in Chapters 4 and 5.

Textbooks, Handbooks and Manuals

Some textbooks act as a basic introduction to archaeology as a whole, dealing with, for example, its history, its theoretical basis, aims and methods, procedures for surveying and excavating, and methods of analysing finds, of dating, and of interpreting results. Examples of this type are Greene [73] (with valuable guides to further reading at the end of each chapter), Branigan [63], Coles [66], Fagan [69], Hole and Heizer [80], and Sharer and Ashmore [85] (with a Mesoamerican, processual, bias).

There are various handbooks, or manuals, usually aimed at the practising archaeologist and/or student. For techniques of excavation, Alexander [61], Barker [62], Hester, Heizer and Graham [76], Joukowsky [81], and Webster [87] give sound practical advice with differing degrees of emphasis, while Taylor [86] is helpful for fieldwork aspects. Opinions vary on the usefulness of such manuals; it can be argued that a few weeks work with an experienced excavator will prove more valuable than any field manual.

For surveying techniques, Fryer [71] is the best basic manual, while Hogg [79] is more detailed. For preparing drawings of finds for publication, Brodribb [64] is a useful guide, and Maney [82] gives a printer's advice to illustrators on how to produce good drawings for publication. For the use of photography in archaeology, Harp [75] is a detailed practical guide. For techniques of conservation, Plenderleith and Werner [83] is the standard guide.

Dictionaries and Encyclopaedias

The basic function of the dictionary is to explain words – a very necessary role in archaeology, whose technical terms can be intimidating. Explanations in some detail are often required and consequently there may be little difference between an archaeological dictionary and an encyclopaedia, which in theory, at least, goes further in the amount of detail it gives. However, titles can be misleading and both types of work are best considered together. Linguistic dictionaries have a different function and are considered separately.

For explanations of archaeological terms of all kinds – techniques, sites, cultures, periods, personalities, etc. – the most complete work is *The Macmillan dictionary of archaeology* [146] covering all aspects of the subject worldwide. Bray and Trump's *The Penguin dictionary of archaeology* [128] (translated into several languages) covers similar ground but excludes classical, medieval and industrial archaeology. A smaller but excellent work concentrating only on terms and techniques applied to science-based archaeology is Champion's *A dictionary of terms and techniques in archaeology* [130], some entries including one bibliographical reference each. An older work, the *Dictionnaire archéologique des techniques* [134] is useful for its numerous illustrations and drawings. Briefer lists of terms are sometimes produced: for example, Victoria Archaeological Survey's *A glossary of useful archaeological terms* [590].

A major role of the archaeological encyclopaedia is to summarize what is known from archaeology about the human past. The most comprehensive encyclopaedia of prehistory is the massive *Handbuch der Archäologie* [138]. Some encyclopaedias have an alphabetical arrangement of brief entries, as, for example Daniel's *Illustrated encyclopedia of archaeology* [132], or, at a more popular level, Cottrell's *Concise encyclopedia of archaeology* [131]. Other encyclopaedias are arranged differently and discuss major themes in more detail – for example, the *Cambridge encyclopedia of archaeology* [143], invaluable as a guide to current trends in archaeological thinking.

Classical archaeology is covered by the *Oxford classical dictionary* [137], Caffarello's *Dizionario archeologico di antichità classiche* [129], the comprehensive Pauly's *Real-Encyclopädie der classischen Altertumswissenschaft* [142] and the excellent, detailed *Princeton encyclopedia of classical sites* [144], which summarizes work done at each of the approximately 3,000 sites covered. The art history and iconography of the classical world is covered by the *Enciclopedia dell'arte antica: classica e orientale* [126]. Daremberg and Saglio's *Dictionnaire des antiquités grecques et romaines* ... [133] covers all aspects of Greek and Roman life, excluding biography and literature.

For Europe, Filip's *Enzyklopädisches Handbuch zur Ur- und Frühgeschichte Europas* [236] gives factual data on pre- and early history, although some of the information needs updating. For Britain, Adkins and Adkins' *A thesaurus of British archaeology* [269] is an excellent, detailed and up-to-date work. For the Germanic world, the *Reallexikon der germanischen Altertumskunde* [322] is a very detailed encyclopaedia covering archaeology and related fields.

For the Near East, the *Reallexikon der Assyriologie und vorderasiatischen Archäologie* [529] is a scholarly encyclopaedia on Assyriology and Near Eastern archaeology. For Israel, Avi-Yonah's *Encyclopedia of archaeological excavations in the Holy Land* [526] gives a detailed, comprehensive summary. Negev's *Archaeological encyclopedia of the Holy Land* [528] describes excavations done at sites named in the Bible. The

Lexikon der Ägyptologie [411] is a scholarly, detailed encyclopaedia on Egyptology.

Archaeological literature, like that of other subjects, shows an increasing tendency to use abbreviations and acronyms rather than full names or titles. Of the several general works which can help to decipher these, the most comprehensive is *Acronyms, initialisms, and abbreviations dictionary*, with its companion volume *Reverse acronyms, initialisms and abbreviations dictionary*, and its supplements *New acronyms, initialisms and abbreviations* (Detroit: Gale); the 8th edition (1983–4) included over 250,000 terms of all kinds covering all subjects.

Linguistic Dictionaries

There are several linguistic dictionaries giving archaeological terms in various languages; some of these are older works which do not give an up-to-date picture of the subject. Réau's *Dictionnaire polyglotte des termes d'art et d'archéologie* [153] covers many languages but is somewhat old-fashioned conceptually. German terminology is covered in Apelt's *Deutsch–englisches Wörterbuch für Kunstgeschichte und Archäologie* [147]. Marois's *English–French, French–English vocabulary of prehistoric archaeology* [150] gives an elementary list of sample terms, with a bias towards stone tools. Other dictionaries linking terms in various languages are listed in Part II [147–155].

In this context, it might be emphasized that Bray and Trump's *The Penguin dictionary of archaeology* [128] has been translated into several languages.

Archaeological Atlases

Archaeological atlases contain maps (and often plans, drawings, etc.) pinpointing significant sites on a world or area basis. Generally regarded as the best in the field is Whitehouse and Whitehouse's *Archaeological atlas of the world* [145] which includes about 5,000 pre- and protohistoric sites. Hawkes's *The atlas of early man* [140] is designed to answer the question 'what happened at the same time as what?'. Hawkes's *Atlas of ancient archaeology* [139] concentrates more on individual sites, as does Finley's *Atlas of classical archaeology* [135].

The proportion of map material in these atlases varies considerably. Hammond's excellent *Atlas of the Greek and Roman world in antiquity* [136] consists almost entirely of maps and plans, but many such works contain additional material; they can include, for example, helpful general introductions to archaeology (Branigan [127]), glossaries (Finley [135], Hawkes [139]), chronological tables (Finley [135], Baines and Málek [410]), lists of museums (Baines and Málek [410]); they may be in the nature of a general survey (Muckelroy [141], Beek [504]); or they may put the emphasis on the general environment of the area (Baly and Tushingham [527]). Information on the sites included will need to be updated by current publications.

References

Cordell, L. S. 1981. Academic Press publications in archaeology. *American Antiquity*, 46, 446–54.

Fagan, B. M. 1982. A hundred volumes of 'A.P. & P.' *Antiquity*, 66:216, 42–5.

Hasso, M. H. 1978. *A bibliometric study of the literature of archaeology*. M.Phil. Thesis, City University (England). 193 pp. + refs.

Lavell, C. 1981. Publication: an obligation: archaeological documentation in Britain today. *Bulletin of the Institute of Archaeology, University of London*, 18, 91–125.

Peters, E. 1981. Archaeology and publishing. In J. D. Evans, B. Cunliffe, and C. Renfrew (eds.), *Antiquity and man: essays in honour of Glyn Daniel*, pp. 195–202. London: Thames and Hudson.

7 Other sources of information

Archaeologists frequently need access to other more specialized kinds of information, some of which are in non-book form. Some of the works discussed earlier (e.g. Day [5]) include examples of these types. This final chapter describes other major sources. It should be noted that, generally speaking, international and British examples are given to illustrate particular types of sources; for other parts of the world, appropriate organizations in Part III should be consulted.

'Grey' Literature

'Grey' literature is the term given to semi-published literature such as reports, theses and translations, which may be hard to identify and locate. Such literature is only partially covered by works discussed earlier. British 'grey' literature is conveniently listed, without annotation, in the British Library Lending Division's publication *British reports, translations and theses received by the British Library Lending Division* (1981–), formerly known as *BLLD Announcement Bulletin*. This lists British report literature and translations produced by British government organizations, industry, universities and learned institutions, and most doctoral theses accepted at British universities during and after 1970. It also covers reports and unpublished translations from the Republic of Ireland and selected British official publications of a report nature that are not published by HMSO. Some archaeology is included.

Government Publications

As noted in Chapter 1, much archaeological material is issued by national governments and their departments. Some of the periodicals listed in Part II are published by the National Board of Antiquities (or its equivalent) of a particular country. In Britain, for example, the Department of the Environment publishes a series of *Archaeological Reports* on particular sites, the *Annual Reports* of the Ancient Monuments Boards for England, Scotland, and Wales, and a series of official guides to ancient monuments and historic buildings. These publications appear in the Department of Environment's *Annual list of publications*, which also includes Statutory Instruments, Departmental Circulars and Press Notices relating to British archaeology. Those publications relating to ancient monuments and historic buildings and obtainable from HMSO are listed in HMSO Sectional List 27 *Ancient Monuments and Historic Buildings* which is regularly updated and includes the publications of the Royal Commissions on the Ancient and Historical Monuments of England, Scotland and Wales; non-HMSO publications are obtainable from the relevant issuing body listed in the Department of the Environment's *Annual list of publications*.

Details of government publications in archaeology in other parts of the world are probably best obtained through the institutions listed in Part III of this *Keyguide*. General information on certain countries can be found in the series *Guides to Official Publications*, published by Pergamon Press.

Legislation on Cultural Property

National legislation on a world scale governing the discovery, ownership, circulation and sale of cultural property was summarized in B. Burnham's *The protection of cultural property: handbook of national legislation* (Paris: International Council of Museums, 1974. 203 pp.). Such legislation varies, often considerably, from country to country, and also changes from time to time. There is a general trend towards expansion of existing legislation, with the result that a greater number of sites can be protected and new categories of remains included. The European Science Foundation has stated basic principles for national legislation on archaeology (*Helinium* [313], 23 (1983), 205–8). On one aspect – the use of metal detectors – the Council of Europe's *Report on metal detectors and archaeology* (Document 4741, 9 June 1981) called for member countries to take steps to control the use of these machines.

UNESCO is currently issuing a series of volumes entitled *La protection du patrimoine culturel mobilier: recueil de textes législatifs* (Paris: UNESCO, 1979–), covering national legislation. A complete archive of cultural property legislation is held on microfiche at the UNESCO–ICOM Documentation Centre in Paris [600]. The latter acts as a reference centre for those seeking advice on the legal and professional aspects of the import, export and transfer of ownership of cultural property. Its periodical *ICOM News* publishes notices of thefts, articles on destruction of cultural property and professional statements and editorials on the ethics of acquisition.

Such legislation can also be found in some monographs: for example, C. R.

McGimsey's *Public archeology* (New York and London: Seminar Press, 1972) includes the texts of United States federal laws concerning archaeological preservation and the legislative support enjoyed by archaeology in each state; Baker [247] outlines existing British laws relating to monuments, wrecks, objects, buildings and historic areas.

Maps and Atlases

Useful practical advice on tracing maps and atlases and keeping up to date with current cartographic publication is given in the chapter on cartobibliography in J. G. Brewer's *The literature of geography: a guide to its organisation and use* (2nd ed. London: Bingley, 1978). A list of selected important map collections is given in Ristow's *World directory of map collections* [183].

For maps and atlases currently available, Winch's *International maps and atlases in print* [184] is the most useful general source, including over 8,000 entries. It includes some archaeological maps and atlases in a 'Historical' section within particular areas of the world: e.g. *Tabula Imperii Romani* (*Map of the Roman Empire*); for Great Britain, the historical and archaeological maps *Southern Britain in the Iron Age, Ancient Britain, Roman Britain, Britain in the Dark Ages, Britain before the Norman Conquest* (AD 871–1066), *Monastic Britain, Hadrian's Wall* and the *Antonine Wall* are listed. However, there are other archaeological maps not listed in Winch [184], e.g. the multi-fascicled *Carte archéologique de la Gaule romaine* (Paris: Centre National de la Recherche Scientifique, 1931–), and appropriate organizations listed in Part III should be consulted for more information.

Gazetteers of Sites

There are gazetteers acting as guides to material discovered, giving such information as the nature of the material, its provenance and present whereabouts. These are particularly valuable for unpublished material. For Britain, for example, there is D. A. Roe's *A gazetteer of British Lower and Middle Palaeolithic sites* (London: CBA Research Report no. 8, 1968), J. J. Wymer's *Gazetteer of Mesolithic sites in England and Wales* and C. J. Bonsall's *Gazetteer of Upper Palaeolithic sites in England and Wales* (the latter two contained in CBA Research Report no. 20, 1977).

Radiocarbon Dates

Results of dating tests carried out in laboratories on archaeological material are published in the periodical *Radiocarbon* [207]. Those relating to Great Britain and Ireland are regularly abstracted from *Radiocarbon* and issued in loose-leaf form as the *Archaeological site index to radiocarbon dates for Great Britain and Ireland* (first published by the CBA in 1971 as a supplement to *British Archaeological Abstracts* [245] and regularly updated since; eventually it will be available in computerized form from AERE Harwell Low Level Measurements Laboratory). There is a similar publication — *Catálogo de Yacimientos arqueológicos con datación mediante carbono-14 de la península ibérica e islas Baleares y Canarias* (Madrid; Instituto Español de Prehistoria, 1978). *The Bulletin de la Société Préhistorique Française* [307] sometimes includes radiocarbon lists. Polach's bibliography *First 20 years of radiocarbon dating: an annotated bibliography 1948–1968* [190] was mentioned in Chapter 5.

Air Photographs

Some countries maintain their own catalogues of air photographs. For Britain, the Air Photographs Unit of the National Monuments Record of the Royal Commission on Historical Monuments (England) has over half a million air photographs of archaeological sites. For details of collections of air photographs and other aspects of aerial archaeology, the periodical *Aerial Archaeology: the Journal for Air Photography and Archaeology* [94] is a good source (concentrating mainly on the UK but also covering some other parts of the world), as is its publisher, Aerial Archaeology Publications [595].

Audio-Visual Aids: pictures, photographs, slides, films, etc.

Many archaeological publications naturally include visual material such as photographs, illustrations, diagrams, etc. and this is noted in Part II only when it is a particularly striking feature – as, for example, in the series *The Making of the Past* [44], Adkins and Adkins's *A thesaurus of British archaeology* [269], and the periodical *Archéologia* [106].

For pictures in general relating to archaeology – photographs, drawings, slides, etc. – Evans and Evans' *Picture researcher's handbook* [182] indicates some useful sources worldwide. The CBA's *Archaeological resources handbook for teachers* [246] includes a section on audio-visual aids: a detailed annotated listing of films, slides and filmstrips on archaeology worldwide. For audio-visual aids in higher education, the two publications of the British Universities Film and Video Council, [180], [181], together form a single file of about 5,000 audio-visual items on all subjects including archaeology. For publications and audio-visual materials available from museums, the directory *World museum publications* [185] includes visual and audio-visual materials along with books; for Great Britain and Ireland, *The bibliography of museum and art gallery publications and audio-visual aids in Great Britain and Ireland* [273] plays a similar role.

For conservation of audio-visual aids, *Art and Archaeology Technical Abstracts* [191] regularly includes sections entitled 'Photographs and other audio-visual materials' and 'Information sources (including motion pictures and slides)'; the supplement to vol. 12(1) (Summer 1975, pp. 181–295) of *AATA* comprised an annotated list of motion pictures concerning techniques, conservation, display, and analysis of works of art and archaeology.

PART II

Bibliographical Listing
of Sources of Information

Bibliographical Listing
of Sources of Information

General Archaeology: worldwide and multi-regional

General bibliographical guides

1 **Arntzen, E.** and **Rainwater, R.** *Guide to the literature of art history.* Chicago:
American Library Association; London: Art Book Company, 1980. 616 pp.
Almost 4,000 entries, nearly all annotated in detail, with emphasis on recent
worldwide material in Western languages. Archaeology is treated selectively,
coverage being limited to basic reference literature and general works of an art
historical nature. Major subjects included are painting, sculpture, architecture,
prints, drawings, photography and the decorative arts. Author–title index;
subject index.

2 **Beaudiquez, M.** *Les Services bibliographiques dans le monde 1975–1979.* Paris:
UNESCO, 1983. 488 pp. + 1980 supplement. (Documentation, libraries and
archives: bibliographies and reference works, 7.) (English ed. in preparation.)
Gives details of the bibliographical services of 121 countries worldwide. The 1980
supplement (114 pp. 1982) published as a supplement to the UNESCO publication *General Information Programme: Unisist Newsletter*, 10:1 (1982).

3 **Besterman, T.** *A world bibliography of bibliographies and of bibliographical
catalogues, calendars, abstracts, digests, indexes, and the like.* 4th rev. ed. Lausanne:
Societas Bibliographica. 1965–66. 5 vols.
An international listing of separately published bibliographies, without annotation, arranged by subject with an author index. Entries under 'Archaeology,
antiquities' occupy 12 pp. (24 columns), of which 8 pp. (15 columns) are devoted
to a country arrangement. Useful starting point for older (pre-1963) bibliographies.
   Supplemented by Toomey, A. F. *A world bibliography of bibliographies,
1964–1974: a list of works represented by Library of Congress printed catalog cards*

(Totowa (New Jersey): Rowman and Littlefield, 1977, 2 vols.) which follows in general Besterman's principles; by *Bibliographic Index* (New York: Wilson, 1937–. Three times a year, cumulating annually. Delay: *c*. one to two years) which lists alphabetically both bibliographies published separately and those included in books, certain periodicals and pamphlets (only bibliographies with fifty or more citations are listed), concentrating on titles in the Germanic and Romance languages; and by *Bibliographische Berichte/Bibliographical Bulletin* (Frankfurt: Klostermann, 1959–. Irreg.), a similar work but with the emphasis on material in East European languages.

4 *COWA surveys and bibliographies.* Editor-in-chief: D. F. Brown. Cambridge (Mass.): Council for Old World Archaeology, 1957–71 (series 1–4).
Each series comprised twenty-two area reports on Old World archaeology from Palaeolithic to recent historical times as seen from an American viewpoint. Areas 1–8 covered Europe; 9–14 Africa; 15–20 Asia; 21 Pacific Islands; 22 Australia. Each area report covered the last two to three years of archaeological activity in the area and consisted of a survey of current work and an annotated bibliography of the more important books and articles. Within each geographical division the entries were divided alphabetically into smaller units including both actual countries, e.g. Afghanistan, and civilizations, e.g. Indus. Each series contained over 4,000 annotated bibliographic items.
   Preceded by Movius, H. L. *Recent publications in Old World archaeology* (Cambridge (Mass.): Peabody Museum, 1948–55, nos. 1–8).

5 Day, A. E. *Archaeology: a reference handbook.* London: Bingley, 1978. 319 pp.
Detailed guide to all aspects of British archaeology – its organization, forms of literature and the bibliographies, etc. that control them, and biographies of eminent antiquarians and archaeologists. Industrial and nautical archaeology are included, and also American and biblical archaeology but the latter two in less detail. Comprises 639 entries for titles of books, articles and periodicals, names of organizations, antiquarians, archaeologists, publishers and series – all in a single alphabetical sequence. Index of titles and authors. No subject approach.

6 Deutsches Archäologisches Institut. *Kataloge der Bibliothek des Deutschen Archäologischen Instituts.* Boston (Mass.): Hall, 1969. 13 vols.
Autoren- und Periodica Kataloge (7 vols.). *Systematischer Katalog* (3 vols.) classifies monographs, periodical and Festschriften articles and special publications into *c*. 1,200 categories beginning with 1956 and continuing an earlier classified catalogue. *Zeitschriften-Autorenkatalog* (3 vols.) lists authors of articles in periodicals and Festschriften on classical archaeology and epigraphy published from 1956 onwards.
   Reproduction of the catalogue cards of one of the world's strongest archaeological libraries. Some 91,000 vols. cover all areas of European and Near Eastern archaeology and philology, from the prehistoric to the Byzantine period.

7 Freedman, R. L. (compiler). *Human food uses: a cross-cultural, comprehensive annotated bibliography.* Westport (Connecticut); London: Greenwood Press, 1981. 589 pp.

Has 9,097 entries, some annotated, of publications of all kinds (over 1,000 series scanned) on various aspects of food in human culture. Arranged alphabetically by author. Includes much archaeological material; detailed key word index lists 343 entries under 'Archeology'.

8 Haas, M. L. Anthropology: a guide to basic sources. *Reference Services Review*, 5:4 (1977), 45–51. Bibliography: pp. 49–51 (73 items).
Lists and describes English language reference works of all types in anthropology as a whole (including archaeology). Updated by Perry, P. J. and Nelson, D. R.: Anthropology: Haas revisited (*Reference Services Review*, 11:3 (1983), 67–70. Bibliography: pp. 69–70 (21 items)).

9 Heizer, R. F. *Archaeology: a bibliographical guide to the basic literature.* New York; London: Garland, 1980. 445 pp. (see also [435])
Unannotated list of 4,818 references on all aspects of archaeology worldwide but with emphasis on the New World and English-language publications. A selective guide to basic sources, some of which are now rather dated. Arranged in five sections: nature and purpose of archaeology; history of archaeology; the work of the archaeologist (the bulk of the book); archaeology as a profession; sources of primary data (i.e. bibliographies, dictionaries and atlases). Author index, but no subject index.

10 Koch, J. E. *Industrial archaeology: a selected bibliography.* Chicago: Council of Planning Librarians, 1977. 17 pp. (Exchange Bibliography, 1382.)
About 200 references, with a few annotations, covering mainly English-language publications of all kinds on industrial archaeology worldwide but with emphasis on the United Kingdom and North America. Arranged alphabetically by author. No index.

11 Metropolitan Museum of Art, New York. *Library catalog of the Metropolitan Museum of Art, New York.* 2nd rev. ed. Boston (Mass.): Hall, 1980. 48 vols.
Catalogue of one of the world's leading art research libraries. Material covers *c.* 5,000 years of art and archaeology from ancient Egypt to the present. Some 220,000 vols. cover archaeology, art history, painting, sculpture, decorative arts, arms and armour, and architecture. A dictionary catalogue of authors, titles and subjects.

12 Nelson, B. R. *A guide to published library catalogs.* Metuchen (New Jersey); London: Scarecrow, 1982. 358 pp.
Describes in some detail 429 multi-volume catalogues of significant collections in all subjects. Arranged in broad subject groups. Subject index includes twenty-nine entries under 'Archaeology', some of these libraries having material in a range of subjects including archaeology. Some entries include a brief history of the library concerned. Subject index; index of libraries.

13 Peabody Museum of Archaeology and Ethnology, Harvard University. *Author and subject catalogs of the library.* Boston (Mass.): Hall, 1963–. 54 vols. + supplements.

Photoreproduction of the catalogue cards from this outstanding collection (over 100,000 vols. in many languages) covering the whole world with emphasis on American archaeology. Believed to be the strongest collection in the USA for prehistoric archaeology generally, anthropology and ethnology. Entries for journal articles (some in Slavic languages), contributions to Festschriften, and proceedings of congresses are included, as well as books, etc.

14 Rounds, D. *Articles on antiquity in Festschriften: the ancient Near East, the Old Testament, Greece, Rome, Roman law, Byzantium: an index.* Cambridge (Mass.): Harvard University Press, 1962. 579 pp.

An index of *c.* 10,000 Festschriften – names of scholars and institutions honoured, names of authors of articles, all significant words in the titles of the articles – arranged in a single alphabetical sequence with numerous cross-references. Covers all periods, except the New Testament period, from the Neolithic onwards.

15 Sheehy, E. P. *Guide to reference books.* 9th ed. Chicago: American Library Association, 1976. 1,033 pp. 1980 supplement, 314 pp.; 2nd supplement, 1982, 252 pp.

International in scope, but with a US slant, covering all types of reference works in all subjects. Classified arrangement, with annotation. Arrangement of the supplements corresponds to that of the main work. Includes a general 'Archaeology and prehistory' section (2 pp.); works on the archaeology of a particular country are listed separately under that country within 'History and Area studies'. The 'Anthropology and Ethnology' section includes some archaeological material. Index comprises author and subject entries and most title entries. The American equivalent of 'Walford' [17].

16 Stansfield, G. *Sources of museological literature.* 2nd rev. ed. London: Museums Association, 1976. 5 pp. (Museums Association Information Sheet.)

Lists the international and national organizations which are mainly concerned with museology and which are the most important publishers of museological literature, together with a selection of their publications. Also covers the most useful indexes, abstracts and bibliographies in the field, and outlines other sources of information. No index.

17 Walford, A. J. (ed.). *Guide to reference material. Vol. 2: Social and historical sciences, philosophy and religion.* 4th ed. London: Library Association, 1982. 822 pp.

International in scope, with emphasis on works published in Britain, covering all types of reference works in all subjects. Classified arrangement, with annotation. The 'Archaeology' section covers 24 pp., arranged first by form (bibliographies, manuals, etc.) then by area. Other archaeological material can be found in the 'Area studies', 'History' and 'Ancient history' sections, and also in the 'Anthropology' section of vol. 1: *Science and Technology.* Author/title/subject index. The British equivalent of 'Sheehy' [15].

Abstracting, indexing, current awareness services

18 *Abstracts in Anthropology.* Farmingdale (New York): Baywood, 1970–. Quarterly.
Worldwide coverage, with emphasis on North America. Archaeology (arranged by regions) is covered along with cultural and physical anthropology, and linguistics. Some 350 periodicals are indexed. Author index; subject index. Delay: one to two years.

19 *Abstracts in German Anthropology.* Göttingen (Association for International Scientific Communication): Edition Herodot, 1980–. Twice a year.
Abstracts of anthropological publications of all kinds in German on a worldwide basis from *c.* sixty periodicals. A general section is followed by sections on archaeology, physical anthropology, regional studies, and films. Author index; subject index. Delay: one to two years.

20 *L'Année Philologique: bibliographie critique et analytique de l'antiquité gréco-latine.*
Paris: Société d'Édition 'Les Belles Lettres', 1924/26– (publ. 1928–). Annual.
Comprehensive annotated listing of publications of all kinds on all aspects of Greek and Roman antiquity from prehistoric to medieval times. Consists of an (ancient) author section and a subject section. Part IV of the subject section 'Antiquités', the most valuable for archaeologists, is arranged by area. Over 1,000 periodicals are consulted. Index of collections; index of ancient authors; geographical index; index of humanists; index of modern authors. Delay: at least two years.
Continues Marouzeau, J. *Dix années de bibliographie classique: bibliographie critique et analytique de l'antiquité gréco-latine pour la période 1914–1924.* (Paris: Société d'Édition 'Les Belles Lettres', 1927–8. 2 vols. 1: *Auteurs et textes*; 2: *Matières et disciplines.* (Collection de bibliographie classique)), which itself continues Lambrino, S. *Bibliographie de l'antiquité classique 1896–1914* (Paris: Société d'Édition 'Les Belles Lettres', 1951. 761 pp. 1 vol. only, arranged alphabetically by ancient authors. (Collection de bibliographie classique)).

21 *Anthropological Index to Current Periodicals in the Museum of Mankind Library (incorporating the former Royal Anthropological Institute Library).* London: Royal Anthropological Institute of Great Britain and Ireland, 1963–. Quarterly.
Worldwide coverage of archaeology, ethnomusicology, physical anthropology, ethnography, linguistics, cultural anthropology, human biology. *c.* 8,000 articles a year from *c.* 600 periodicals, many of them archaeological. Main arrangement is geographical. Annual author index. Cumulative author index to vols. 1–9 (1963–71) and subject index to vols. 1–5 (1963–7) are available on cards for reference in the Museum of Mankind Library, 6 Burlington Gardens, London W1X 2EX. Delay: most items published within last few months.

22 *Anthropological Literature: an Index to Periodical Articles and Essays.* Pleasantville (New York): Redgrave, 1979–. Quarterly.
Index to articles in over 1,000 periodicals and other publications received by the Tozzer Library, Peabody Museum of Archaeology and Ethnology, Harvard

University. Arranged in five sections: cultural/social; archaeology; biological/ physical; linguistics; general method/theory. Covers archaeology up to Roman times for relevant parts of the world except for the Near East for which articles up to Islamic times are included. Author index; archaeological site and culture index; ethnic and linguistic group index; geographic index. Delay: one to two years. Its arrangement and lack of detailed subject index make it less useful than *Anthropological Index* [21].

23 *Antiquaries Journal: Journal of the Society of Antiquaries of London.* Neasden (England): (Society of Antiquaries of London) Oxford University Press, 1921–. Twice a year. En. (see also [226])
Includes two valuable bibliographical sections: 'List of accessions' to the Society's library, worldwide, arranged by alphabetical subject headings; and 'Periodical literature', a listing of the contents of British and non-British journals.

24 *Archäologische Bibliographie. Beilage zum Jahrbuch des Deutschen Archäologischen Instituts.* Berlin: de Gruyter, 1913–. (publ. 1914–). Annual.
Comprehensive unannotated bibliography of books and articles, international in scope. Covers the whole Mediterranean from prehistory to late antiquity, with the emphasis on classical archaeology. Some 1,000 periodicals are scanned. Arranged in three main sections: general; Greek and Roman culture; other cultures. Author index; subject index; book review index; place index. Delay: one to two years. The best current bibliography for classical archaeology.
　　Preceded by the bibliographies in *Jahrbuch des Deutschen Archäologischen Instituts* (1886–88) and in *Archäologischer Anzeiger* (1889–1912).

25 *Art Index.* New York: H. W. Wilson, 1929– (publ. 1930–). Quarterly with annual cumulations.
Worldwide coverage of serial literature on all aspects of art including archaeology, art history and museology. Some 200 serials are indexed, including several leading archaeological ones. Arranged in a single alphabetical author/subject sequence, with full bibliographical details. Includes book reviews, listed separately. Delay: usually three to six months.

26 *Bulletin de la Société Préhistorique Française.* Paris: Société Préhistorique Française, 1904–. Monthly. Fr. In two sections: *Comptes rendus des séances mensuelles: Études et travaux.* (see also [292] and [307])
Includes regular bibliographies comprising the Society's library's intake of materials.

27 *Bulletin Signalétique 525: Préhistoire et Protohistoire.* Paris: Centre National de la Recherche Scientifique, 1970–. Quarterly with annual cumulative index.
List of articles, most with abstracts, covering world prehistory from the origins of man to the appearance of writing. Coverage of France and adjacent countries is especially detailed. Some 450 archaeological and *c.* 200 multi-disciplinary journals are covered. Arranged by general sections, then geographically. Index of cultures; index of geographical areas; index of sites and regions; subject index; author index. Delay: most items published within last two years. A product from

the data base FRANCIS (subfile 525) which is searchable online through QUESTEL/TÉLÉSYSTÈMES.

28 *Bulletin Signalétique 526: Art et Archéologie.* Paris: Centre National de la Recherche Scientifique, 1970–. Quarterly with annual cumulative index.
List of articles, most with abstracts, on the ancient civilizations of the Near East, Asia, America, and Islam. Some 400 archaeological and *c.* 200 multi-disciplinary journals are covered. Arranged by general sections, then geographically. Subject index; author index. Delay: most items published within last two years. A product from the data base FRANCIS (subfile 526) which is searchable online through QUESTEL/TÉLÉSYSTÈMES.

29 Canadian Museums Association. *Bibliography: an extensive listing of published material on the subjects of museology, museography and museum and art gallery administration.* [Ottawa]: Canadian Museums Association, 1976–. Loose-leaf insertions.
Attempts to be comprehensive, listing all major source materials while remaining currently relevant. Arranged in twenty-eight subject categories, of which archaeology is one. Entries listed alphabetically by author or title within each category.

30 *Fasti Archaeologici: Annual Bulletin of Classical Archaeology.* Florence: (International Association for Classical Archaeology) Sansoni, 1946– (publ. 1948–.) Annual.
Unannotated list of all types of publications on classical archaeology from prehistory to late antiquity. About 150 periodicals are scanned. A general section precedes geographical subdivisions. Indexes: authors, ancient and modern; geographical names; subjects; lexicalia (words in ancient languages, the meaning of which is discussed in the text); literary and epigraphic sources. Delay: six to seven years.

31 *Germania: Anzeiger der Römisch-Germanischen Kommission des Deutschen Archäologischen Instituts.* Berlin: de Gruyter, 1917–. Annual De. Cumulative index: vols.1–36 (1917–58). (see also [312])
Includes a list of additions to the library of the Römisch-Germanische Kommission.

32 *Historical Metallurgy: Journal of the Historical Metallurgy Society.* Coleford (England): Historical Metallurgy Society Ltd, 1963–. Twice a year. En. Cumulative index: vols. 1–7 (1963–73). (see also [114])
Includes abstracts of publications on historical metallurgy, worldwide.

33 *Index Islamicus 1906–1955: a catalogue of articles on Islamic subjects in periodicals and other collective publications.* Compiled by J. D. Pearson and J. F. Ashton. Cambridge (England): Heffer, 1958. 897 pp. + supplements 1956–60, 1961–65, 1966–70, 1971–75.
Unannotated listing of articles, Festschriften and other collective works covering the whole field of Islamic studies (except for pure science and technology) on a world scale from the 7th century AD to the present. Restricted to material in

Western languages, including Russian. Nearly 1,000 periodicals, including a wide range of archaeological ones, are currently covered. Classified arrangement. Author index.

Continued by *Quarterly Index Islamicus* (London: Mansell, 1977–. Quarterly), which follows the same principles but has no author index (delay: one to three years).

Index Islamicus 1976–1980. Part 1, *Articles*. Compiled by J. D. Pearson. Part 2, *Monographs*. Compiled by J. D. Pearson and W. Behn. London: Mansell, 1983. Total 944 pp.

A five-year cumulation, with additional entries, of the *Quarterly Index Islamicus* mentioned in the previous entry. Author index.

34 *International Bibliography of Social and Cultural Anthropology/Bibliographie Internationale d'Anthropologie Sociale et Culturelle*. London and New York: Tavistock, 1955– (publ. 1958–). Annual. (International Bibliography of the Social Sciences.)

Selective, unannotated listing of scientific publications in anthropology worldwide. Some 700 periodicals are consulted. Arranged by type of anthropology. The 'Archaeology' section (B51) is small (*c*. 300–400 items in each vol.) and is arranged by general works, then geographically. Author index; subject index (Fr. and En.). Delay: twelve to thirty months.

35 *Numismatic Literature*. New York: American Numismatic Society, 1947–. Twice a year.

Abstracts of articles on coins from earliest to modern times, worldwide. Includes coin reports from excavations. General sections are followed by a geographical arrangement. Nearly 1,000 periodicals are scanned. Subject index; author index. Delay: one to two years.

36 *Recently Published Articles*. Washington: American Historical Association, 1976–. Three times a year.

The most current and comprehensive bibliography of periodical literature covering all periods and fields of history worldwide. Over 3,000 periodicals are scanned and over 15,000 references a year are listed, without annotation. Some archaeology in the 'Ancient' and 'Medieval' sections which precede the main geographical arrangements. No indexes. Delay: most items published within last year. Formerly (1895–1975) a section of the periodical *American Historical Review*.

37 *Sprawozdania Archeologiczne*. Warsaw: (Polska Akademia Nauk, Instytut Historii Kultury Materialnej) Ossolineum, Publishing House of the Polish Academy of Sciences, 1955–. Irreg. Pl. (summaries and contents page in En.) (see also [365])

Includes 'Archaeological abstracts – the Neolithic of East-Central Europe' (in En., covering Bulgaria, Czechoslovakia, Hungary, Poland, Romania, USSR, Yugoslavia).

38 *Technology and Culture: the International Quarterly of the Society for the History of Technology.* Chicago: (Society for the History of Technology) University of Chicago Press, 1960–. Quarterly. (see also [123])
The second part each year includes a current bibliography on the history of technology covering a wide range of subjects from ceramic technology to marine transportation.

39 *UNESCO List of Documents and Publications.* Paris: UNESCO, 1972– (publ. 1973–). Quarterly with annual cumulations. Five-year cumulation (1972–76) publ. 1979.
Comprehensive bibliography of everything published recently by UNESCO. Each issue consists of two parts – Part 1: a listing in number order, giving a full bibliographic description for each item; Part II: subject index, personal author index, meeting and corporate body index, title and series index. Delay: only a few months. A good deal of archaeological material is included.

Continues *Bibliography of publications issued by UNESCO or under its auspices; the first twenty-five years: 1946–1971* (Paris: UNESCO, 1973. 385 pp.) which has a classified arrangement with 'Archaeology. Antiquities. Manuscripts' at 930.26, and title and author indexes.

Series

40 *Ancient Civilisations* (formerly: *Archaeologia Mundi*). Geneva: Nagel, 1961–. Irreg. En.
Series covering many parts of the world, each volume sumptuously illustrated. Eighteen vols. published by 1983.

41 *Ancient Peoples and Places.* London: Thames and Hudson, 1956–. Irreg. En.
An extensive series with 101 vols. published by 1983. Vols. summarize in an authoritative and readable way archaeological knowledge on an ancient people (e.g. the Scythians, the Phoenicians, etc.), an ancient place (e.g. Mexico, Babylon, etc.) or other topics (e.g. writing, food in antiquity, etc.).

42 *Archaeological Guides.* London: Faber and Faber, 1967–. Irreg. En.
Series of guides to areas rich in archaeological remains. Each vol. includes list of sites to be visited. Particularly useful for the traveller. Nine titles published by 1983.

43 *British Archaeological Reports.* Oxford: British Archaeological Reports, 1974–. Irreg. En. (occasionally Fr. De.).
The British series (1974–) covers all aspects of British archaeology; the International (formerly Supplementary) series (1978–) covers all aspects of world archaeology and related subjects. Most of the titles are either theses or excavation reports. Over 200 titles by 1983.

44 *The Making of the Past.* Oxford: Elsevier-Phaidon, 1975–. Irreg. En.
A more popular series, richly illustrated, aimed basically at the layman. Each volume covers a specific period and region of the world. Nine titles published by 1983.

45 *Museums and Monuments*. Paris: UNESCO, 1952–. Irreg. En. Fr. Es.
Series concerned with the protection and preservation of monuments and works of art. Some vols. deal with particular places (e.g. Cuzco (vol. 3), Lebanon (vol. 6), Syria (vol. 7)); others cover a general topic (e.g. underwater archaeology (vol. 13), preserving and restoring monuments and historic buildings (vol. 14)).

46 *New Approaches in Archaeology* (formerly: *Perspectives in Archaeology*).
   London: Duckworth, 1978–. Irreg. En.
Applies modern archaeological thinking to specific problems. Five titles published by 1983.

47 *New Aspects of Antiquity*. London: Thames and Hudson, 1967–. Irreg. En.
Series of monographs of archaeologists describing their own recent work. Much of the material is new in book form. Sixteen titles published by 1983.

48 *New Directions in Archaeology*. Cambridge (England): Cambridge University Press, 1978–. Irreg. En.
Examines the interrelationships of archaeology in different parts of the world in terms of common sets of ideas, models of explanation and problems of interpretation and technique. Seven titles published by 1983.

49 *New Studies in Archaeology*. Cambridge (England): Cambridge University Press, 1976–. Irreg. En.
Series covering many different aspects of archaeology, with nine titles published by 1983.

50 *Studies and Documents on Cultural Policies*. Paris: UNESCO, 1970–. Irreg. En. Fr. Es.
Each vol. shows how cultural policies are planned and implemented in various individual Member States of UNESCO. Useful for archaeologists concerned with the organization of cultural affairs in different countries.

51 *Studies in Archaeology*. New York and London: Academic Press, 1972–. Irreg. En.
Wide-ranging series, with sixty-four titles published by 1983.

52 *Technical Handbooks for Museums and Monuments*. Paris: UNESCO, 1977–. Irreg. En. Fr. Es.
A series giving practical and technical guidance on the protection of cultural property. Each vol. includes a select bibliog. Covers such topics as the guarding of cultural property, museum collection storage, procedures and conservation standards for museum collections in transit and on exhibition, protection of the underwater heritage (a basic text, produced by five authors, international in scope and covering all periods. In four parts: archaeology in an underwater environment; conservation of the underwater heritage (includes an Appendix listing the main laboratories specializing in the conservation of underwater archaeological material); museological problems associated with the underwater heritage (includes an Appendix listing the best-known museums dealing with the

underwater heritage); law and the underwater heritage; and a guide for the collection of traditional musical instruments.

Surveys

53 *Aufstieg und Niedergang der Römischen Welt: Geschichte und Kultur Roms im Spiegel der neueren Forschung.* Berlin: de Gruyter. Teil 1: *Von den Anfängen Roms bis zum Ausgang der Republik*; ed. by H. Temporini. Bands 1–4. 1972–3. Teil 2: *Principat*; ed. by H. Temporini and W. Haase. Bands 1– 1974–.
Detailed history of the Roman world, including much archaeology.

54 *Cambridge Ancient History.* London: Cambridge University Press.
Vol. 1(1): *Prolegomena and prehistory.* 3rd ed. 1970; ed. by I. E. S. Edwards and others. 780 pp. Bibliography: pp. 619–72. Index.
Vol. 1(2): *Early history of the Middle East.* 3rd ed. 1971; ed. by I. E. S. Edwards and others. 1,081 pp. Bibliography: pp. 877–993. Index.
Vol. 2(1): *History of the Middle East and the Aegean region, c. 1800–1380 BC.* 3rd ed. 1973; ed. by I. E. S. Edwards and others. 891 pp. Bibliography: pp. 720–817. Index.
Vol. 2(2): *History of the Middle East and the Aegean region, c. 1380–1000 BC.* 3rd ed. 1975; ed. by I. E. S. Edwards and others. 1,151 pp. Bibliography: pp. 911–1,036. Index.
Vol. 3(1): *The prehistory of the Balkans; and the Middle East and the Aegean world, tenth to eighth centuries BC.* 2nd ed. 1982; ed. by J. Boardman and others. 1,079 pp. Bibliography: pp. 906–1,007. Index.
Vol. 3(3): *The expansion of the Greek world, eighth to sixth centuries BC.* 2nd ed. 1982; ed. by J. Boardman and N. G. L. Hammond.
Standard, scholarly work, each chapter by a specialist. Many of the individual chapters appeared earlier as fascicles.

55 Clark, G. *World prehistory in new perspective.* 3rd ed. Cambridge (England): Cambridge University Press, 1977. 574 pp. Further reading: pp. 510–33.
Major survey of world prehistory.

56 Fagan, B. M. *People of the earth: an introduction to world prehistory.* 3rd ed. 1980. 431 pp. Notes [serving as a bibliography]: pp. 369–92. Bibliography and archaeology [i.e. the methods and theory of the subject itself]: pp. 393–7.
Worldwide survey from the origins of mankind to the beginnings of literate civilization, with a preliminary section on the study of archaeology itself.

57 Hudson, K. *World industrial archaeology.* Cambridge (England): Cambridge University Press, 1979. 247 pp. (New Studies in Archaeology.) Select bibliography: pp. 237–41.
Discusses the aims and academic status of industrial archaeology, appropriate techniques, and the range of current work, taking each major industry in turn with fully illustrated examples from many countries.

58 Muckelroy, K. *Maritime archaeology.* New York and London: Cambridge

University Press, 1978. 280 pp. (New Studies in Archaeology.) Bibliography: pp. 255–67.
A comprehensive view of archaeology underwater. Discusses the scope and theoretical basis of this sub-discipline.

59 Müller-Karpe, H. *Handbuch der Vorgeschichte.* Munich: Beck, 1966–. To be completed in five vols. Vol. 1: *Altsteinzeit.* 2nd ed. 1977; vol. 2: *Jungsteinzeit.* 1968; vol. 3: *Kupferzeit.* 1974; vol. 4: *Bronzezeit.* 1980.
Detailed survey of prehistory worldwide on a vast scale. Each volume comprises a series of chapters, well documented, including 'Regesten Wichtiger Funde', numerous plates and indexes for subjects, names and localities. Bias towards Europe, with unevenness of treatment apparent for the coverage of particular areas.

60 Trump D. H. *The prehistory of the Mediterranean.* London: Allen Lane, 1980. 320 pp. Bibliography: p. 302.
Synthesis of the whole of Mediterranean prehistory from the first farmers in the Levant to the rise of Classical Greece and Rome.

Textbooks, handbooks, manuals

61 Alexander, J. *The directing of archaeological excavations.* London: Baker; New York: Humanities Press, 1970. 304 pp. Bibliography: pp. 287–93.
Discusses the general principles involved and the special problems connected with the excavation of different types of sites.

62 Barker, P. A. *Techniques of archaeological excavation.* New ed. London: Batsford, 1982. 279 pp. Bibliography: pp. 264–72.
Comprehensive guide covering every stage from fieldwork to publication.

63 Branigan, K. *Reconstructing the past: a basic introduction to archaeology.* London: David and Charles, 1974. 126 pp.
General introduction to archaeology for the layman, explaining how and why the archaeologist works in the way that he does.

64 Brodribb, C. *Drawing archaeological finds for publication.* London: Baker, 1970. 50 pp.
An aid for students and amateur archaeologists to prepare drawings of finds for publication.

65 Clarke, D. L. *Analytical archaeology.* 2nd ed. revised by B. Chapman. London: Methuen, 1978. 547 pp. Bibliography: pp. 497–513.
One of the most important works on archaeological theory yet published. Attempts to define regularities in the processes of material culture change.

66 Coles, J. M. *Field archaeology in Britain.* London: Methuen, 1972. 276 pp.
Students' guide to some of the techniques of observation and recording of material remains, to the processes of recovery and conservation, and to the aims and methods of archaeology.

67 Council for British Archaeology. Publications Committee. *Signposts for archaeological publication: a guide to good practice in the presentation and printing of archaeological periodicals and monographs.* 2nd ed. London: Council for British Archaeology, 1979. 36 pp. Select bibliography: pp. 20–3.
Gives guidelines on the production and dissemination of archaeological material, paying particular attention to the problem of high publication costs. Aimed basically at editors, but anyone with writing or publishing responsibilities will benefit.

68 Doran, J. E. and **Hodson, F. R.** *Mathematics and computers in archaeology.* Edinburgh: Edinburgh University Press, 1975. 392 pp. Bibliography: pp. 349–70.
Useful for those involved in using or understanding the results of mathematical or computer methods in archaeology.

69 Fagan, B. M. *In the beginning: an introduction to archaeology.* 4th ed. Boston (Mass.) Little, Brown and Co., 1981. 574 pp. Bibliography: pp. 506–23. Glossary.
Discusses the history and methods of archaeology and its significance today. Includes a useful 'Suggested readings in world archaeology'.

70 Fowler, P. J. *Approaches to archaeology.* London: Black, 1977. 203 pp. Further reading: pp. 194–5.
Discusses some of the principles, recent developments and present trends.

71 Fryer, D. H. *Surveying for archaeologists.* 4th ed. Durham: Durham University Excavation Committee, 1971. 39 pp.
The best *basic* manual on surveying, giving enough information to allow an amateur archaeologist to make an intelligible survey.

72 Gaines, S. (ed.). *Data bank applications in archaeology*; contributors L. Bourrelly [and others]. Tucson: University of Arizona Press, 1981. 152 pp.
Discusses successful applications of computers for managing archaeological data in North America, Britain and France, and also general considerations for archaeologists contemplating the computerization of almost any type of data.

73 Greene, K. *Archaeology: an introduction: the history, principles and methods of modern archaeology.* London: Batsford, 1983. 190 pp. Bibliography: pp. 177–80.
A general introduction to archaeology aimed at beginners or non-specialists with a passing acquaintance with the subject. Each chapter concludes with a guide to further reading.

74 Grinsell, L. V., Rahtz, P. and **Williams, D. P.** *The preparation of archaeological reports.* 2nd ed. London: Baker, 1974. 105 pp. Some publications recommended for study, references and bibliography: pp. 95–102.
Gives practical advice on the form of publication, the preliminaries and initial stages, the body of an excavation report (text and illustrations), the body of a non-excavational report, distribution maps, and the final stages.

75 Harp, E. (ed.). *Photography in archaeological research.* Albuquerque: University of New Mexico Press, 1975. 403 pp. References: pp. 369–73.
Detailed, practical guide to the archaeologist's use of photography at all stages of an excavation for acquiring and recording data, analysing and interpreting discoveries, and illustrating and communicating results.

76 Hester, T. R., Heizer, R. F. and **Graham, J. A.** *Field methods in archaeology.* 6th ed. Palo Alto (California): Mayfield, 1975. 414 pp. Bibliography: pp. 319–89.
A manual giving advice on surveying, methods of excavation, recording data, stratigraphy, photography, chronological methods, etc. Includes appendices on choosing archaeology as a profession, and on state and federal regulations concerning archaeological sites.

77 Hodder, I. *Symbols in action: ethnoarchaeological studies of material culture.* Cambridge (England): Cambridge University Press, 1982. 254 pp. (New Studies in Archaeology.) Bibliography: pp. 230–8.
Describes work carried out among communities of farmers and pastoralists in Africa, with the object of seeing how the distribution of material culture items relates to human social ordering and activity. Illustrations, tables, etc.

78 Hodder, I. and **Orton, C.** *Spatial analysis in archaeology.* Cambridge (England): Cambridge University Press, 1976. 278 pp. (New Studies in Archaeology.) Bibliography: pp. 249–63.
Discusses applications to archaeology of modern statistical and quantitative techniques.

79 Hogg, A. H. A. *Surveying for archaeologists and other fieldworkers.* London: Croom Helm, 1980. 315 pp. (Croom Helm Studies in Archaeology.)
Very detailed description of surveying techniques.

80 Hole, F. and **Heizer, R. F.** *Prehistoric archaeology: a brief introduction.* New York: Holt, Rinehart and Winston, 1977. 490 pp. Suggestions for further reading: pp. 391–415; these references are included in the Bibliography: pp. 416–68. Glossary.
Discusses the theoretical basis of archaeology, procedures for surveying and excavating, methods of analysing finds, methods of dating and ways of interpreting results.

81 Joukowsky, M. *A complete manual of field archaeology: tools and techniques of field work for archaeologists.* Englewood Cliffs (New Jersey): Prentice-Hall, 1980. 640 pp. Bibliography: pp. 543–607.
Very detailed work with large expensive excavations as the frame of reference.

82 Maney, A. S. *The preparation of archaeological illustration for reproduction.* [Stonehurst (England)]: Association of Archaeological Illustrators and Surveyors [1979]. 4 pp. (Association of Archaeological Illustrators and Surveyors. Technical Papers, 1.)

Advice from a printer to illustrators on how to produce good drawings for publication and reduce expenses at the production stage.

83 Plenderleith, H. J. and **Werner, A. E. A.** *The conservation of antiquities and works of art: treatment, repair and restoration.* 2nd ed. London: Oxford University Press, 1971. 413 pp.
Standard guide to conservation techniques.

84 Schiffer, M. B. *Behavioral archaeology.* New York: Academic Press, 1976. 240 pp. (Studies in Archaeology.) References: pp. 200–15.
Deals with the interrelationships between human behaviour and material culture.

85 Sharer, R. J. and **Ashmore, W.** *Fundamentals of archaeology.* Menlo Park (California): Benjamin/Cummings, 1979. 636 pp. Suggestions for further reading: pp. 571–6; these references are included in the Bibliography: pp. 577–600. Glossary.
Textbook with a Mesoamerican bias. Discusses the techniques, methods and frameworks of prehistoric archaeology, including chapters on data acquisition, data processing and analysis, and synthesis and interpretation.

86 Taylor, C. *Fieldwork in medieval archaeology.* London: Batsford, 1974. 176 pp. References: pp. 154–9; Select bibliography of medieval and later field monuments: pp. 160–8.
Gives practical advice on the techniques of field archaeology – the discovery, recording and interpretation of sites by visual examination alone without excavation. The examples (from certain parts of England) are used to illustrate general principles.

87 Webster, G. *Practical archaeology: an introduction to archaeological fieldwork and excavation.* 2nd ed. London: Black, 1974. 176 pp.
Students' guide to the practical aspects of archaeology introducing the basic techniques of excavation, with a final chapter on publication. Excludes experimental field methods.

Guides to periodicals

88 *History periodicals directory.* Editors: E. H. Boehm and others. Santa Barbara (California); Oxford (England): ABC-Clio, 1981–. 5 vols. (projected).
International guide to periodicals in history interpreted in its broadest sense (includes archaeology). Includes all current titles and those that have ceased publication since 1960. Arranged alphabetically by title within country of publication. Details include a brief summary of the subject scope. Title index to each vol.

89 *Ulrich's international periodicals directory: a classified guide to current periodicals, foreign and domestic.* New York and London: Bowker, 1932–. Annual.
The authoritative worldwide list of serials in all subjects currently in print and published more frequently than once a year. Currently *c.* 65,000 serials in *c.* 400

subject areas are covered; the 'Archaeology' section lists *c.* 250 serials. There is a subheading 'Abstracting, Bibliographies, Statistics' for each major subject section. Includes details such as year of origin, frequency, publisher's name and address, corporate author, where abstracted or indexed. Its companion volume *Irregular serials and annuals: an international directory* (8th ed. New York & London: Bowker, 1983. 1,633 pp.) lists serials, annuals, continuations and conference proceedings in all subjects currently in print and published irregularly or less frequently than twice a year. Currently *c.* 32,000 serials in *c.* 400 subject areas are covered; the 'Archaeology' section lists *c.* 500 serials. Both the above are supplemented by *Ulrich's Quarterly* (New York and London: Bowker, 1977–. Quarterly) which gives up-to-date information on new serial titles and title changes and cessations, and is arranged in the same way. Complemented by *Sources of serials* (2nd ed. New York and London: Bowker, 1981. 1,840 pp.) which arranges by corporate author and publisher all the serials in the Bowker serials bibliography database. All the above material is available online through DIALOG.

90 Wellington, J. S. *Dictionary of bibliographic abbreviations found in the scholarship of classical studies and related disciplines.* Westport (Connecticut); London: Greenwood, 1983. 408 pp.
Collects and explains the abbreviations of journals, serials and standard works used most frequently by classicists. In two parts: list of abbreviations; bibliographic descriptions.

Periodicals

91 *Acta Praehistorica et Archaeologica.* Berlin: (Berliner Gesellschaft für Anthropologie, Ethnologie und Urgeschichte) Spiess, 1970–. Annual. De. (occasionally En.).
Worldwide coverage, with emphasis on Eastern Europe. Book reviews. Vol. 9/10 (1978/9) included a list of abbreviations of titles of international periodicals, series, monographic sets, and dictionaries of European and Oriental archaeology in two parts: by abbreviation and by full title.

92 *Advances in Archaeological Method and Theory.* New York: Academic Press, 1978–. Annual. En.
Worldwide synthesis of recent methodological and theoretical advances. Articles act as critical reviews, synthesize recent progress and provide new ideas.

93 *Advances in World Archaeology.* New York: Academic Press, 1982–. Annual. En. (abstracts in Fr. De. Ru.).
Aims to provide syntheses of current archaeological knowledge worldwide. Each vol. comprises chapters each covering a particular part of the world, each with references.

94 *Aerial Archaeology: the Journal for Air Photography and Archaeology.* East Dereham (England): Aerial Archaeology Publications, 1977–. Annual. En.
Worldwide coverage of archaeological air reconnaissance, interpretation, photographic techniques, computer enhancement, transcription of archaeological

evidence, details of archives of air photographs, summary reports of projects, etc. Book reviews.

95 *American Journal of Archaeology: the Journal of the Archaeological Institute of America.* New York: Archaeological Institute of America, 1885–. Quarterly. En. Cumulative indexes: vols. 1–11 (1885–96); 2nd series vols. 1–10 (1897–1906); vols. 11–70 (1907–66).
Mediterranean and the Near East. Excellent plates. Regular features include 'News Letter from Greece', 'Archaeology in Asia Minor', 'News Letter from North Africa', 'Chronologies in Old World Archaeology', and 'Americanist Archaeology'. Some issues are devoted to specific topics, e.g. sculpture, vase painting. Book reviews, books received, obituaries. Annual list of recent dissertations (North American).

96 *Annual Review of Anthropology.* Palo Alto (California): Annual Reviews Inc., 1972–. Annual. En.
Coverage includes archaeology on a world scale, with 'state of the art' articles.

97 *L'Anthropologie.* Paris: Masson, 1890–. Quarterly. Fr. Cumulative indexes: vols. 21–40 in vol. 40 (1930); vols. 41–60 (1931–56).
International journal important for prehistory. Book reviews. Includes 'Bulletin bibliographique', listing the contents of other journals in the field.

98 *Antiquity: a Periodical Review of Archaeology.* Cambridge (England): Antiquity Publications Ltd, 1927–. Three times a year. En. Cumulative indexes: vols. 1–25 (1927–51); vols. 26–50 (1952–76).
Worldwide coverage from the Neolithic to the Iron Age. Notes and news, book chronicle, lengthy book reviews (a particular feature); editorials comment on issues of the day, publications, and personalities, together with obituaries.

99 *Archaeoastronomy: Supplement to Journal for the History of Astronomy.* Chalfont St Giles (England): Science History Publications, 1979–. Annual. En.
Research on prehistoric astronomy. Includes state of the subject surveys, e.g. on Mesoamerican studies, megalithic studies. Book reviews.

100 *Archaeoastronomy: the Bulletin of the Center for Archaeoastronomy.* (formerly: *Archaeoastronomy Bulletin.*) Maryland: University of Maryland, Center for Archaeoastronomy, 1977–. Quarterly. En.
Semi-popular articles on astronomical observations and records of prehistoric peoples, especially in North America. Reviews of current literature and conference reports.

101 *Archaeological Reports.* London: Council of the Society for the Promotion of Hellenic Studies, 1955–. Annual. En. Site indexes: 1954–66; 1966–76.
Summaries of archaeological work in the Mediterranean area, with emphasis on Greece, Cyprus, Southern Italy and Sicily, Central Italy and Etruria, the Black Sea, Western and Southern Asia Minor.

102 *Archaeological Review from Cambridge.* Cambridge (England): Department of Archaeology, 1981–. Twice a year. En.
Provides a forum for the review and discussion of current research and theoretical developments in archaeology and related disciplines. Book reviews.

103 *Archaeology; a Magazine dealing with the Antiquity of the World.* New York: Archaeological Institute of America, 1948–. Every two months. En. Cumulative indexes: vols 1–10 (1948–57); vols. 11–26 (1958–73).
Semi-popular magazine covering archaeology worldwide. Includes sections on current exhibitions (mainly USA), news, archaeology films, new books, guides to archaeological sites (both USA and elsewhere). Photographs a particular feature.

104 *Archaeology Abroad.* London: Archaeology Abroad Service, 1972–. Annual. En.
Gives details of British Schools and Institutes of Archaeology abroad and the work currently being done by them, grants and studentships available, and helpers required. Also details of other excavations worldwide needing helpers, study tours and courses, publications and insurance. The Service also produces a *Newsheet.*

105 *Archaeonautica.* Paris: (Service des Fouilles et Antiquités) Centre National de la Recherche Scientifique, 1977–. Irreg. Fr.
Underwater archaeology worldwide.

106 *Archéologia.* Dijon: Archéologia, 1964–. Monthly. Fr. Cumulative index: nos. 1–161 (1964–81) in no. 161.
International, semi-popular journal, with emphasis on French archaeology. Photographs a special feature.

107 *Archives de l'Institut de Paléontologie Humaine.* Paris: Masson, 1927–. Irreg. Fr.
Coverage is mainly France but many other parts of the world are covered too, e.g. Middle East.

108 *Asian Perspectives: a Journal of Archaeology and Prehistory of Asia and the Pacific.* Honolulu: (University of Hawaii) University Press of Hawaii, 1957–. Twice a year. En.
Includes articles and reports of work in progress in all aspects of prehistory for India, Southeast Asia, China, Japan, Indonesia, Australia, and the Pacific. Book reviews.

109 *Bulletin of the Institute of Archaeology, University of London.* London: University of London, Institute of Archaeology, 1958–. Annual. En.
Multi-regional journal, with each paper carrying its own abstract. Book reviews. Includes lists of titles of MA and MSc theses and undergraduate reports.

110 *Current Anthropology: a World Journal of the Sciences of Man.* Chicago: University of Chicago Press, 1960–. Five times a year. En.

International journal covering research, theory and critical analyses in anthropology and related areas. Includes abstracts of its own articles. Book reviews. Includes 'Recent publications', a listing of the anthropological content of periodicals and symposia, and a list of books received.

111 *Early Man News.* Tübingen: (International Union for Quaternary Research) Commission for the Palecology of Early Man of INQUA, 1976–. Annual. En.
Reports on current field research worldwide on the palaeoecology of early man.

112 *Epigraphische Studien.* Cologne: Rheinland-Verlag, 1967–. Irreg. De.
International journal of epigraphic studies.

113 *Hesperia: Journal of the American School of Classical Studies at Athens.* Athens: American School of Classical Studies at Athens, 1932–. Quarterly. En. Gr. Cumulative index: vols. 1–35 (1932–66).
Research papers and excavation reports of the School, describing some of the most significant work in classical archaeology in Greece, Italy and Turkey. *Supplements* also published.

114 *Historical Metallurgy: Journal of the Historical Metallurgy Society.* Coleford (England): Historical Metallurgy Society Ltd, 1963–. Twice a year. En. Cumulative index: vols 1–7 (1963–73). (see also [32])
History of metallurgy, forging and production, worldwide. Book reviews. Includes abstracts of publications in the field, arranged geographically.

115 *Industrial Archaeology Review.* Neasden (England): (Association for Industrial Archaeology) Oxford University Press, 1976–. Three times a year. En.
Industrial archaeology with emphasis on Great Britain, from the mid 17th century to the present. 'Notes and news'. Book reviews.

116 *International Journal of Nautical Archaeology and Underwater Exploration.* London: (Council for Nautical Archaeology) Academic Press, 1972–. Quarterly. En.
Worldwide coverage of the latest exploration, discoveries and technical innovations in the field. Many articles relate archaeology to other scientific disciplines. 'Notes and news.' Book reviews. List of books and periodicals received.

117 *Journal of Anthropological Archaeology.* New York: Academic Press, 1982–. Quarterly. En.
International journal devoted to the development of theory and methodology for the understanding of the organization, operation and evolution of human societies, with no geographical or temporal limitations.

118 *Journal of Field Archaeology.* Boston (Mass.): (Association for Field Archaeology) Boston University, 1974–. Quarterly. En.
Worldwide coverage of significant archaeological projects, stressing the interdisciplinary nature of archaeology and the increasing involvement of archaeologists in legal matters. Includes 'Antiquities market' (news of illicit trade in antiquities), 'Perspectives' (a forum for discussion), 'Staffing opportunities',

'Preservation and rescue', news items. Also regular lists of archaeometrists and 'Archaeometric Clearinghouse'. Vol. 5 (1978) pp. 361–70 included a world list of archaeozoologists. Includes abstracts of papers. Book reviews.

119 *Journal of Mediterranean Anthropology and Archaeology*. Xanthi (Greece): Anthropological Museum of the International Demokritis Foundation, 1981–. Twice a year. En. Fr. De.
Anthropology and archaeology of the Mediterranean area including the latest results of research in biogenetics, classical archaeology, palaeodemography, palaeoecology, the palaeoenvironment, palaeopathology, palaeopopulation genetics, prehistoric archaeology and interdisciplinary studies.

120 *Old World Archaeology Newsletter*. Middletown (Connecticut): c/o Classics Dept, Wesleyan University, 1977–. Three times a year. En.
Contains a miscellany of information from anyone working on Old World archaeology. Includes book news, news of grant organizations, excavation and study opportunities, details of state antiquities organization in e.g. Germany (*OWAN*, 2:1 (1978)), Austria (*OWAN*, 3:2 (1979)).

121 *Quarterly Review of Archaeology*. Williamstown (Massachusetts): 1980–. Quarterly. En. Index to vols. 1–3 in Dec. 1982.
Devoted entirely to the review of archaeological literature of all kinds – mainly site reports, articles, monographs and theses. Coverage is worldwide, with emphasis on the Americas.

122 *Quaternaria: Quaternary Natural and Cultural History/Storia Naturale e Culturale del Quaternario*. Rome: Istituto Italiano di Paleontologia Umana, 1954–. Annual. En. Fr. De. It. Es.
Cultural and natural history of the Quaternary worldwide. Book reviews.

123 *Technology and Culture: the International Quarterly of the Society for the History of Technology*. Chicago: (Society for the History of Technology) University of Chicago Press, 1959–. Quarterly. En. Cumulative index: vols. 1–10 (1959–69). (see also [38])
Development of technology and its relations with society and culture. The second part each year includes a current bibliography on the history of technology. Book reviews.

124 *Tools and Tillage: a Journal on the History of the Implements of Cultivation and other Agricultural Processes*. Copenhagen: National Museum, 1968–. Annual. En. (summaries in De.).
History of agriculture from its beginnings to the industrial era. Worldwide with emphasis on Europe. Book reviews.

125 *World Archaeology*. Henley-on-Thames (England): Routledge and Kegan Paul, 1969–. Three times a year. En.
International journal which synthesizes current thinking on matters of general interest to archaeologists worldwide. Includes abstracts of its own papers. Each

issue is devoted to a particular theme, e.g. archaeology and musical instruments, island archaeology, etc. (theme titles of past issues are listed in the journal itself).

Dictionaries, encyclopaedias, atlases

126 Bandinelli, R. B. (ed. in chief). *Enciclopedia dell'arte antica: classica e orientale.* Rome: Istituto della Enciclopedia Italiana, 1958–73. 8 vols. + supplements 1970–73. Bibliographies at the end of most articles.
Covers the art history and iconography of the classical world, from prehistory to about AD 500.

127 Branigan, K. (consultant ed.). *The atlas of archaeology.* London: Macdonald, 1982. 240 pp. No bibliography.
An excellent introduction, summarizing the history, development and methods of archaeology, is followed by a regional arrangement (on almost a world scale) with emphasis on specific sites. Aimed at the general reader rather than the scholar. Numerous illustrations, drawings, maps, plans, etc. Gazetteer. Glossary. Index.

128 Bray, W. and **Trump, D. H.** *The Penguin dictionary of archaeology.* 2nd rev. ed. Harmondsworth: Penguin Books, 1982. 283 pp. + maps (16 pp.). (Penguin Reference Books.) No bibliography.
Over 1,600 entries in a single alphabetical sequence, with many cross-references, for sites, cultures, periods, techniques, terms and personalities of archaeology worldwide. Excludes classical, medieval and industrial archaeology. Aimed at the non-specialist as well as the serious student. Illustrations. Regional index. Maps. Translated as:
Lexikon der Archäologie; ed. and translated by J. Rehork (Reinbek (West Germany): Rowohlt, 1977. 2 vols.).
Diccionario de arqueologia; translated by J. Barberá Farrás (Barcelona: Labor, 1976. 276 pp.).
Dizionario di archeologia; (Milan: Mondadori, 1974).

129 Caffarello, N. *Dizionario archeologico di antichità classiche.* Florence: Olschki, 1971. 532 pp.
Gives clear, authoritative definitions and derivations of terms in classical art and archaeology. Some drawings and photographs.

130 Champion, S. *A dictionary of terms and techniques in archaeology.* Oxford: Phaidon, 1980. 144 pp. Bibliography: pp. 142–4.
An introduction for non-professional archaeologists to the terms and techniques of modern scientific archaeology, alphabetically arranged. Some entries include one bibliographical reference each to aid a search for further information. Numerous photographs, drawings, plans, maps, etc.

131 Cottrell, L. (ed.). *The concise encyclopedia of archaeology.* 3rd rev. ed. London: Hutchinson, 1974. 430 pp. Further reading: pp. 413–25.
A single alphabetical sequence of entries for famous archaeologists, surveys of regional archaeology, great discoveries, technical terms, scientific processes,

places, peoples, cities, civilizations, ancient languages and their decipherment, on a worldwide scale. Emphasis is on archaeology outside classical Greece and Rome and medieval Europe. Aimed at the 'intelligent amateur'. Classified list of entries.

132 Daniel, G. (consultant ed.). *The illustrated encyclopedia of archaeology.* Editor: E. Paintin. London: Macmillan, 1978; New York: Crowell, 1977. 224 pp. No bibliography.

Some 1,000 entries, alphabetically arranged, covering the whole field in general terms from prehistoric times to the 20th century. Aimed at the general reader, the student and the professional. Photographs and maps. Index.

133 Daremberg, C. and **Saglio, E.** *Dictionnaire des antiquités grecques et romaines d'après les textes et les monuments* . . . Paris: Hachette, 1877–1919 (reprinted 1969). 5 vols. + index.

Scholarly work covering all aspects of Greek and Roman life, customs and institutions, but excluding biography and literature. Arranged alphabetically by topic, with very detailed bibliographical references. Numerous drawings and plans. Indexes of subjects, Greek words, Latin words, and modern authors.

134 *Dictionnaire archéologique des techniques.* Paris: Éditions de l'Accueil, 1963–4. 2 vols. Bibliography: pp. 1,081–4.

The 'techniques', alphabetically arranged, are mostly general topics (e.g. métallurgie, navigation, urbanisme, cartes, etc.) divided by area (Precolumbian America, Far East and Central Asia, India, Western Asia, Egypt, Greece, Rome and Central Europe) with a 'Prehistory' section where appropriate. Maps, chronological chart. Numerous illustrations, drawings, plates, etc. Index.

135 Finley, M. I. (ed.). *Atlas of classical archaeology.* London: Chatto and Windus, 1977. 256 pp.

Covers the Greek and Roman world from c. 1000 BC to c. AD 500. An Introduction is followed by an arrangement by area (e.g. Roman Britain, North Africa, etc.). Each section has a general introduction preceding details of selected sites (nearly 100 in total) having visible classical remains, with references. Numerous photographs, maps, plans, etc. Aimed at both students and travellers. Chronological table, list of Roman emperors, Glossary, Greek vase types, Greek architectural orders, Index.

136 Hammond, N. G. L. (ed. in chief). *Atlas of the Greek and Roman world in antiquity.* Park Ridge (New Jersey): Noyes, 1981. 56 pp.

Detailed, scholarly topographical atlas of Greek and Roman lands. Covers the period from the Neolithic to the 6th century AD. Consists almost entirely of maps and plans (30 pp.) and a gazetteer (24 pp.). Includes over 10,000 sites, many identifications being no more than probable. Appendices of Greek colonies, British towns and other features, and towns in Gaul, Germany and the Alps.

137 Hammond, N. G. L. and **Scullard, H. H.** (eds.). *The Oxford classical dictionary.* 2nd ed. Oxford: Clarendon, 1970. 1,198 pp. General bibliography: pp. 1,151–3.

An indispensable first source of reference for information on all aspects of the classical world, including archaeology. Entries arranged alphabetically with references. Index of names, etc. which are not titles of entries in the main work.

138 Hausmann, U. (ed.). *Handbuch der Archäologie, im Rahmen des Handbuchs der Altertumswissenschaft.* New ed. Munich: Beck, 1969–. Irreg. A comprehensive encyclopaedia of prehistory. Forms Abteilung 6 of the massive co-operative work *Handbuch der Altertumswissenschaft.*

139 Hawkes, J. (ed.). *Atlas of ancient archaeology.* London: Heinemann, 1974. 272 pp.
Examines world cultures down to the classical period. Each section deals with one region (Africa, British Isles, France, etc.), with an introduction and map followed by a description of important sites (nearly 200 in total). Each site is illustrated with plans and/or drawings and has a short bibliography. A chronological chart of Palaeolithic and other hunting cultures indicates the approximate relative age of the sites described in the Atlas. Aimed at travellers as well as students. Glossary. Index.

140 Hawkes, J. *The atlas of early man.* London: Macmillan, 1976. 255 pp. No bibliography.
Covers the whole world within the time-span 35,000 BC (marking approximately the emergence of modern man) to AD 500. This period is divided into eight sections, each consisting of a general account of developments worldwide during the period covered, followed by separate accounts of technology, architecture and art, and ends with a summary chart giving the main information in tabular form. Aimed at the general reader. With 15 pp. of maps plotting all the sites mentioned in the text and a gazetteer. Many photographs and drawings. Index.

141 Muckelroy, K. (ed.). *Archaeology under water: an atlas of the world's submerged sites.* New York; London: McGraw-Hill, 1980. 192 pp. Further reading (with annotations): pp. 188–9.
Presents a synopsis of material finds and summarizes the state of underwater archaeology in 1980. Prologue discusses the worldwide aspects of the subject, followed by sections on: techniques and approaches, Mediterranean wreck sites and classical seafaring, European shipwrecks over 3,000 years, shipwrecks in the wake of Columbus, structures under water, and preservation: past, present and future. Aimed at both the archaeologist and the general reader. Many drawings, maps and photographs. Index.

142 Pauly, A. F. von and **Wissowa, G.** (eds.). *Pauly's Real-Encyclopädie der classischen Altertumswissenschaft.* Revised ed. by K. Ziegler. Stuttgart: Metzler, 1894–1967. Series 1: A–Q (24 vols.); Series 2: R–Z (10 vols.); Supplements 1903–.
Comprehensive multi-volume scholarly work covering all aspects of classical antiquity. The standard starting point for classical archaeology. Lengthy articles, each including a detailed bibliography. Supplements are linked to the main set.
Der Kleine Pauly: Lexikon der Antike auf der Grundlage von Pauly's Real-Encyclopädie der

classischen Altertumswissenschaft; ed. by K. Ziegler and others (Munich: Drucken-müller, 1964–75. 5 vols.) is a condensation of the above, with new advances in scholarship reflected and updated bibliographical references where necessary.

143 Sherratt, A. (ed.). *The Cambridge encyclopedia of archaeology.* Cambridge (England): Cambridge University Press, 1980. 495 pp. Bibliography: pp. 453–65. Further reading pp. 466–7.
A comprehensive overview of the whole field, presenting a concise synthesis of archaeological knowledge worldwide from earliest man to the European conquest of the Americas. Comprises a series of sixty-four chapters on separate topics written by fifty-five contributors. Part 1 summarizes the development of modern archaeology. Arrangement is primarily chronological, secondly areal. Chronological tables, maps, plans. Index.

144 Stillwell, R. and others (eds.). *The Princeton encyclopedia of classical sites.* Princeton (New Jersey): Princeton University Press, 1976. 1,041 pp.
A monumental, scholarly work giving information on *c.* 3,000 sites that show remains from classical times. Period covered is *c.* 750 BC to the 6th century AD. Sites are arranged alphabetically with detailed bibliographies at the end of each article. Information given includes location, summary of excavation expeditions and work done at the site. Glossary. Maps. Map indexes.

145 Whitehouse, D. and **Whitehouse, R.** *Archaeological atlas of the world,* with 103 maps drawn by J. Woodcock and S. Schotten. London: Thames and Hudson; San Francisco: W. H. Freeman, 1975. 272 pp.
The best archaeological atlas, comprising 103 maps covering the whole world pinpointing *c.* 5,000 pre- and protohistoric sites. Maps are arranged in seven sections, the first covering Palaeolithic sites in the Old World, the rest devoted to a particular area of the world and prefaced by a commentary. Each map is accompanied by explanatory notes with suggestions for further reading. An introduction briefly surveys the origin and growth of archaeological research. Aimed at the professional as well as the interested amateur. Index of sites with map grid references.

146 Whitehouse, R. (ed.). *The Macmillan dictionary of archaeology.* London: Macmillan, 1983. 597 pp. Further reading: pp. 592–7.
The most complete archaeological dictionary, covering all aspects of the subject worldwide. Aimed at both the non-specialist and the scholar. Illustrations. Chronological tables. Subject index (terms used in the work are listed here under general headings).

Language dictionaries

147 Apelt, M. L. *Deutsch–Englisches Wörterbuch für Kunstgeschichte und Archäologie/ German–English dictionary: art history–archaeology.* Berlin: Schmidt, 1978. 240 pp.

148 Jaźdzewski, K. (ed.). *Glossarium archaeologicum.* (Union Internationale des Sciences Préhistoriques et Protohistoriques) Bonn: Habelt; Warsaw: Éditions Scientifiques de Pologne, 1962–. Irreg.

Polyglot dictionary of archaeological terms. Each fascicule covers *c.* twenty terms translated into *c.* twenty-five European languages.

149 Kostrzewski, J. *Słowniczek prehistoryczny niemiecko–polski.* Warsaw: Książnica Polska, 1921. 87 pp. (De.→Pl.)

150 Marois, R. *English–French, French–English vocabulary of prehistoric archaeology.* Montreal: Les Presses de L' Université du Québec, 1972. 42 pp. + 43 pp. Elementary list of sample terms, with a bias towards stone tools.

151 Niemann, J. W. *Polnisch–deutsches Fachwörterbuch für die Vorgeschichte.* Breslau: Priebatsch, 1938. 70 pp. (Pl.→De.)

152 Novotný, B. *Príručný archeologický nemecko–slovenský slovník. Deutsch–slowakisches archäologisches Handwörterbuch.* Bratislava: Slovenské Pedagogické Nakladatel'stvo, 1967. 90 pp. (De.→Sl.)

153 Réau, L. *Dictionnaire polyglotte des termes d'art et d'archéologie.* Osnabrück: Zeller, 1977. 961 pp. (Reimpression, greatly extended, of the edition published in Paris: Presses Universitaires de France, 1953.)
Languages covered are French, Czech, Danish, Dutch, English, German, Italian, Latin, Polish, Portuguese, Russian, Spanish, Swedish. Conceptually old-fashioned.

154 Rukówna, J. *Słowniczek prehistoryczny francusko–polski i polsko–francuski.* Poznań: Polskiego Towarzystwo Prehistorycznego, 1951. 88 pp. (Pl.⇄Fr.)

155 Višňovská, D. *Polśko–slovenský archeologický slovník.* Bratislava: SPN, 1967. 187 pp. (Pl.→Sl.)

Theses

156 *Dissertation abstracts international.* Ann Arbor (Michigan): University Microfilms, 1938–. Monthly.
Abstracts of doctoral dissertations submitted to University Microfilms by over 450 institutions in North America and some European ones. Most North American universities co-operate in the scheme, but the number of European universities, especially Eastern European, is still relatively small. In three sections – A: *Humanities and social sciences*; B: *Sciences and engineering*; C: *European abstracts*. Author index, keyword index, both cumulating annually.
  A retrospective index (9 vols., 1970) covers vols. 1–29 (1938–69). First eight vols. are arranged by subject; archaeology is covered in vol. 5 (Social sciences). Vol. 9 is a cumulative author index. This retrospective index has been superseded by *Comprehensive dissertation index 1861–1972* (Ann Arbor (Michigan): University Microfilms International, 1973. 37 vols. + supplements, 1973 to the present and five-year cumulation 1973–77) which can be searched online through DIALOG. This is the definitive list of North American doctoral theses.

157 *Index to theses accepted for higher degrees in the universities of Great Britain and Ireland*

and the Council for National Academic Awards. London: Aslib, 1950/51– (publ. 1953–). Twice a year.

Excludes higher degrees awarded solely in respect of published work or dissertations submitted in partial fulfilment of the requirements for a higher degree in conjunction with a written examination. Arranged under broad subject headings; 'Archaeology' is a sub-heading under 'History'. Subject index, author index.

Preceded by *Retrospective index to theses of Great Britain and Ireland 1716–1950* (Santa Barbara (California): American Bibliographical Center–Clio Press, 1975–77. 5 vols. + an addenda issue) which lists these under subject headings. 'Archaeology and antiquities' is included in vol. 1: *Social sciences and humanities.*

158 Thompson, L. S. *A bibliography of dissertations in classical studies: American, 1964–1972; British, 1950–1972; with a cumulative index, 1861–1972.* Hamden (Connecticut): Shoe String, 1976. 296 pp. Continues Thompson, L. S. *A bibliography of American doctoral dissertations in classical studies and related fields* (Hamden (Connecticut): Shoe String, 1968. 250 pp.).

Listed are theses covering all aspects of the culture of Greece and Rome, including archaeology, from prehistoric times to AD 500. British theses are taken from the *Aslib Index* [157]. A cumulative index (author, subject, title, topographical) serves both vols. Index of Greek words; index of Latin words.

159 University of London. Institute of Archaeology. *Archaeological theses in progress in British universities.* London: London Institute of Archaeology in conjunction with the Council for British Archaeology. 1976 + supplements.

Theses are listed under geographical headings, with a general section at the end. Information given is title, author, university, degree and period of study. Includes theses at all levels from BA to PhD. No index.

Directories (biographical, organizational, research in progress, meetings)

160 *The archaeologists' year book: an international directory of archaeology and anthropology.* Poole (England): Dolphin, 1977. 312 pp.

Gives basic details (names, addresses, names of staff, topics covered, etc.) on museums; university and archaeology departments; institutes, schools and centres; government departments; councils, committees, trusts and units; societies and associations; research groups; grant-making institutions. There are separate sections for British and non-British institutions. List of useful addresses, book reviews. Index (of individuals' names). Partly out of date but still useful.

161 British Library Lending Division. *Index of Conference Proceedings Received.* Boston Spa (England): British Library Lending Division, 1964–. Monthly, with annual, five- and ten-year cumulations.

A worldwide list of conference proceedings received by the BLLD covering all subjects. Arranged alphabetically by subject keywords taken from the title of the conference proceedings. Information given includes the date of the meeting, its title and where it was held. Delay: most meetings listed were held within the last two or three years but publication delays can be considerable. A microfiche cumulation is available covering eighteen years (1964–81); includes *c.* 250 conferences under 'Archaeology' and related headings. Available online through BLAISE as CONFERENCE PROCEEDINGS INDEX.

162 Centre National de la Recherche Scientifique. Institut de Recherche et d'Histoire des Textes. *Répertoire international des médiévistes/International directory of medievalists.* 5th ed. Munich: Saur, 1979. 2 vols. 811 pp.
Contains 5,527 bio-bibliographies for medievalists, some of whom are archaeologists, in forty-three countries. Each entry includes the individual's name, title, business and private addresses, telephone number, his research speciality, and a list of his published and planned works. Period covered is from late antiquity to the beginning of the Reformation.

163 Comas, J. *Historia y bibliografía de los congresos internacionales de ciencias antropológicas: 1865–1954.* Mexico City: Dirección General de Publicaciones, 1956. 490 pp.
Describes the activities and publications of four major international organizations in anthropology – the International Congress of Anthropology and Prehistoric Archaeology, the International Institute of Anthropology, the International Congress of the Prehistoric and Protohistoric Sciences (later to become the UISPP [608]), and the International Congress of Anthropological and Ethnological sciences – as well as those of several smaller bodies. Includes a classified subject bibliography of *c.* 3000 papers published in the reports of the more important congresses.

164 *Commonwealth universities yearbook: a directory to the universities of the Commonwealth and the handbook of their Association.* London: Association of Commonwealth Universities, 1914–. Annual. 4 vols.
Gives detailed information about universities in Commonwealth countries, which are listed alphabetically. Details includes address, names of all officers, teaching staff (arranged by department), administrative and other staff, and general information including details of courses available. Appendices include details of university admission requirements and a select bibliography. Abbreviations for universities, degrees, etc. General index (institutions and topics, subjects of study); names index.

165 *Current Research in Library and Information Science.* (formerly: *Radials Bulletin.*) London: Library Association, 1974–. Quarterly.
Current awareness service giving regularly updated information on current developments in research and development work in librarianship, information science, archives, documentation and the information aspects of other fields including archaeology. Until 1982 only UK projects were listed but from 1983 coverage is international. Name index; subject index.

166 *Fifth international directory of anthropologists.* Chicago and London: University of Chicago Press, 1975. 496 pp. (Current Anthropology Resource series.)
Gives biographical information on 4,373 scholars worldwide, alphabetically arranged. Details given include name, position, research interests and publica-

tions. Geographical index; chronological index; subject/methodological index; institutional location/residence index.

167 *The grants register.* London: Macmillan, 1969–. Every two years.
International directory of scholarships, fellowships, grants and similar financial aids available to students at or above graduate level and those who require further professional or advanced vocational training. Arranged alphabetically by grant-giving body with information on the type of assistance offered. Subject index (1983–85 ed. included over seventy entries under 'Archaeology'); index of awards and awarding bodies. Bibliography (2 pp.) lists other sources of financial support.

168 Hudson, K. and **Nicholls, A.** (eds.). *The directory of museums.* 2nd ed. London: Macmillan, 1981. 681 pp.
An extensive list of *c.* 30,000 museums worldwide. Information given for each museum includes name, address and a brief description of the collections. Arranged alphabetically by country, and within each country alphabetically by place preceded by a brief summary of the national situation. Also included: a brief note on the museum world today, criteria for the directory, glossary, and a select bibliography of national museum directories and articles (pp. 677–81).

169 Hyamson, A. M. *A dictionary of universal biography of all ages and of all peoples.* 2nd rev. ed. London: Routledge and Kegan Paul, 1951. 691 pp.
An index to the biographies of over 100,000 individuals (pre-*c.* 1950) prominent in all fields worldwide, including many archaeologists and antiquarians.

170 *Index to Social Sciences and Humanities Proceedings.* Philadelphia (Pennsylvania): Institute for Scientific Information, 1982–. Quarterly, with annual cumulations.
Lists published conference proceedings and the individual papers appearing in them. Various social science and humanities subjects are covered, including archaeology. The 1982 issues covered *c.* 1,000 proceedings and the *c.* 15,000 papers they contained; no. 2 (1982) indexed six conferences under 'Archaeology' and eight under 'Anthropology'. Author/editor index; sponsor index; meeting location index; subject index; corporate index. Delay: most proceedings published within last year.

171 *International directory of arts.* Frankfurt: Müller, 1952/3–. Annual. 2 vols.
Detailed lists of addresses and other information worldwide on all aspects of art, the fine art trade and museum organizations. Arranged in subject groups: museums and art galleries; universities, academies, colleges; associations; artists; collectors; art and antique dealers; numismatics; galleries; auctioneers; restorers; art publishers; art periodicals; antiquarian and art booksellers; and within these groups by countries.

172 *International handbook of universities and other institutions of higher education.* Paris: International Association of Universities, 1959–. Every three years.
Gives information about university institutions in all countries outside the

Commonwealth except for the USA. Countries are listed alphabetically. Detail includes name and address; list of faculties, departments, institutes, schools and colleges; brief notes on history, admission requirements, degrees and diplomas, etc. Individual staff are not listed, apart from senior officers. Index (of institutions).

173 *Museums of the world*. 3rd rev. ed. Munich: Saur, 1981. 623 pp.
Lists nearly 18,000 museums worldwide. Information given for each museum includes name, address, museum type, year of founding, and a summary of collections and facilities. Arranged alphabetically by country, and within each country alphabetically by place. List of national and international museum associations. Name index (persons, places, collections); subject index.

174 *Obituaries from The Times 1951–75*. Compiled by F. C. Roberts. Reading (England): Newspaper Archive Developments, 1975–79. 3 vols.
Selected obituaries from *The Times*. Each vol. includes an index to all obituaries and tributes appearing in *The Times* during the period covered. For more recent obituaries, the *Times Index* must be used.

175 *Research Centers Directory*. Detroit (Michigan): Gale Research, 1960–. Irreg.
Guide to university-related and independent non-profit research centres in the USA and Canada. Subjects covered include archaeology and related fields; 1983 vol. subject index listed 126 centres under 'archeology' (out of a total of 6,314). Arranged by broad subject field. Details include address, name of director, scope of research, publications and any special library facilities. Institutional index; alphabetic index of research centres; subject index. Updated by *New Research Centers: A Periodic Supplement* (Detroit (Michigan): Gale Research, 1965–. Quarterly), arranged on similar lines, with cumulative indexes by institution and centre. Complemented by *International Research Centers Directory* (Detroit (Michigan): Gale Research, 1982–), similar to the above, but covering countries other than the USA and Canada. Name and keyword index; country index.

176 *World guide to libraries: Internationales Bibliotheks-Handbuch*. 6th ed. Munich: Saur, 1983. 1218 pp. (Handbook of International Documentation and Information, 8.)
The most comprehensive listing of libraries worldwide. Contains over 42,000 libraries, including national, university and college, general research libraries, public libraries with holdings of 30,000 vols. or more and special libraries with 3,000 vols. or more. Basic information given includes address, name of head, and number of vols. Arranged by continent, then by country, then by type of library, finally by town/city. Alphabetical index of libraries.

177 *World guide to scientific associations and learned societies*. 2nd ed. Munich: Verlag Dokumentation, 1978. 510 pp. (Handbook of International Documentation and Information, 13.)
Includes over 11,000 national and international associations and societies from all subject fields, arranged alphabetically within a country and continent division. Each entry includes the name of the organization, the year of

foundation, address, the name of the president or director and secretary and the number of members. List of key words. Subject index (158 organizations are listed under 'Archaeology', with a great bias towards the UK).

178 *World guide to universities/Internationales Universitäts Handbuch.* Compiled by M. Zils. 2nd ed. New York: Bowker. Vol. 1 (2 parts): Europe, 1976; vol. 2 (2 parts): Africa, the Americas, Asia, Oceania, 1978.
Lists and describes universities and their staff on a world scale.

179 *The world of learning.* London: Europa Publications, 1947–. Annual. 2 vols.
A world directory of academies, learned societies, research institutes, libraries and archives, museums and art galleries, universities, colleges, arranged alphabetically by country. Details include address, names of principal officials (staff below Reader level are not included), a list of publications, descriptions of activities, and (where available) numbers of teachers, students or members. Section on international scientific, educational and cultural organizations, and a list of abbreviations. Index of over 24,000 institutions, but no index of persons.

Guides to non-book material

180 British Universities Film and Video Council. *Audio-visual materials for higher education*; ed. by J. Ballantyne. 4th ed. London: British Universities Film and Video Council, 1979–80. 4 parts + supplements.
Annotated list of *c.* 3,500 titles of audio-visual materials, including much archaeology, currently in distribution, appraised by specialists, and suitable for degree-level or research work. Classified arrangement. Title index; subject index. Distributors' addresses. Other useful catalogues and sources. Slide suppliers. Computer software: a select list of bibliographies, catalogues and projects. Data files for this and the *HELPIS catalogue* [181] form a single file of *c.* 5,000 audio-visual materials, searchable online through BLAISE.

181 British Universities Film and Video Council [*HELPIS*] *Higher education learning programmes information service catalogue*; ed. by O. Terris. 7th ed. London: British Universities Film and Video Council, 1982. 276 pp.
Annotated list of *c.* 2,000 audio-visual materials, including much archaeology, intended for degree-level use produced in institutions of higher education in the UK. The material has not been appraised (unlike that in [180]). Classified arrangement. Title index; subject index. Distributors' addresses. Data files for this and *Audio-visual materials for higher education* [180] form a single file of *c.* 5,000 audio-visual materials, searchable online through BLAISE.

182 Evans, H. and **Evans, M.** *Picture researcher's handbook: an international guide to picture sources – and how to use them.* 2nd ed. London: Saturday Ventures, 1979. 328 pp.
International directory of selected libraries, museums, institutes, government agencies, commercial firms and studios, from which illustrations may be obtained. Information given includes brief indication of scope, address, hours, availability, etc. Subject index (thirty-nine entries under 'archeology'); alphabetical index of collections.

183 Ristow, W. W. (ed.). *World directory of map collections*; compiled by the Geography and Map Libraries Sub-Section [of IFLA]. Munich: Verlag Dokumentation, 1976. 326 pp. (IFLA publications, 8.)
Lists nearly 300 map collections in forty-six countries, with information on size and type of collection, reference services available, etc.

184 Winch, K. L. (ed.). *International maps and atlases in print.* 2nd ed. London: Bowker, 1976. 882 pp.
Contains over 8,000 detailed entries on maps and atlases (including historical ones) worldwide available from about 700 publishers. Arranged by continent and country, with maps and atlases listed separately. Index of geographical names.

185 *World museum publications 1982: a directory of art and cultural museums, their publications and audio-visual materials.* New York and London: Bowker, 1982. 731 pp.
Lists the permanent collections of over 10,000 museums and major art galleries worldwide and the publications and audio-visual materials available from them. The 'Geographic guide to museums' lists the institutions by country. The 'Museum publications and audio-visual materials index' lists over 30,000 publications and audio-visual items by museum and gallery name. Three other indexes for authors and titles.

Archaeological Science

General bibliographical guides

186 Armelagos, G. J., Mielke, J. H., and **Winter, J.** *Bibliography of human paleopathology.* Amherst (Massachusetts): University of Massachusetts, Department of Anthropology, 1971. 175 pp. (Research Reports, no. 8.)
Unannotated list of sources for the study of disease in prehistoric and ancient societies, arranged by author. Brief introduction on the development of the subject. No index.

187 Bleck, R.-D. *Bibliographie der archäologisch-chemischen Literatur.* Weimar (West Germany): Museum für Ur- und Frühgeschichte Thüringens. (Beiheft zu 'Alt-Thüringen'.) Vol. 1: 1966. 253 pp.; vol. 2: 1968. 195 pp.; vol. 3: 1971. 269 pp.
Has 5,846 entries, some annotated, of publications of all kinds on the scientific investigation of cultural and artistic products of all periods, chemical conservation methods and the history of chemical technology. Each vol. arranged alphabetically by author, with a subject index.

188 Gaudel, P. *Bibliographie der archäologischen Konservierungstechnik.* 2nd ed. Berlin: Hessling, 1969. 374 pp. (Berliner Jahrbuch für Vor- und Frühgeschichte. Ergänzungsbande, 2.)
Lists 1,803 publications, with detailed annotations, on the recovery, restoration, conservation and copying of archaeological remains. Name index; subject index; topographic index; list of firms and manufacturers; list of trade names.

189 Hester, T. R. and **Heizer, R. F.** *Bibliography of archaeology 1: experiments, lithic technology, and petrography.* Reading (Pennsylvania): Addison-Wesley, 1973–. 56 pp. (loose-leaf). (Addison-Wesley Modular Publications, 29. An Addison-Wesley Module in Anthropology.)

Unannotated bibliography in three sections (each sub-divided): experiments and replications with the aim of learning the processes by which prehistoric forms of artefacts were fashioned; analysis of chipped stone technology; identification of rocks or minerals used for artefacts.

190 Polach, D. *First 20 years of radiocarbon dating: an annotated bibliography 1948–1968.* Canberra: Australian National University, Radiocarbon Dating Research Laboratory, 1979. 136 pp.

Random selection of 1,000 entries out of several thousand collated for a definitive bibliography (to be published). Arranged in fourteen categories, five of which comprise archaeological material on a regional basis. Author index; subject index.

Abstracting, indexing, current awareness services

191 *Art and Archaeology Technical Abstracts.* London: International Institute for Conservation of Historic and Artistic Works, 1966–. Twice a year.

Worldwide listing, with abstracts, of publications of all kinds dealing with the technical examination, investigation, analysis, restoration, preservation and technical documentation of objects and monuments having historic or artistic significance. Following a section on general methods and techniques, arrangement is by the material comprising the objects under study or treatment, e.g. wood, glass and ceramics, etc. *c.* 400 periodicals are abstracted. Some numbers include as supplements annotated bibliographies on specific topics, e.g. the preservation of natural stone. Author index for each number; subject index for each vol. Delay: usually *c.* 6–12 months.

Preceded by *I.I.C. abstracts: abstracts of the technical literature on archaeology and the fine arts* (London: International Institute for Conservation of Historic and Artistic Works, vols. 1–5, 1955–65). Publications (similar to those in *AATA*) listed under various headings. Author index; subject index; cumulative subject index to vols. 1–10 (1955–73) of *I.I.C. abstracts* and *AATA* forms a supplement to *AATA* 11:1 (1974). Cumulative author and abbreviated title index to vols. 1–10 (1955–73) of *I.I.C. abstracts* and *AATA* forms a supplement to *AATA* 12:2 (1975).

Technical literature on art and archaeology before 1955 is covered back to 1932 by the following two publications:

Gettens, R. J. and **Usilton, B. M.** *Abstracts of technical studies in art and archaeology, 1943–1952.* Washington: Smithsonian Institution, 1955. (Smithsonian Institution publications, 4,176; Freer Gallery of Art Occasional Papers, 2(2).) 408 pp.

Lists, with abstracts, 1,399 papers that appeared in approximately the ten year period prior to *I.I.C. abstracts.* Arranged under headings: museology; materials, construction, and conservation of objects; technological examination of objects and analysis of materials; each with subdivisions. Index.

Usilton, B. M. *Subject index to 'Technical Studies in the field of the fine arts' vols. 1–10, 1932–42.* Pittsburgh (Pennsylvania): Tamworth, 1964. 44 pp.
The key to the more than 160 articles and 450 abstracts that appeared in the above periodical.

192 *Bibliographie zur Archäo-Zoologie und Geschichte der Haustiere.* Berlin: (International Council for Archaeozoology) Akademie der Wissenschaften der DDR, Zentralinstitut für Alte Geschichte und Archäologie, 1971–. Annual.
Unannotated references from a wide variety of sources on archaeozoology and the history of domestic animals. Arranged in three sections: 'Archäo-Zoologie'; 'Archäologie'; 'Rezent-Zoologie'. Delay: one to two years. No indexes.

193 Muséum National d'Histoire Naturelle. *Bibliographie: palynologie.* Paris: Éditions du Muséum, 1958–. Annual.
Unannotated bibliography on palynology from a wide range of sources worldwide, alphabetically arranged by author. Index. Delay: *c.* 6–12 months.
    Previously a Supplement to *Pollen et Spores* (1959–73), which in turn continued *Palynologie: bibliographie* (1958–59).

Textbooks, handbooks, manuals

194 Brothwell, D. R. and **Higgs, E.** (eds.). *Science in archaeology: a survey of progress and research.* 2nd ed. London: Thames and Hudson, 1969. 720 pp. References at the end of each chapter.
Series of essays illustrating the range of scientific techniques applied to excavations and the information derived from them. An introductory chapter on scientific studies in archaeology is followed by sections on dating, the environment (subdivided into climate, soils, plants, animals), man, microscopy and radiography, artefacts, statistics, prospecting. Index of sites; general index.

195 Fleming, S. J. *Dating in archaeology: a guide to scientific techniques.* London: Dent, 1978. 272 pp. Notes and bibliography: pp. 240–67.
A guide to scientific dating methods in archaeology drawing on a wide range of data, with chapters on dendrochronology, radiocarbon, radioactive decay techniques, thermoluminescence, fission track, obsidian, archaeomagnetic, chemical methods of dating bone, and new scientific techniques applied to art history.

196 Shackley, M. *Environmental archaeology.* London: Allen and Unwin, 1981. 228 pp. Detailed references at the end of each chapter.
Guide to environmental archaeology; also a reference work giving details of procedures and laboratory techniques.

197 Tite, M. S. *Methods of physical examination in archaeology.* London: Seminar Press, 1972. 419 pp. (Studies in Archaeological Science.) References at the end of each chapter.
Describes and assesses the many methods of physical examination used for locating buried features and for age determination, and describes the wide range of physical techniques available.

Periodicals and series

198 *Advances in Computer Archaeology.* (formerly: *Newsletter of Computer Archaeology.*) Tempe: Arizona State University, Department of Anthropology, 1983–. Twice a year. En.
Computer applications in archaeology, emphasizing topics such as potential use of new software and hardware, and applications of mini-micro computing.

199 *Archaeo-Physika.* Cologne: Rheinland-Verlag GmbH, 1965–. Irreg. De. En. Fr.
Various aspects of archaeological science, e.g. magnetic prospecting in archaeology, techniques of data analysis, etc. Bibliographies.

200 *Archaeometry.* Oxford: University of Oxford, Research Laboratory for Archaeology and the History of Art, 1958–. Twice a year. En. Cumulative index: vols. 1–15 (1958–73).
International research journal dealing with the involvement of the physical sciences in archaeology and art history. Includes abstracts of its own papers. Sometimes includes introductory review articles.

201 *Journal of Archaeological Science.* London: Academic Press, 1974–. Quarterly. En.
International journal covering material which combines archaeology and other sciences including the physical, biological and earth sciences, and mathematics. Book reviews, book notes. Includes abstracts of its own papers.

202 *Lithic Technology.* (formerly: *Newsletter of Lithic Technology.*) San Antonio: University of Texas at San Antonio, Center for Archaeological Research, 1972–. Three times a year. En.
Technology of stone tools worldwide.

203 *MASCA Journal.* (formerly: *MASCA Newsletter.*) Philadelphia: University Museum, Applied Science Center for Archaeology, University of Pennsylvania, 1965–. Twice a year. En.
Emphasis on the spectrum of sciences applicable to archaeology. Book reviews.

204 *Ossa: International Journal of Skeletal Research.* Stockholm: University of Stockholm, Osteological Research Laboratory, 1974–. En. (summaries in En. and Ru.).
Human and animal osteology. Reports on work using skeletal remains for the exploration of e.g. prehistoric and present man, his domestic animals, his environment and its changes, etc.

205 *PACT: Journal of the European Study Group on Physical, Chemical and Mathematical Techniques applied to Archaeology.* Rixensart (Belgium): European Study Group on Physical, Chemical and Mathematical Techniques applied to Archaeology, 1977–. Annual. En. Fr.
Mainly reports of congresses and symposia on scientific techniques applied to archaeology.

206 *Quaternary Research: an Interdisciplinary Journal.* New York: Academic Press, 1970–. Every two months. En.
International interdisciplinary journal dealing with the Quaternary Period. Book reviews.

207 *Radiocarbon.* New Haven (Connecticut): American Journal of Science, 1959–. Three times a year. En.
International journal publishing compilations of carbon 14 dates produced by various laboratories, and technical and interpretative articles on all aspects of carbon 14. Book reviews.

208 *Revue d'Archéometrie: Bulletin de Liaison du Groupe des Méthodes Physiques et Chimiques de l'Archéologie.* Rennes: Université de Rennes, 1977–. Annual. Fr.
Archaeometric studies worldwide. Includes abstracts of its own papers (Fr. and En.).

209 *Science and Archaeology.* Stafford (England): Research Centre for Computer Archaeology, 1970–. Annual. En. Cumulative indexes: vols. 1–10 in vol. 10 (1973); vols. 11–20 in vol. 20 (1977).
Scientific techniques in archaeology worldwide with emphasis on computer applications in processing geophysical survey data, statistical studies, information retrieval, distribution maps, publication. Book reviews.

210 *Studies in Archaeological Science.* New York and London: Academic Press, 1971–. Irreg. En.
Each volume covers some specialized aspect, e.g. land snails in archaeology, fish remains in archaeology, animal diseases in archaeology, etc. Twelve titles published by 1983.

211 *Studies in Conservation: the Journal of the International Institute for Conservation of Historic and Artistic Works.* London: International Institute for Conservation of Historic and Artistic Works, 1952–. Quarterly. En. Fr. Cumulative indexes: vols. 1–12; vols. 13–22.
Conservation and restoration of material remains (including monuments, libraries and archival materials, the technology and composition of different types of object, the nature of deteriorative processes and their prevention, and all aspects of storage and display). Includes abstracts. Book reviews.

Europe
(in general; excluding USSR)

General bibliographical guides

212 Borroni, F. *'Il Cicognara': bibliografia dell'archeologia classica e dell'arte italiana.* Florence: Sansoni, 1954–67. 2 vols. in 37 parts.
Comprehensive listing, with some annotations, of the sources of classical archaeology and Italian art, with emphasis on Greece and Italy. Vol. 1: *Opere bibliografiche citate;* Vol. 2: *Archeologia classica.* Each volume is arranged in many sections, and chronologically within each section. Index of places, editions and

printings, printers, publishers and engravers; analytical index; index of subjects; index of facsimiles; general index.

213 Coulson, W. D. E. *Annotated bibliography of Greek and Roman art, architecture, and archaeology.* New York and London: Garland, 1975. 140 pp.
Arranged in seven sections, with helpful annotations: general works, aims, methods and history of archaeology; prehistoric Greek archaeology; Archaic, Classical and Hellenistic Greek art, architecture, and archaeology; the Etruscans; Roman art, architecture, and archaeology; miscellaneous. Appendices comprise a list of books on ancient urbanism and urban planning, a list of useful hardcover editions above $10, and a useful select list of German and French publications on classical subjects, including excavation reports. No index.

214 Gerlach, G. and **Hachmann, R.** *Verzeichnis vor- und frühgeschichtlicher Bibliographien.* Berlin: de Gruyter, 1971. 273 pp. (Deutsches Archäologisches Institut (Frankfurt). Römisch-Germanische Kommission. Bericht, 50, Beiheft.)
Comprehensive list of 3,103 unannotated bibliographies for European pre- and early history (excluding Greece and Portugal), both those published separately and those included in publications. Arranged by country with introductory remarks for each country. An essential guide to pre-1970 European archaeological bibliographies.

215 Greenwood, J. Industrial archaeology in Western Europe: a bibliography. *Industrial Archaeology Review*, 6:2 (1982), 125–39.
Industrial archaeology in Western Europe, excluding the British Isles. A general section is followed by a country arrangement, under which societies are listed first, followed by books and articles on the industrial archaeology of that country.

216 Schmider, B. *Bibliographie analytique de préhistoire pour le paléolithique supérieur européen (publications parues entre 1850 et 1968 conservées à la bibliothèque du Musée de l'Homme).* Paris: Centre de Documentation Humaines. n.d. 2 vols.
Vol. 1: *Index* (authors, geographical areas, cultures, materials).
Vol. 2: *Catalogue des publications analysées.*
Lists 4,999 numbered items, unannotated, on the European Upper Palaeolithic.

217 Willerding, U. Bibliographie zur Paläo-Ethnobotanik des Mittelalters in Mitteleuropa 1945–1977. Teil 1: *Zeitschrift für Archäologie des Mittelalters*, 6 (1978), 173–223; Teil 2: *Zeitschrift für Archäologie des Mittelalters*, 7 (1979), 207–25.
Detailed unannotated bibliography of publications on palaeoethnobotany in the middle ages in Europe 1945–77, with indexes. Part 1 is the bibliography; Part 2 gives a survey of finding places of medieval seed materials, and an English summary.

Abstracting, indexing, current awareness services
218 *Archeologické Rozhledy.* Prague: (Československá Akademie Věd, Archeolo-

gicky Ustav) Academia, Publishing House of the Czechoslovak Academy of Sciences, 1949–. Every two months. Cz. Sl. (occasionally En. Fr. De.) (summaries in En. Fr. De.). (see also [360])
Includes lists of contents of periodicals covering archaeology in Europe.

219 *Ausgrabungen und Funde: Archäologische Berichte und Informationen.* Berlin: (Akademie der Wissenschaften der DDR, Zentralinstitut für Alte Geschichte und Archäologie) Akademie-Verlag, 1956–. Every two months. De. (see also [305])
Certain issues include 'Neue Schriften: Bibliographie zur Ur- und Frühgeschichte' – a list of books and articles on mainly European pre- and early history arranged by subject, area and period.

220 *Bulletin Signalétique 530: Répertoire d'Art et d'Archéologie (de l'époque paléochrétienne à 1939).* Paris: Centre National de la Recherche Scientifique, 1910–. Quarterly with annual cumulative index.
Covers all kinds of publications, most with abstracts, on mainly European art and archaeology from the palaeochristian era to 1939. Over 2,000 serials are examined. Arranged by general sections, then chronologically. Index of artists; subject index; author index. Delay: most items published within last two years. A product from the data base FRANCIS (subfile 530) which is searchable online through QUESTEL/TÉLÉSYSTÈMES.

221 *International Medieval Bibliography.* Leeds (England): International Medieval Bibliography, 1967– (publ. 1968–). Twice a year.
Unannotated listing of articles on the whole range of medieval European studies published in journals, Festschriften, colloquium papers and collected essays. Period covered: *c.* AD 500–1500. Currently *c.* 1,000 serials are covered, including a wide range of archaeological ones. Arranged by topic (archaeology is one such topic) and subdivided by area. Author index; general index. Delay: usually only a few months.

222 *Zeitschrift für Archäologie des Mittelalters.* Cologne: Rheinland-Verlag, 1973–. Annual. De. Fr. En. (see also [235])
Each volume includes a bibliography of medieval archaeology, 1945 to the present, usually for one European country or German state.

Surveys

223 Krzysztof, J. K. and **Kozlowski, S. K.** *Pradzieje Europy od XL do IV tysiaclecia p.n.e. (Prehistory of Europe from the 40th to the 4th millennium BC).* Warsaw: Panstwowe Wydawnictwo Naukowe, 1975. 504 pp.
Surveys Upper Palaeolithic and Mesolithic Europe. Valuable for its non-Western standpoint.

224 Milisauskas, S. *European prehistory.* New York: Academic Press, 1978. 345 pp. (Studies in Archaeology.) References: pp. 295–315.
A survey of the Neolithic, Bronze and Iron Ages, with the emphasis on Central and Eastern Europe.

225 Phillips, P. *The prehistory of Europe.* London: Allen Lane, 1980. 314 pp. Bibliography: pp. 269–97.
Survey of recent developments in European prehistory to the dawn of the Christian era, arranged chronologically.

Periodicals and series

226 *Antiquaries Journal: Journal of the Society of Antiquaries of London.* Neasden (England): (Society of Antiquaries of London) Oxford University Press, 1921–. Twice a year. En. Cumulative indexes: vols. 1–10 (1921–30); vols. 11–20 (1931–40); vols. 21–30 (1941–50); vols. 31–40 (1951–60); vols. 41–50 (1961–70). (see also [23])
Prehistory, history and archaeology of Europe, with emphasis on Great Britain. Includes notes, book reviews, obituaries, 'List of accessions' to the Society's library, and 'Periodical literature' (listing the contents of British and non-British journals).

227 *Archaeologia: or, Miscellaneous Tracts relating to Antiquity.* London: Society of Antiquaries of London, 1770–. Irreg. En. Cumulative indexes: vols. 1–50 (1770–1887); 51–100 (1888–1966).
Prehistory, history and archaeology of Europe with emphasis on Great Britain.

228 *Archaeologia Atlantica.* Bad Bramstedt (West Germany): Morland Editions, 1975–. Irreg. En. Fr. De.
Prehistory and early history of Western European countries bordering the Atlantic. Notes and news.

229 *Études Celtiques.* Paris: Centre National de la Recherche Scientifique, 1936–. Annual. En. Fr. De. It. Es. Cumulative index: vols. 1–10 (1936–64) in vol. 10:3 (1965).
History of the early Celts in Ireland, Wales and continental Europe; includes archaeology, epigraphy, philology, numismatics, toponymy. Includes 'Bibliographie' (book reviews) and 'Périodiques' (summary of the contents of periodical articles).

230 *Frühmittelalterliche Studien: Jahrbuch des Instituts für Frühmittelalterforschung der Universität Münster.* Berlin: (Universität Münster, Institut fur Frühmittelalterforschung) de Gruyter, 1967–. Annual. De.
History, culture and archaeology of European early middle ages. Book reviews.

231 *Inventaria Archaeologica: an illustrated card-inventory of important associated finds in archaeology.* Founded by M.-E. Mariën. Issued under the auspices of the Union Internationale des Sciences Préhistoriques et Protohistoriques (UISPP). *Austria*: Heft 1–. Antwerpen: De Sikkel, 1956. Bonn: Habelt, 1958–. *Belgium*: Fasc. 1–. Anvers: De Sikkel, 1953–. *Czechoslovakia*: Heft 1–. Bonn: Habelt, 1961–. *Denmark*: Set 1–. Bonn: Habelt, 1965–. *France*: Fasc. 1–. Anvers: De Sikkel and others, 1954–. *Germany*: Heft 1–. Bonn: Habelt, 1954–. *Great Britain*: Set 1–. London: Garraway, 1955–59. London: British Museum, 1960–. *Hungary*: Heft 1–. Bonn: Habelt, 1962–. *Italy*: Fasc. 1–. Florence: Sansoni, 1961–. *Netherlands*:

Set 1–. Bonn: Habelt, 1971–. *Norway*: Set 1–. Bonn: Habelt, 1966. *Poland*: Fasc.
1–. Lodz: Pańtswowe Wydawnictwo Nauk, 1958–. *Romania*: Fasc. 1–. Bucharest: Académie de la République Socialiste de Roumanie, 1966–. *Spain*: Fasc.
1–. Madrid: Instituto Español de Prehistoria, 1958–. *Yugoslavia*: Fasc. 1–.
Bonn: Habelt. Zagreb: Soc. Arch. de Yougoslavie, 1957–.
International project aimed at publishing compact accounts of important
associated finds, illustrated by drawings in line, in the form of printed cards.

232 *Mesolithic Miscellany*. Madison (Wisconsin): Union International des Sciences Préhistoriques et Protohistoriques, Commission 14, 1980–. Twice a year.
En.
Newsletter including brief research reports on the European Mesolithic. Book
reviews. List of recent publications.

233 *Oxford Journal of Archaeology*. Oxford: (Institute of Archaeology, Oxford)
Blackwell, 1982–. Twice a year. En.
Origins and development of European society from prehistoric to medieval
times. Notes section. Includes abstracts of its own papers.

234 *Praehistorische Zeitschrift*. Berlin: de Gruyter, 1909–. Twice a year. De.
European cultural history, archaeology and art from prehistoric times to the
early middle ages. Book reviews.

235 *Zeitschrift für Archäologie des Mittelalters*. Cologne: Rheinland-Verlag, 1973–.
Annual. De. Fr. En. (see also [222])
Archaeology during the middle ages in Europe. Book reviews. Each vol. includes
a bibliography of medieval archaeology, 1945–present, usually for one European
country or German state.

Encyclopaedia

236 Filip, J. *Enzyklopädisches Handbuch zur Ur- und Frühgeschichte Europas*. Stuttgart: Kohlhammer, 1966–69. 2 vols.
A compendium of factual data on European prehistory and early history,
arranged alphabetically. Entries under sites, countries, people, periodical titles,
etc. Includes photographs, illustrations, drawings, maps, etc.

Directories (biographical, organizational, research in progress, meetings)

237 *Directory of European associations*. Part 2: *National learned, scientific and technical
societies*; ed. by I. G. Anderson. 2nd ed. Beckenham (England): CBD Research,
1979. 399 pp.
Gives information on national and important regional European associations,
including well over 100 archaeological and related organizations. Excludes the
British Isles (for which see *Directory of British associations* [270]). Arranged
alphabetically by subject and by country within each subject. Details include
name, year of foundation, address and telephone number, field of interest,
activities, publications, etc. Subject index; index of abbreviations of names of
associations; index of names of associations. Introductory matter and subject
index also in Fr. and De.

238 Lewanski, R. C. *Subject collections in European libraries.* 2nd ed. London and New York: Bowker, 1978. 495 pp.
Gives information such as address, number of vols., special collections and restrictions on access for over 100 major European archaeological libraries, in addition to those in other subject fields. Arranged by the Dewey Decimal classification scheme, with a subject index.

239 Verhaeghe, F. *Archaeology, natural science and technology: the European situation; a survey prepared for the European Science Foundation.* Strasbourg: European Science Foundation, [1979]. 3 vols.
Excellent inventory of existing facilities (institutes, organizations, university departments, laboratories, etc.) in natural science in archaeology in Western Europe (except for Yugoslavia and Portugal). Includes the name and address of each unit (695 in total) and a summary of its work including any databanks, archives or publications. Arranged alphabetically by country with Nordic countries treated separately. Also includes a report surveying the situation in each of the fields covered, with a separate report on the Nordic countries. The fields are: archaeological prospection and surveying (air photography, geophysical and geochemical prospection, photogrammetric work, archaeomagnetism, underwater archaeology); excavations and study of finds (archaeological legislation, earth sciences, analysis of materials, palaeobotany, archaeozoology, physical anthropology, archaeometry); training; archaeological documentation, databanks, archives, publications; conservation. Geographical index. Subject index.

240 *Zusammenstellung.* Compiled by Prof. O. Kleenan. Bonn: Universität Bonn, Institut für Vor- und Frühgeschichte, 1967–. Twice a year.
Lists the prehistoric and protohistoric institutes, with addresses, for West Germany, Austria, Switzerland, Netherlands, Belgium, Luxemburg, with details of courses and seminars for the following term. Some issues include lists of prehistory theses in preparation; occasional issues have lists of completed theses. Each issue also includes details of prehistory organizations (institutes, museums, individuals, etc.) in one German state or foreign country (a list of areas covered in previous issues is included in each issue). Index of persons.

British Isles
(United Kingdom, Ireland)

General bibliographical guides

241 *Archaeological bibliography for Great Britain and Ireland.* London: Council for British Archaeology, 1950–80. Annual.
Comprehensive list of articles from *c.* 150–200 British and Irish periodicals and monographs on the archaeology of the British Isles from the earliest times to AD 1600. Arranged in two parts: topographical section arranged by county, period and subjects; bibliography (authors' list) giving bibliographical details. Subject index. Delay: two to three years. Preceded by *Archaeological bulletin for the British Isles* (London: Council for British Archaeology, 1940–49), arranged in the same way, which in turn succeeded the *Reports of the Congress of Archaeological Societies*

(London: Congress of Archaeological Societies, 1905–39) which included an *Index of reports of the Earthworks Committee for the years 1905–26*. This succeeded *Index of archaeological papers published in 1891–1910* (London: Constable, 1892–1914), an annual listing, by author, of articles in selected British archaeological society periodicals, with a subject index, which in turn was preceded by Gomme, G. L. (ed.) *Index of archaeological papers 1665–1890* (London: Constable, 1907. 921 pp.), an index by author to articles in ninety-four British archaeological and historical periodicals which include some non-British as well as British material. For 1901 onwards Mullins, E. L. C. *A guide to the historical and archaeological publications of societies in England and Wales, 1901–1933* (London: Athlone, 1968. 863 pp.) lists the contents of the publications of over 400 local and national historical and archaeological societies. This was continued by Supplements 1–13 (1929–1942/ 46) of the *Bulletin of the Institute of Historical Research* (London: Longmans, 1930–48).

242 Bonser, W. *An Anglo-Saxon and Celtic bibliography (450–1087)* Oxford: Blackwell; Berkeley: University of California Press, 1957. 2 vols.
List of 11,975 items, some with brief notes, from 376 periodicals (mainly British), collective works and monographs, on Anglo-Saxon and Celtic history (in the widest sense) in the British Isles. Vol. 1: general topics and historical source material; political history; local history; constitutional history and law; social and economic history; ecclesiastical history and religion; geography and place-names; general culture; archaeology; numismatics and seals; epigraphy; art. Vol. 2: index of authors; subject and topographical index.

243 Bonser, W. *A prehistoric bibliography*. Extended and ed. by J. Troy. Oxford: Blackwell, 1976. 441 pp.
Unannotated list of 9,020 articles from *c.* 200 British archaeological and local history society periodicals on British prehistory. Arranged in five sections: men and methods in archaeology; field archaeology; specific sites; material finds; culture; with the three middle sections divided geographically according to the regional group structure of the Council for British Archaeology. Useful but marred by a large number of errors and corrections. Index of authors and subjects.

244 Bonser, W. *A Romano-British bibliography (55 BC–AD 449)*. Oxford: Blackwell, 1964. 2 vols.
List of 9,370 items, some with brief notes, from 253 periodicals (mainly British) and collective works, on British history from 55 BC to AD 449. Vol. 1, part 1: general topics; history; army, fleet and defence; social and economic; religion; geography; general archaeology; numismatics; art. Part 2: sites arranged geographically. Vol. 2: indexes of authors, subjects, personal names, place-names.

Abstracting, indexing, current awareness service

245 *British Archaeological Abstracts*. London: Council for British Archaeology, 1968–. Twice a year.
Indicates the most significant material currently being published on British archaeology in over 200 British, Irish and foreign periodicals, monograph series,

monographs, reference works, etc. Large general section, worldwide in scope, precedes sections arranged by period, then by subject. Annual author and subject index. From 1983, gives titles only but also includes minor items which were formerly given in the *Archaeological bibliography for Great Britain and Ireland* [241]. Delay: *c.* 10 months.

Handbook

246 Corbishley, M. J. (ed.). *Archaeological resources handbook for teachers.* 2nd ed. London: Council for British Archaeology, 1983. 152 pp.
Provides guidelines for teaching archaeology in schools and gives information on resources available, with the emphasis on British archaeology. An introduction on the Council for British Archaeology and teaching archaeology in schools is followed by sections on books, finding out in archaeology, examinations, museums, central government archaeology, audio-visual aids, post-school education, careers, and professional units.

Surveys

247 Baker, D. *Living with the past: the historic environment.* Bletsoe (England): privately published, 1983. 174 pp. Select bibliography: pp. 169–71.
Covers the philosophy and organization of conservation of ancient monuments and historic buildings in Britain.

248 Megaw, J. V. S. and **Simpson, D. D. A.** *Introduction to British prehistory: from the arrival of 'Homo sapiens' to the Claudian invasion.* Leicester: Leicester University Press, 1979. 575 pp. Bibliography: pp. 503–44.
Descriptive outline of British prehistory, including Ireland.

249 Ritchie, G. and **Ritchie, A.** *Scotland: archaeology and early history.* London: Thames and Hudson, 1981. (Ancient Peoples and Places, 99.) 192 pp. Select bibliography: pp. 183–6.
Covers the archaeology of Scotland from the earliest settlement to the 9th century AD.

250 Thomas, N. *A guide to prehistoric England.* 2nd ed. London: Batsford, 1976. 270 pp.
An introduction is followed by a Gazetteer, arranged by county with descriptions of individual sites and monuments.

Periodicals and series

251 *Archaeologia Cambrensis: Journal of the Cambrian Archaeological Association.* Aberystwyth: Cambrian Archaeological Association, 1846–. Annual. En. Cumulative indexes: 1846–1900; 1901–60.
Archaeology of Wales from prehistoric times to the present. Includes section on periodical literature in Wales for the previous year. Book reviews.

252 *Archaeological Journal.* London: Royal Archaeological Institute, 1844–. Annual. En. Cumulative indexes: vols. 1–25 (1844–68); vols. 26–50 (1869–93); vols. 51–75 (1894–1918).

Archaeology and architectural history, with emphasis on the United Kingdom. Book reviews.

253 *Archaeology in Britain.* London: Council for British Archaeology, 1972–. Annual. En.
The annual report of the CBA. An introduction discusses developments of the past year and regular features include notes on the work of official bodies in Britain such as the Royal Commissions, the Department of the Environment, etc. and of national bodies such as the CBA, the Museums Association, summaries of research projects, notes on the activities of county and regional groups, excavation trusts and units.

254 *Britannia: a Journal of Romano-British and Kindred Studies.* London: Society for the Promotion of Roman Studies, 1970–. Annual. En. Cumulative index: vols. 1–10 (1970–79).
Concerned specifically, but not exclusively, with Roman Britain. Includes notes, a survey of Roman Britain during the preceding year, and book reviews.

255 *Bulletin of the Board of Celtic Studies, University of Wales.* Cardiff: University of Wales Press, 1921–. Quarterly. En. We.
Interdisciplinary studies of the history, law, archaeology, art, language and literature of Celtic peoples.

256 *CBA Newsletter and Calendar.* London: Council for British Archaeology, 1977–. Nine times a year. En.
Gives general archaeological news, lists of excavations requiring volunteer workers, information on courses, conferences, study tours, CBA publications, lectures, appointments, etc. Continues *CBA Calendar of Excavations* (1951–76).

257 *Council for British Archaeology Research Reports.* London: Council for British Archaeology, 1955–. Irreg. En.
Various aspects of British archaeology.

258 *Current Archaeology.* London: Selkirk, 1967–. Every two months. En.
Semi-popular treatment of British archaeology from earliest times to the middle ages. Book reviews.

259 *Discovery and Excavation in Scotland.* Edinburgh: Council for British Archaeology (Scotland), 1956–. Annual. En.
Lists by counties all discoveries, excavations and surveys made in Scotland during the previous year. Includes 'Scottish bibliography', a listing by period of publications relating to Scotland.

260 *The Journal of Irish Archaeology.* (formerly: *Irish Archaeological Research Forum.*) Belfast: Queen's University, Joint Conservation Laboratory, 1983–. Quarterly. En.
All aspects of archaeology with particular reference to Ireland.

261 *Journal of the British Archaeological Association.* London: British Archaeological

Association, 1843–. Annual. En. Cumulative indexes: vols. 1–30 (1846–74); new series vols. 1–25 (1895–1919); recently, every four or five years.
Archaeology, art and architectural history of Western Europe, with emphasis on the United Kingdom, from Roman times to the 19th century. Book reviews.

262 *Journal of the Royal Society of Antiquaries of Ireland.* Dublin: Royal Society of Antiquaries of Ireland, 1849–. Annual. En. Cumulative indexes: vols. 1–19 (1849–89) as vol. 20; vols. 21–40 (1891–1910); vols. 41–60 (1911–30).
Irish history, archaeology and antiquities of all periods. Book reviews.

263 *Medieval Archaeology: Journal of the Society for Medieval Archaeology.* London: Society for Medieval Archaeology, 1957–. Annual. En. Cumulative index every five years.
British archaeology from the end of Roman rule to the middle ages. Includes notes and news, book reviews and a survey of excavations undertaken during the preceding year ('Medieval Britain').

264 *Post-Medieval Archaeology: Journal of the Society for Post-Medieval Archaeology.* London: Society for Post-Medieval Archaeology, 1967–. Annual. En. Cumulative indexes: vols. 1–5 (1967–71); vols. 6–10 (1972–76).
Archaeology of post-medieval Britain before industrialization. Includes notes and news, book reviews and a survey of post-medieval Britain during the preceding year (excavations and periodical literature).

265 *Proceedings of the Prehistoric Society of London.* London: Prehistoric Society, 1935–. Annual. En. Cumulative indexes: vols. 1–30 (1935–64); vols. 31–40 (1965–74).
Prehistory and archaeology of Europe from the Neolithic to the Iron Age with emphasis on Great Britain and Ireland. Lengthy book reviews. Continued *Proceedings of the Prehistoric Society of East Anglia* (1908–35).

266 *Proceedings of the Royal Irish Academy: Section C: Archaeology, Celtic Studies, History, Linguistics, Literature.* Dublin: Royal Irish Academy, 1836–. Irreg. En. Ir. Cumulative indexes: 1836–61; 1907–32; 1932–53.
History and archaeology of Ireland. Includes abstracts of papers.

267 *Proceedings of the Society of Antiquaries of Scotland.* Edinburgh: National Museum of Antiquities of Scotland, 1851–. Annual. En. Cumulative indexes: vols. 1–24 (1851–90); vols. 25–48 (1890–1914); vols. 49–81 (1914–47); vols. 82–105 (1947/8–1972/4)
Archaeology and history of Scotland from prehistoric times to the present.

268 *Ulster Journal of Archaeology.* Belfast: Ulster Archaeological Society, 1853–. Annual. En. Cumulative indexes: 3rd series vols. 7–12 (1944–49); vols. 13–20 (1950–67).
Local history, archaeology and antiquities of the northern counties of Ireland, primarily from ancient times to the middle ages. Book reviews.

Thesaurus

269 Adkins, L. and **Adkins, R. A.** *A thesaurus of British archaeology.* Newton Abbot (England): David and Charles; Totowa (New Jersey): Barnes and Noble, 1982. 319 pp. Bibliography: pp. 285–96.

Excellent, detailed work explaining the technical terms and jargon found in British archaeology (excluding Ireland). Covers the Palaeolithic to medieval periods. Arranged by period, with a further chapter on archaeological techniques and a final 'Miscellaneous' chapter. Text includes sources for further reading, with full details given in the Bibliography. Numerous drawings and diagrams. Index (very full).

Also published as *The Handbook of British archaeology* (London: Macmillan, 1983).

Directories (organizational, research in progress)

270 *Directory of British associations and associations in Ireland.* Ed. by G. P. Henderson and S. P. A. Henderson. 7th ed. Beckenham (England): CBD Research, 1982. 486 pp.

Standard guide for information on British national and local associations, societies, institutes in all fields including well over 100 archaeological ones. Arranged alphabetically by the name of the association and gives address, activities, details of meetings, total membership, etc. Abbreviations index; subject index.

271 *Directory of grant-making trusts.* 8th ed. Tonbridge (England): Charities Aid Foundation, 1983. 958 pp.

Directory of registered charities and foundations in Britain. 8th ed. included thirty-eight trusts listed under the classification 'Archaeology'. Geographical index of trusts; alphabetical index of subjects; alphabetical index of trusts.

272 *Research in British universities, polytechnics and colleges.* 3rd ed. Boston Spa (England): British Library, 1982. 3 vols.

The national register of current research in science and social science. Arranged in broad subject groups; vol. 2 (Biological Sciences) and vol. 3 (Social Sciences) both include 'Archaeology and Anthropology', with some overlap. Vol. 3 also includes research in government departments and other institutions. Each vol. also contains name and keyword indexes.

Guide to non-book material

273 Roulstone, M. (ed.). *The bibliography of museum and art gallery publications and audio-visual aids in Great Britain and Ireland 1979/80.* Cambridge (England): Chadwyck-Healey, 1980. 560 pp.

Lists the publications and audio-visual aids (i.e. books, guides, catalogues, bulletins, reports, slides, postcards, photographs, films, records, microform, tapes, etc.) produced by 955 British museums and art galleries. Arranged alphabetically by institution. Geographical index; author index; subject index.

Scandinavia

(Denmark, Finland, Greenland, Iceland, Norway, Sweden)

General bibliographical guides

274 Bakka, L. Norsk arkeologisk bibliografi, 1957–1976. *Universitetets Oldsaksamling. Årbok* 1977/8. 192 pp.
Bibliography of publications on Norwegian archaeology, continuing earlier works listed in Lamm [276].

275 Becker, C. J. Litteratur om Danmarks forhistorie, 1969–1973. In *Fortid og Nutid*, 28:3 (1980), 473–81.
Bibliography of publications on Danish archaeology, continuing earlier works listed in Lamm [276].

276 Lamm J. P. Bibliografisk hjälpreda vid sökandet efter nordisk arkeologisk litteratur. In *Fornvännen*, 71 (1976), 205–6.
Gives a complete list of all Nordic archaeological bibliographies published up to 1976.

Abstracting, indexing, current awareness services

277 *Nordic Archaeological Abstracts.* Viborg (Denmark): Viborg Stiftsmuseum, 1974– (publ. 1975–). Annual.
Covers publications of all kinds dealing with the archaeology (of all periods) of the Nordic countries, including Greenland and Iceland, and the work of Nordic archaeologists abroad. Arranged by period, then by subject, preceded by a large general section. Some 250 periodicals and irregular serials are covered. Indicates other Nordic archaeological and related bibliographies. Index of authors and scholars. Subject index. Site indexes. Maps. Chronological table. Delay: *c.* two years.

278 *Swedish Archaeological Bibliography.* Stockholm: Svenska Arkeologiska Samfundet, 1939– (publ. 1951–). Irreg.
Records work published by Swedish archaeologists both in Sweden and abroad. Six vols. published to date for the period 1939–75, each vol. covering several years. Each vol. includes narrative surveys, selective and critical, arranged by period, topic and area. Index of publications acts as a detailed bibliography, each vol. listing over 1,000 references. Vols. 5 and 6 also include list of seminar papers and licentiate theses. Delay: *c.* two or three years.

Survey

279 Huurre, M. *9000 vuotta Suomen esihistoriaa (9000 years of Finnish prehistory).* Helsinki: Otava, 1979. 235 pp.
Synthesis of Finnish prehistory from the earliest settlements to the middle ages.

Periodicals

280 *Aarbøger for Nordisk Oldkyndighed og Historie.* Copenhagen: Kongelige Nordiske Oldskriftselskab, 1836–. Annual. Da. (summaries in En. and De.). Cumulative indexes: 1836–63; 1866–1933.
Archaeology and anthropology of the Nordic countries, with emphasis on Denmark, from prehistoric times to the middle ages.

281 *Acta Archaeologica.* Copenhagen: Munksgaard, 1930–. Annual. En. De. Fr. Cumulative index: vols. 1–50 (1930–79) in vol. 50.
Emphasis is on Scandinavian archaeology of all periods. Also covers Asia Minor, Northern Africa, Europe.

282 *Antikvariskt Arkiv.* Stockholm: Kungliga Vitterhets Historie och Antikvitets Akademien, 1954–. Irreg. Sw. De. En.
Scandinavian archaeology.

283 *Árbók hins Íslenzka Fornleifafélags.* Reykjavík: Ísafoldarprentsmidja, 1881–. Annual. Ic. (summaries in En.). Cumulative index: 1955–79.
Icelandic archaeology and history.

284 *Finskt Museum.* Helsinki: Finska Fornminnesföreningen, 1894–. Annual. En. De. Sw. Cumulative index: vols. 1–20 (1894–1943).
Prehistoric and historic archaeology, ethnography and cultural history with emphasis on Finland.

285 *Fornvännen: Tidskrift för Svensk Antikvarisk Forskning/Journal of Swedish Antiquarian Research.* Stockholm: Kungliga Vitterhets, Historie och Antikvitets Akademien, 1906–. Quarterly. Da. En. De. No. Sw. (summaries in En.).
Swedish archaeology, including reports on recent finds and projects. Includes lists of recent Swedish doctoral theses on archaeology and related subjects. Book reviews.

286 *Journal of Danish Archaeology.* Odense: Odense University Press, 1982–. Annual. En.
Reports on the most important results achieved in Denmark and by Danish archaeologists working abroad. Includes 'Recent excavations and discoveries'. Book reviews.

287 *Kungliga Vitterhets, Historie och Antikvitets Akademiens Årsbok.* Stockholm: Kungliga Vitterhets, Historie och Antikvitets Akademien, 1926–. Annual. Sw.
Swedish history and archaeology. Includes brief reports on the most significant fieldwork.

288 *Norwegian Archaeological Review.* Oslo: Universitetsforlaget, 1968–. Twice a year. En. Cumulative index: vols. 1–10 in vol. 11 (1978).
Concentrates on articles of special interest to Scandinavian archaeological research, with emphasis on Europe, but includes also articles on methodology and theory based on results from other parts of the world as well as Scandinavia. Book reviews.

289 *Suomen Muinaismuistoyhdistyksen Aikakauskirja/Finska Fornminnesföreningens Tidskrift.* Helsinki: Suomen Muinaismuistoyhdistys/Finska Fornminnesföreningen, 1874–. Irreg. En. Fi. Fr. De. Sw. Cumulative index: vols. 1–52 (1874–1953).
Prehistory, archaeology, art and cultural history of northern Europe.

290 *Viking: Tidsskrift for Norrøn Arkeologi.* Oslo: Norsk Arkeologisk Selskap, 1937–. Annual. No. (summaries in En.).
Norwegian archaeology.

Western Europe
(Belgium, France, Germany, Luxemburg, Netherlands, Switzerland)

General bibliographical guides

291 Gandilhon, R. and **Samaran, C.** *Bibliographie générale des travaux historiques et archéologiques, publiés par les sociétés savantes de la France. Période 1910–40.* Paris: Imprimerie Nationale, 1944–61. 5 vols.
Lists books and articles on historical and archaeological subjects published by French learned societies between 1910 and 1940. A note on each society and its publications precedes an analysis of the contents of each volume's publications. Arranged alphabetically by département, then by place of publication, then by society.

Continues *Bibliographie annuelle des travaux historiques et archéologiques publiés par les sociétés savantes de la France, 1901–10* (Paris: Imprimerie Nationale, 1906–14. 3 vols.), listing in total 42,612 items, which in turn continues Lasteyrie du Saillant, R.C., Comte de. *Bibliographie générale des travaux historiques et archéologiques, publiés par les sociétés savantes de la France* (Paris: Imprimerie Nationale, 1888–1918. 6 vols.; vols. 1–4 cover publications to 1885, vols. 5–6 1886–1900).

292 Montandon, R. *Bibliographie générale des travaux palethnologiques et archéologiques (époques préhistorique, protohistorique, et gallo-romaine).* Paris: Leroux, 1917–38. 5 vols. and 3 supplements.
Comprehensive bibliography of over 30,000 entries, arranged geographically. Since 1952, continued in the *Bulletin de la Société Préhistorique Française* [26].

Abstracting, indexing, current awareness services

293 *Helinium: Revue consacrée à l'Archéologie des Pays-Bas, de la Belgique et du Grand-Duché de Luxembourg.* Wetteren (Belgium): Éditions Universa, 1961–. Three times a year. En. Nd. Fr. (see also [313])
Includes a detailed, classified current bibliography for the Netherlands, Belgium and Luxemburg.

294 *Résumés d'Archéologie Suisse.* Lausanne: Université de Lausanne, Institut d'Archéologie et d'Histoire Ancienne, 1981–. Annual.
Abstracts of Swiss archaeology in the Roman period. Index of authors; index of subjects; index of cantons; index of place names. Delay: most items published within last year.

Surveys

295 De Laet, S. J. *Prehistorische Kulturen in het zuiden der Lage Landen.* Wetteren (Belgium): Éditions Universa, 1979. 689 pp. Each chapter has its own bibliography.

Prehistory of the southern Low Countries from the first appearance of man to the Iron Age.

296 Piggott, S., Daniel, G. and **McBurney, C.** (eds.). *France before the Romans.* London: Thames and Hudson, 1974. 240 pp. Bibliography: pp. 224–31. Survey of French prehistory.

297 *La Préhistoire française.* Paris: Éditions du Centre National de la Recherche Scientifique, 1976.
Tome 1: *Les civilisations paléolithiques et mésolithiques de la France.* 2 vols. 1,537 pp.
Tome 2: *Les civilisations néolithiques et protohistoriques de la France.* 924 pp.
Authoritative overview of French prehistory. Bibliographies at the end of each section.

298 Schweizerische Gesellschaft für Ur- und Frühgeschichte (ed.) *Ur- und Frühgeschichtliche Archäologie der Schweiz.* Basle: Schweizerische Gesellschaft für Ur- und Frühgeschichte. Band 1: *Die ältere und mittlere Steinzeit.* 1968; Band II: *Die jüngere Steinzeit.* 1969; Band III: *Die Bronzezeit.* 1971; Band IV: *Die Eisenzeit.* 1974; Band V: *Die römische Epoche.* 1975; Band VI: *Das Frühmittelalter.* 1979.
Major survey of Swiss prehistory and archaeology.

Periodicals

299 *Archaeologia Belgica.* Brussels: Service National des Fouilles, 1950–. Irreg. Fr. Nd.
Belgian archaeology of all periods.

300 *Archäologie der Schweiz/Archéologie Suisse/Archeologia Svizzera.* Basle: Schweizerische Gesellschaft für Ur- und Frühgeschichte, 1978–. Quarterly. Fr. De. It.
History and archaeology of Switzerland from earliest times to the middle ages.

301 *Archäologie. Zeitschrift.* Berlin: (Akademie der Wissenschaften der DDR, Zentralinstitut für Alte Geschichte und Archäologie) VEB Deutscher Verlag der Wissenschaften, 1967–. Twice a year. De. (contents page in En. Fr. Ru.).
Archaeology of the Germanic area. Book reviews.

302 *Archäologisches Korrespondenzblatt: Urgeschichte, Römerzeit, Frühmittelalter.* Mainz: Römisch-Germanischen Zentralmuseum, Mainz, 1971–. Quarterly. De. Cumulative indexes: vols. 1–5 (1971–5); vols. 1–10 (1971–80)
German archaeology from prehistoric times to the early middle ages.

303 *Archéologie: Chronique Semestrielle.* Brussels: Centre National de Recherches Archéologiques en Belgique, 1938–. Twice a year. Nd. Fr. De.
Belgian archaeology through to the middle ages. Surveys activities of Belgian archaeological societies and the National Service for Excavations. Lists of publications and research. Book reviews.

304 *Archéologie Médiévale.* Caen (France): Centre de Recherches Archéologiques Médiévales, 1971–. Annual. Fr.
Medieval archaeology, with the emphasis on France. Book reviews. Each issue includes 'Chronique des fouilles médiévales en France', an annual round up of medieval excavations in France.

305 *Ausgrabungen und Funde: Archäologische Berichte und Informationen.* Berlin: (Akademie der Wissenschaften der DDR, Zentralinstitut für Alte Geschichte und Archäologie) Akademie-Verlag, 1956–. Every two months. De. (see also [219])
German archaeology of all periods, including reports on current excavations. Certain issues include 'Neue Schriften: Bibliographie zur Ur- und Frühgeschichte', a list of books and articles on mainly European prehistory and early history arranged by subject, area and period.

306 *Berichten van de Rijksdienst voor het Oudheidkundig Bodemonderzoek/Proceedings of the State Service for Archaeological Investigations in the Netherlands.* The Hague: Rijksdienst voor het Oudheidkundig Bodemonderzoek, 1950–. Annual. Nd. En. De.
Dutch archaeology of all periods.

307 *Bulletin de la Société Préhistorique Française.* Paris: Société Préhistorique Française, 1904–. Monthly. Fr. In two sections: *Comptes rendues des séances mensuelles; Études et travaux.* (see also [26])
Prehistory, with emphasis on France. Includes regular bibliographies comprising the Society's library's intake of material. Book reviews.

308 *Bulletin–Koninklijke Nederlandse Oudheidkundige Bond.* The Hague: Koninklijke Nederlandse Oudheidkundige Bond – Royal Netherlands Archaeological Society, 1899–. Five times a year. Nd. (summaries in En.). Cumulative index: 1899–1931.
Archaeology and historic preservation of Dutch monuments and artefacts.

309 *Bulletins de l'Institut Archéologique du Luxembourg: Archéologie–Art–Histoire–Folklore.* Arlon (Belgium): Institut Archéologique du Luxembourg, 1925–. Quarterly. Fr.
Archaeology of all periods in Luxemburg. Book reviews.

310 *Gallia: Fouilles et Monuments Archéologiques en France Métropolitaine.* Paris: Centre National de la Recherche Scientifique, 1943–. Twice a year. Fr. Cumulative indexes: vols. 1–20 (1943–62); vols. 21–30 (1963–72). Also *Supplément* (1943–).
Archaeology of France to the end of the 7th century. Includes reports of current excavations and research.

311 *Gallia Préhistoire: Fouilles et Monuments Archéologiques en France Métropolitaine.* Paris: Centre National de la Recherche Scientifique, 1958–. Twice a year. Fr.

Cumulative indexes: vols. 1–5 (1958–62); vols. 6–15 (1963–72). Also *Supplément* (1963–).
Prehistoric archaeology in France.

312 *Germania: Anzeiger der Römisch-Germanischen Kommission des Deutschen Archäologischen Instituts.* Berlin: de Gruyter, 1917–. Annual. De. Cumulative index: vols. 1–36 (1917–58). (see also [31])
Prehistory, early history, archaeology of Europe, with emphasis on Germany. Includes a list of additions to the library of the Römisch-Germanischen Kommission. Lengthy book reviews.

313 *Helinium: Revue consacrée à l'Archéologie des Pays-Bas, de la Belgique et du Grand-Duché de Luxembourg.* Wetteren (Belgium): Éditions Universa, 1961–. Three times a year. En. Nd. Fr. (see also [293])
Archaeology of the Netherlands, Belgium and Luxemburg. Includes a detailed, classified, current bibliography for these countries; also 'Kroniek' (now in En.), a rundown of excavation and other news arranged by province. Book reviews.

314 *Jahrbuch der Schweizerischen Gesellschaft für Ur- und Frühgeschichte.* Frauenfeld (Switzerland): Huber and Co., 1908–. Annual. De. Fr. It. Cumulative indexes: vols. 1–25 (1908–33) in 1934; vols. 26–50 (1934–63) in 1969.
Prehistory, early history and archaeology, with emphasis on Switzerland. Book reviews.

315 *Jahrbuch des Römisch-Germanisches Zentralmuseum Mainz.* Bonn: Habelt, 1954–. Annual. De.
Archaeology of the Germanic area. Book reviews.

316 *Mainzer Zeitschrift: Mittelrheinisches Jahrbuch für Archäologie, Kunst und Geschichte.* Mainz: Mainzer Altertumsverein, 1906–. Annual. De.
Regional history, archaeology and art of central Rhineland Palatinate. Includes details of finds.

317 *Münchner Beiträge zur Vor- und Frühgeschichte.* Munich: C.H. Beck'sche Verlagsbuchhandlung, 1950–. Irreg. De.
Prehistory and early history of Europe with emphasis on Germany.

318 *Nouvelles de l'Archéologie.* Paris: Nouvelles de l'Archéologie, 1979–. Three times a year. Fr.
News of French archaeology – its organization and conduct of research, research in progress, employment, meetings, publications, etc.

319 *Palaeohistoria: Acta et Communicationes Instituti Bio-Archaeologici Universitatis Groninganae.* Rotterdam: (Biologisch-Archaeologisch Instituut, Rijksuniversiteit Groningen) Balkema, 1951–. Annual En. De.
Prehistory and archaeology, with emphasis on the Netherlands.

320 *Römisch-Germanische Forschungen.* Mainz: Philipp von Zabern, 1928–. Irreg. De.
Roman Germany.

321 *Zeitschrift für Archäologie.* Berlin: (Zentralinstitut für Alte Geschichte und Archäologie, Akademie der Wissenschaften der DDR) Deutscher Verlag der Wissenschaften, 1967–. Twice a year. De.
Archaeology of the Germanic countries. Book reviews.

Encyclopaedia

322 Hoops, J. *Reallexikon der germanischen Altertumskunde.* 2nd rev. ed. edited by H. Beck and others. Berlin: de Gruyter, 1968–.
Very detailed, scholarly, multi-volume encyclopaedia of archaeology and related fields concentrating on the Germanic world from the emergence of the Germanic tribes to the establishment of Christianity. Articles arranged alphabetically, with bibliographies. First published 1911–19 (4 vols.).

Directory (biographical, organizational, research in progress)

323 Centre de Recherches Archéologiques. *Répertoire de la recherche archéologique française.* Valbonne (France): Centre de Recherches Archéologiques, 1982–. 2 vols. Regularly updated.
Lists all archaeological research being done in France and by French excavators abroad. Arranged geographically, with details of organizations, individuals, research in progress. Index of names; index of subjects; list of archaeological libraries; lists of personnel.

Western Mediterranean
(Italy, Malta, Portugal, Spain)

General bibliographical guide

324 Fernandez, J. *Bibliografía arqueológica de las islas Pitiusas.* Ibiza: Museo Arqueológico, 1980. 71 pp. (Trabajos del Museo Arqueológico de Ibiza, 3.) Summaries in En. Fr. and De.
Annotated list of the main works covering the archaeology of the islands of Ibiza and Formentera. Arranged alphabetically by author in two sequences: general works; specialized works (i.e. those covering only the two islands).

Surveys

325 *Historia de España.* Ed. by J. M. J. Zamora. Rev. ed. Madrid: Espasa-Calpe, c. 1982. Tome 1: *España Primitiva* (vol. 1: *La Prehistoria*; vol. 2: *La Protohistoria*; vol. 3: *La Historia prerromana*); Tome 2: *España Romana* (vol. 1: *La conquista y la explotación económica*; vol. 2: *La sociedad, el derecho y la cultura*).
A projected forty-tome history of Spain.

326 Pericot-Garcia, L. *The Balearic Islands*; translated [from the Spanish

MSS] by M. Brown. London: Thames and Hudson, 1972. 184 pp. (Ancient Peoples and Places, 81.) Bibliography: pp. 135–42.
Comprehensive study of Balearic archaeology.

327 *Popoli e civiltà dell'Italia antica.* General editor: M. Pallottino, and others. Rome: Biblioteca di Storia Patria, 1974–78. 7 vols.
Italian history and archaeology. Covers all aspects of pre-Roman Italy and adjacent islands.

328 Reich, J. *Italy before Rome.* Oxford: Elsevier-Phaidon, 1979. 151 pp. (The Making of the Past.) Bibliography: p. 137.
A brief account of pre-Roman Italy.

329 Trump, D. H. *Malta: an archaeological guide.* London: Faber and Faber, 1972. 171 pp. (Archaeological Guides.) Bibliography: pp. 165–6.
Authoritative guidebook to Malta's remains of all periods.

Periodicals

330 *Ampurias: Revista de Prehistòria, Arqueologia y Etnologia.* Barcelona: Diputació de Barcelona, Institut de Prehistòria i Arqueologia, 1939–. Annual. Es.
Prehistory, archaeology and ethnology of Catalonia. Book reviews.

331 *Archivo Español de Arqueología.* Madrid: Consejo Superior de Investigaciones Científicas, Instituto Español de Arqueología, 1925–. Twice a year. Es.
Prehistory, archaeology and antiquities of Spain and the Mediterranean area. Book reviews.

332 *Arqueologia e História: Publicações da Associação dos Arqueólogos Portugueses.* Lisbon: Associação des Arqueólogos Portugueses, 1865–. Annual. Fr. Es. Pt. Cumulative index: 1865–1921.
History and archaeology of Portugal. Book reviews.

333 *Arqueólogo Português.* Lisbon: Museu Nacional de Arqueologia e Etnologia, 1895–. Irreg. Pt. Es. (summaries in Fr.). Cumulative index: vols. 1–30 (1895–1938).
Prehistory, archaeology, history, ethnology, museology of Portugal. Book reviews.

334 *Atti della Accademia Nazionale dei Lincei: Notizie degli Scavi di Antichità, Comunicate alla Accademia dal Ministero della Pubblica Istruzione.* Rome: Accademia Nazionale dei Lincei, 1873–. Annual. It.
Reports on Italian excavations.

335 *Bibliotheca Praehistorica Hispana.* Madrid: Instituto Español de Prehistoria, 1958–. Irreg. Es.
Spanish archaeology.

336 *Bollettino d'Arte*. Rome: Ministero della Pubblica Istruzione, Direzione Generale della Antichità e Belle Arti, 1907–. Quarterly. It.
Italian art and archaeology; occasional area surveys of current excavations. Thematic supplements (e.g. underwater archaeology).

337 *Bullettino di Paletnologia Italiana*. Rome: Museo Preistorico-Etnografico 'Luigi Pigorini', 1875–. Annual. It. (summaries in En. Fr. De.).
Prehistory, early history and paleoethnology of Italy. Book reviews.

338 *Excavaciones Arqueológicas en España*. Madrid: Ministerio de Cultura, 1962–. Irreg. Es.
Reports on excavations in Spain.

339 *Madrider Mitteilungen*. Berlin: (Deutsches Archäologisches Institut, Abteilung Madrid) Kerle, 1960–. Annual. De.
Prehistory, archaeology and history of Spain from ancient times to the middle ages. Includes annual list of accessions to the Institute's library at Madrid and Lisbon.

340 *Noticiario Arqueológico Hispánico*. Madrid: Museo Arqueológico Nacional, 1952–. Twice a year. Es. Originally contained two series: *Prehistoria* and *Arquelogía*.
History and archaeology of Spain during ancient times and the middle ages, emphasizing recent work.

341 *Papers of the British School at Rome*. London: British School at Rome, 1902–. Annual. En.
History, archaeology and literature of Italy and other parts of the Mediterranean up to modern times. Supplementary vols. also published.

342 *Portugalia: Revista do Instituto de Arqueologia da Faculdade de Letras da Universidade do Porto*. Porto: Instituto de Arqueologia, Faculdade de Letras da Universidade do Porto, 1980–. Annual. Pt.
Portuguese archaeology. Book reviews.

343 *Revista de Guimarães: Publicação da Sociedade Martins Sarmento*. Guimarães (Portugal): Sociedade Martins Sarmento, 1884–. Annual. Pt. Es.
Portuguese archaeology of all periods.

344 *Rivista di Archeologia Cristiana*. Rome: Pontificio Istituto di Archeologia Cristiana, 1924–. Twice a year. En. Fr. De. It. Es. Cumulative index: vols. 1–40 (1924–64).
Archaeology of Rome with emphasis on early Christian antiquities, art and symbolism. Book reviews.

345 *Rivista di Scienze Preistoriche*. Florence: (Consiglio Nazionale delle Ricerche) Rivista di Scienze Preistoriche, 1946–. Annual. It. (summaries in En. and Fr.). Cumulative index: vols. 1–30 (1946–75) in vol. 31 (1976).

Prehistory, archaeology, epigraphy, anthropology, art and culture of Italy.
Includes a summary of excavations in Italy during the past year.

346 *Sibrium.* Varese (Italy): Centro di Studi Preistorici ed Archeologici, 1953–.
Every two years. It. Cumulative index: vols. 1–10 in vol. 10 (1970).
Italian archaeology. Book reviews.

347 *Sicilia Archeologica.* Trapani (Sicily): Ente Provinciale per Il Turismo di
Trapani, Corso Italia, 1968–. Three times a year. It.
Archaeology of Sicily.

348 *Studi Etruschi.* Florence: (Istituto di Studi Etruschi ed Italici) Casa Editrice
Leo S. Olschki, 1927–. Annual. It. Cumulative indexes: vols. 1–5 (1927–31);
vols. 1–30 (1927–62).
All aspects of Etruscan studies; includes an annual bibliography.

Central Europe
(Austria, Czechoslovakia, Hungary, Poland)

General bibliographical guides

349 Banner, J. *Bibliographia archaeologica hungarica, 1793–1943.* Szeged (Hungary): Institutum Archaeologicum Universitatis de Nicolao Horthy nominate
Szegediensis, 1944. (Fontes Rerum Archaeologicarum Hungaricarum, 1.) 573
pp. Text in Hu. (explanations in De.).
Gives good retrospective coverage of Hungarian archaeology, in a classified
arrangement. Brief subject index; author index; list of periodicals; list of
museums.

350 *Bibliography of Polish prehistorical and mediaeval archaeology for the years
1970–1974.* Warsaw: Polish Academy of Sciences, 1977.
Provides a complete list of works in Polish and foreign languages published in
Poland and works by Poles published abroad. Complements *Polish Archaeological
Abstracts* [353].

351 Jakabffy, I. *A Közép-Duna-Medence régészeti bibliográfiája 1967–1977 (Archaeological bibliography of the Middle Danubian basin 1967–1977).* Budapest: Akadémiai Kiadó, 1981. 375 pp. List of contents and preface also in Fr. De. and Ru.
Unannotated bibliography of over 8,000 items on the archaeology of the Middle
Danubian basin up to the 11th century. Arrangement is basically chronological.
Index of authors.
  Continuation of work of the same title by Banner, J. and Jakabffy. I. (1954.
581 pp.), with Supplements 1954–59 (1961. 250 pp.) and 1960–66 (1968. 242
pp.).

Abstracting, indexing, current awareness services

352 *Archaeológiai Értesítő/Archaeological Bulletin.* Budapest: Magyar Tudomanyos

Akademia, 1868–. Twice a year. Hu. (summaries in En. Fr. De. Ru.). (see also [358])
Includes list of current Hungarian archaeological literature.

353 *Polish Archaeological Abstracts.* Warsaw: Polish Academy of Sciences, Institute of the History of Material Culture, 1972–. Annual.
Covers publications of all kinds on Polish archaeology from Palaeolithic to the end of the 15th century AD, excluding classical archaeology. Arranged by period, then by subject, preceded by a large general section. Some seventy periodicals are covered. Preface includes list of other sources for Polish archaeology. Author index. Delay: *c.* two years.

Survey

354 *Prahistoria ziem polskich.* Wrocław: Zakład Narodowy im. Ossolińskich Wydawnictwo Polskiej Akademii Nauk. Tom 1: *Paleolit i mezolit.* 1975; Tom 2: *Neolit.* 1979; Tom 3: *Wczesna epoka brązu.* 1978; Tom 4: *Od środkowej epoki brązu do środkowego okresu lateńskiego.* 1979; Tom 5: *Późny okres lateński i okres rzymski.* 1981.
Polish prehistory.

Periodicals

355 *Acta Archaeologica Academiae Scientiarum Hungaricae.* Budapest: (Magyar Tudo-manyos Akademia) Akadémiai Kiadó, Publishing House of the Hungarian Academy of Sciences, 1951–. Quarterly. En. Fr. De. Ru.
Hungarian archaeology from prehistoric times to the middle ages. Book reviews.

356 *Archaeologia Austriaca: Beiträge zur Paläanthropologie, Ur- und Frühgeschichte Österreichs.* Vienna: (Universität Wien, Institut für Ur- und Frühgeschichte) Deuticke, 1948–. Annual. De. Cumulative indexes: vols. 1–20 (1948–56); vols. 21–40 (1957–66); vols. 41–50 (1967–71).
European archaeology up to the middle ages, with emphasis on Austria. Book reviews. Also a supplement *Archaeologia Austriaca. Beiheft.* (1957–. Irreg.) covering Austrian archaeology.

357 *Archaeologia Hungarica.* Budapest: Akadémiai Kiadó, 1926–. Irreg. De. Fr. En.
Hungarian archaeology.

358 *Archaeológiai Értesítö/Archaeological Bulletin.* Budapest: (Magyar Régészeti és Müvészettörténeti Társulat) Magyar Tudomanyos Akademia, 1868–. Twice a year. Hu. (summaries in En. Fr. De. Ru.). (see also [352])
Archaeology of Hungary and adjacent areas. Book reviews. Includes list of current Hungarian archaeological literature.

359 *Archeologia Polski.* Wrocław: (Polska Akademia Nauk, Instytut Historii Kultury Materialnej) Ossolineum, Publishing House of the Polish Academy of Sciences, 1957–. Twice a year. Pl. (summaries in En. Fr. De.).
Polish archaeology. Book reviews.

360 *Archeologické Rozhledy.* Prague: (Československá Akademie Věd, Archeologicky Ustav) Academia, Publishing House of the Czechoslovak Academy of Sciences, 1949–. Every two months. Cz. Sl. (occasionally En. Fr. De.) (summaries in En. Fr. De.). (see also [218])
Czech archaeology. Book reviews. Lists of contents of periodicals covering archaeology in Europe. Two issues a year include *Communications* of the Comité pour la Sidérurgie Ancienne de l'UISPP [596].

361 *Informator Archeologiczny.* Warsaw: Polska Akademia Nauk, Instytut Historii Kultury Materialnej, 1968–. Annual. Pl.
Gives preliminary reports of field studies in Poland and abroad by Polish expeditions.

362 *Jahreshefte–Österreichisches Archäologisches Institut.* Vienna: Österreichisches Archaologisches Institut, 1965–. Annual. De.
Austrian archaeology of all periods. Includes news of the Institut.

363 *Památky Archeologické/Archaeological Memoirs.* Prague: (Československá Akademie Věd, Archeologicky Ustav) Academia, Publishing House of the Czechoslovak Academy of Sciences, 1854–. Twice a year. Cz. De. (summaries in En. Fr. De. Ru. Es.).
Czech archaeology. Book reviews.

364 *Slovenská Archeológia.* Bratislava (Slovenská Akademia Vied, Archeologický Ústav) Veda, Publishing House of the Slovak Academy of Sciences, 1953–. Twice a year. De. Sl. (summaries in De. Ru.).
Slovak archaeology. Book reviews.

365 *Sprawozdania Archeologiczne.* Warsaw: (Polska Akademia Nauk, Instytut Historii Kultury Materialnej) Ossolineum, Publishing House of the Polish Academy of Sciences, 1955–. Irreg. Pl. (summaries and contents page in En.). (see also [37])
Polish archaeology. Includes summaries of investigations anu discoveries in the section 'Survey of recent field research' (En.); also 'Archaeological abstracts – the Neolithic of East-Central Europe' (covering Bulgaria, Czechoslovakia, Hungary, Poland, Romania, USSR, Yugoslavia). (En.). Book reviews. .

366 *Wiadomości Archeologiczne: Organ Muzealnictwa i Konserwatorstwa Archeologicznego.* Warsaw: Państwowe Muzeum Archeologiczne, 1893–. Twice a year. Pl. (summaries in En. Ru.). Cumulative index: 1873–1954 (as vol. 21).
Polish archaeology. Book reviews.

South-East Europe
(Albania, Bulgaria, Cyprus, Greece, Romania, Yugoslavia)

General bibliographical guides

367 Comşa, E. *Bibliografia Neoliticului de pe teritoriul României: I–II.* Bucharest: Muzeul de Istorie, 1976–77. 2 vols. (Biblioteca muzeologică 2 and 3.)

Over 3,000 unannotated references on the Romanian Neolithic, alphabetically arranged by author. Author index; place index; theme index.

368 Comşa, E. *Bibliografia Paleoliticului şi Mezoliticului de pe teritoriul României.* Bucharest: Muzeul de Istorie, 1978. (Biblioteca muzeologica.) 136 pp.
Over 1,000 unannotated references on the Romanian Palaeolithic and Mesolithic, alphabetically arranged by author. Author index; place index; theme index.

369 Georgieva, S. and **Velkov, V.** *Bibliographie de l'archéologie Bulgare (1879–1966).* 2nd ed. Sofia: Éditions de l'Académie Bulgare des Sciences, 1974. 477 pp. Bu. (preface and contents page in Fr.).
Lists 9,523 unannotated entries covering Bulgarian archaeology and related topics. Author index; geographic index.

370 Jakabffy, I. *A Közép-Duna-Medence régészeti bibliográfiája 1967–1977 (Archaeological bibliography of the Middle Danubian basin 1967–1977).* (see [351])

371 Jubani, B. *Bibliografi e arkeologjisë dhe historisë së lashtë të Shqipërisë (1945–1971)/Bibliographie de l'archéologie et de l'histoire antique de l'Albanie.* Tirana: Universiteti i Tiranës Instituti i Historisë, 1972. 222 pp.
Annotated list of 709 entries on Albanian archaeology and ancient history, alphabetically arranged by author. Entries listed in the original language, with annotations in Al., then repeated with titles translated into Fr. and annotations in Fr.

Abstracting, indexing, current awareness service

372 *Bulletin d'Analyses de la Littérature Scientifique Bulgare: Histoire, Archéologie et Ethnographie/Zentralblatt der Bulgarischen Wissenschaftlichen Literatur: Geschichte, Archäologie und Ethnographie.* Sofia: Bulgarian Academy of Sciences Scientific Information Centre, 1958–. Quarterly. De. (for archaeology); Fr. (for history and ethnography). Delay: *c.* one year.
Abstracts of articles on Bulgarian archaeology from a small number of journals, mostly Bulgarian.

Surveys

373 Alexander, J. *Jugoslavia before the Roman conquest.* London: Thames and Hudson, 1972. (Ancient Peoples and Places, 77.) 175 pp. Bibliography: pp. 143–7.
Survey of Yugoslavia from Palaeolithic times to the Roman conquest.

374 Hoddinott, R. F. *Bulgaria in antiquity: an archaeological introduction.* London: Benn, 1975. 368 pp. Select bibliography: pp. 343–5.
Survey of Bulgaria from the Thracian era to the Byzantine withdrawal.

375 Karageorghis, V. *Cyprus: from the Stone Age to the Romans.* London: Thames

and Hudson, 1982. (Ancient Peoples and Places, 101). 207 pp. Select bibliography: pp. 197–8.
Covers the development of Cyprus's culture in all its aspects.

376 *Praistorija Jugoslavenskih Zemalja.* Editor: D. Basler and others. Sarajevo: Akademija Nauka i Umjetnosti Bosne i Hercegovine, 1979. Vol. 1: *Paleolitsko i Mezolitsko doba*; vol. 2: *Neolitsko doba*; vol. 3: *Eneolitsko doba*. Bibliographies (each *c.* 20–30 pp.) at the end of each vol.
Major survey of Yugoslavian prehistory.

Periodicals

377 *Annual of the British School at Athens.* London: British School at Athens, 1894–. Annual. En. Cumulative indexes: vols. 1–16 (1894–1909/10); vols. 17–32 (1910/11–1931/2); vols. 33–48 (1932/3–1953); vols. 49–68 (1954–1973).
History, archaeology and art of Greece. Supplementary vols. also published.

378 *Archaeologia Iugoslavica.* Belgrade: L'Association des Sociétés Archéologiques de Yougoslavie, 1954–. Annual. Sl. En. Fr. De.
Yugoslavian archaeology.

379 *Archaiologiki Ephimeris.* Athens: En Athinais Archaiologiki Hetaireia, 1837–. Annual. Gr.
Greek art and archaeology. Book reviews.

380 *Archaiologikon Deltion.* Athens: Hypourgeion Politismou kai Epistimon. Geniki Dieuthunsi Archaiotiton kai Anasteloseos, 1915–. Annual. Gr. (occasionally En.).
Greek archaeology.

381 *Arheologija.* Sofia: Centre for Research in History, Institute of Archaeology and Museum, 1959–. Quarterly. Bu. (summaries in Fr.).
Bulgarian archaeology.

382 *Arheološki Vestnik/Acta Archaeologica.* Ljubljana: Slovenska Akademija Znanosti in Umetnosti, Institut za Arheologijo, 1950–. Every two months. Sl. (contents page in Sl. and De.).
Yugoslav archaeology. Book reviews.

383 *Athens Annals of Archaeology/Archaiologika Analekta ex Athinon.* Athens: General Directorate of Antiquities and Restoration, 1968–. Twice a year. En. Gr.
New research in Greek archaeology.

384 *Biblioteca de Arheologie.* Bucharest: (Academia de Stiinte Sociale si Politice, Institutul de Arheologie) Editura Academiei Republicii Socialiste România, 1957–. Irreg. Rm. (summaries in Fr.).
Romanian archaeology of all periods.

385 *Iliria: Revistë Arkeologjike.* Tirana: Akademia e Shkencave e RPSSH, Qendra e Kërkimeve Arkeologjike, 1971–. Twice a year. Al. (summaries in Fr.). Albanian archaeology. Includes 'Résultats des fouilles' (summary of excavations).

386 *Studies in Mediterranean Archaeology.* Göteborg: Paul Åströms Förlag, 1962–. Irreg. De. En. Fr.
Mediterranean archaeology with emphasis on Greece, Crete and Cyprus.

387 *Studii şi Cercetări de Istorie Veche şi Arheologie.* Bucharest: (Academia Republicii Socialiste România, Institutul de Arheologie) Editura Academiei Republicii Socialiste România, 1950–. Quarterly. Rm. (summaries in Fr.).
Balkan archaeology. Book reviews.

Directory (biographical)

388 Åstrom, P. *Who's who in Cypriote archaeology: biographical and bibliographical notes.* Göteborg: Åström, 1971. 88 pp. (Studies in Mediterranean Archaeology, 23.)
Includes only scholars active in the field in 1971.

Africa
(in general)

General bibliographical guides

389 *Africa south of the Sahara: index to periodical literature, 1900–1970;* compiled in the African Section, General Reference and Bibliography Division, Reference Department, Library of Congress. Boston (Mass.): Hall, 1971. 4 vols. – vol. 1: *Africa (general) – Central Africa;* vol. 2: *Central African Republic – Ivory Coast;* vol. 3: *Kenya – Somalia;* vol. 4: *South Africa – Zambia.* Literary index, + 1st supplement (1973), 598 pp. 2nd supplement (1981) available on microfilm.
Reproduction of over 80,000 catalogue cards compiled from various European sources and indexing of periodicals received at the Library of Congress; 1st supplement added *c.* 14,000. Most articles listed are within the last twenty years. Over 1,500 periodicals (including many archaeological ones) were scanned for the main work, nearly 1,000 for the 1st supplement. An 'Africa–general' section is followed by a geographical arrangement and by subjects within areas. Archaeology is a subsection of 'History' but some archaeological material can also be found under 'Anthropology and Ethnology', divided by ethnic groups or languages. Many cross-references.

390 Duignan, P. (ed.). *Guide to research and reference works on sub-Saharan Africa;* compiled by H. F. Conover and P. Duignan, and others. Stanford (California): Hoover Institution Press, Stanford University, 1971. (Hoover Institution bibliographical series: XLVI.) 1,115 pp.
The most complete guide to the literature of Africa south of the Sahara, although some of the works listed are rather dated. The 3,127 annotated

references are arranged in four parts: a guide to research organizations, libraries and archives and the book trade; various forms of bibliographies; a subject guide (including sections on prehistory (6 pp.) and anthropology (12 pp.); an area guide. Index of authors, editors, compilers, titles, subjects, areas.

Abstracting, indexing, current awareness service

391 *International African Bibliography: current books, articles, and papers in African Studies.* London: (School of Oriental and African Studies, University of London) Mansell, 1971–. Quarterly.
Unannotated coverage of all authoritative publications on the whole of Africa and adjacent islands, excluding Egypt. Subject scope is mainly arts and humanities but with some overlap into the sciences; archaeology is well covered. Over 1,000 periodicals, including many archaeological ones, are scanned. A section covering Africa as a whole and divided by subject (archaeological material is listed under 'History') is followed by sections arranged geographically by region and country. Index of authors and personalities in African studies; ethnic groups index; language index (all annual). Delay: *c.* one to two years.

Previously published as 'Bibliography of current publications' in the periodical *Africa* (1928–70). The *Cumulative bibliography of African Studies* (Boston (Massachusetts): Hall, 1973. 5 vols.) cumulates all references in the above two publications up to 1972. *International African bibliography 1973–1978* (London: Mansell, 1982) includes *c.* 3,000 items not previously listed in the quarterly issues.

Surveys

392 *The Cambridge history of Africa.* Cambridge (England): Cambridge University Press. Vol. 1: *From the earliest times to c. 500 BC*; ed. by J. D. Clark. 1982. 1,180 pp. Detailed bibliography: pp. 971–1,087.
Complete and authoritative overview of African prehistory from the first hominids to the spread of iron technology *c.* 500 BC. Arranged in twelve chapters, some dealing with the whole of Africa, others with particular areas. Series of critical bibliographical essays (pp. 941–70) corresponding to the chapters give numerous bibliographical sources, including references to specific sites. Index.

Vol. 2: *From c. 500 BC to AD 1050*; ed. by J. D. Fage. 1978. 857 pp. Detailed bibliography: pp. 719–70.
Comprehensive coverage of African protohistory. Arranged in eleven chapters, all but the first dealing with particular areas. Series of bibliographical essays (pp. 685–718) (similar to those in vol. 1). Index.

Vol. 3: *From c. 1050 to c. 1600*; ed. by R. Oliver. 1977. 814 pp. Detailed bibliography: pp. 702–47.
Comprehensive coverage of this period, for which archaeological remains are a major historical source. Arranged in nine chapters, each dealing with a particular area. Series of bibliographical essays (pp. 670–701) (similar to those in vol. 1). Index.

393 *General history of Africa.* Paris: UNESCO; London: Heinemann, 1981. Vol. 1: *Methodology and African prehistory*; ed. by J. Ki-Zerbo. 846 pp. Detailed bibliography: pp. 753–800.

Chapters on methodology are followed by several on prehistory, arranged geographically. General index; index of persons; index of places; index of ethnonyms; index of dynasties.

Vol. 2: *Ancient civilizations of Africa*; ed. by G. Mokhtar. 821 pp. Detailed bibliography: pp. 742–85.
Covers the period from the end of the Neolithic (*c.* 8000 BC) to the early 7th century AD. Arranged geographically. Subject index; index of persons; index of places; index of ethnonyms; index of dynasties.

394 Phillipson, D. W. *African archaeology.* Cambridge (England): Cambridge University Press (forthcoming; includes a bibliography of *c.* 500 items).

395 Phillipson, D. W. *The later prehistory of Eastern and Southern Africa.* London: Heinemann, 1977. 323 pp.
Synthesis of the prehistory of Eastern and Southern Africa during the last 20,000 years.

Periodicals

396 *The African Archaeological Review.* Cambridge (England): Cambridge University Press, 1983–. Annual. En.
All aspects of the archaeology of Africa and neighbouring islands except for specialized human biology and topics relating primarily to North African civilizations and their extra-African interests. Includes reports on research in progress, abstracts of theses and a list of publications received.

397 *Nyame Akuma: Newsletter of the Society of Africanist Archaeologists in America.* Edmonton: University of Alberta, Department of Anthropology, 1972–. Twice a year. Fr. En.
Newsletter of African archaeology. Includes short reports on current research in almost all periods of African archaeology, except for the classical period in North Africa and the Pharaonic periods in Egypt. Book reviews.

North Africa

(Algeria, Djibouti, Egypt, Ethiopia, Libya, Morocco, Somalia, Sudan, Tunisia)

General bibliographical guide

398 Pratt, I. A. *Ancient Egypt: sources of information in the New York Public Library.* New York: New York Public Library, 1925–42. 2 vols.
Unannotated list of 17,500 books and articles in the New York Public Library, covering the period to the conquest of Egypt by the Arabs in AD 639. Author index.

Abstracting, indexing, current awareness services

399 *Annual Egyptological Bibliography/Bibliographie Égyptologique Annuelle.* Leiden: (International Association of Egyptologists) Brill, 1947– (publ. 1948–). Annual.

Annotated list of publications of all kinds (currently *c.* 850 in each vol.) on Egyptology; *c.* 45 periodicals are scanned. Alphabetically arranged by author. No subject index, but ten-yearly indexes (1947–56) (Leiden: Brill, 1960. 494 pp.) comprise author index, and many specialized indexes, e.g. topography, pharaohs, hieroglyphs, divinities, Biblical references and Hebrew words, classical authors, subject index. Delay: *c.* four years.

400 *Archéologie de l'Afrique Antique: Bibliographie des ouvrages parus en ... et complément des années antérieures.* Aix-en-Provence: Centre de Recherches Archéologiques, 1979–. Annual.
Unannotated list of publications on North African archaeology from *c.* fifty periodicals and collective works. Classified arrangement. Author index. Delay: *c.* one to three years.

Survey

401 Johnson, P. *The civilization of Ancient Egypt.* London: Weidenfeld and Nicolson, 1978. 240 pp. Bibliography: pp. 235–6.
Brief survey of ancient Egypt.

Periodicals

402 *Antiquités Africaines.* Paris: Centre National de la Recherche Scientifique, 1967–. Annual. Fr.
History and archaeology of North Africa from the Protohistoric period to the Arab conquest.

403 *Bulletin d'Archéologie Algérienne.* Algiers: Ministère de l'Information et de la Culture de la République Algérienne Démocratique et Populaire, 1962–. Irreg. Fr.
Archaeology of Algeria. Includes a 'Bibliographie analytique de l'Afrique antique', and a summary of recent excavation.

404 *Bulletin d'Archéologie Marocaine.* Rabat: Division de l'Archéologie des Monuments Historiques, des Sites et des Musées, 1956–. Annual. Fr.
Moroccan archaeology of all periods.

405 *Journal of Egyptian Archaeology.* London: Egypt Exploration Society, 1914–. Annual. En. (occasionally Fr. De.). Cumulative indexes: vols. 1–20; 21–40.
Scholarly journal covering all branches of Egyptology. Book reviews.

406 *Karthago: Revue d'Archéologie Africaine.* Paris: Centre d'Études Archéologiques de la Méditerranée Occidentale, 1950–. Every two years. Fr.
North African archaeology. Includes 'Informations et Bibliographie' (a summary of excavation work done and a list of publications).

407 *Kush: Journal of the Sudan Antiquities Service.* Cheltenham (England): Greenaway: 1953–. Irreg. En. (summaries in Fr. and De.).
Archaeology of the Sudan.

408 *Libyan Studies*. London: Society for Libyan Studies, 1969–. Annual. En.
Current research on Libyan topics including much archaeology. Book reviews.

409 *Libyca: Anthropologie, Préhistoire, Ethnographie*. Paris: (Centre de Recherches
Anthropologiques, Préhistoriques et Ethnographiques, Algiers) Flammarion,
1953–. Annual. Fr.
North African prehistory and anthropology. Includes 'Chronique' (a bibliography and details of the activities of CRAPE).

Dictionaries, encyclopaedias, atlases

410 Baines, J. and **Málek, J.** *Atlas of ancient Egypt*. Oxford: Phaidon, 1980. 240
pp. Bibliography: pp. 231–2.
Surveys the most important sites with ancient Egyptian monuments along with
general aspects of Egyptian civilization. Arranged in three parts: the cultural
setting; a journey down the Nile; aspects of Egyptian society. Parts 1 and 3 are
arranged by theme and period; Part 2 by site. Text is supplemented by numerous
photographs, drawings, maps, plans, etc. List of museums with Egyptian
collections. Chronological table. Glossary. Gazetteer. Index. Aimed at the
general reader as well as the student.

411 Helck, W. and **Otto, E.** (eds.). *Lexikon der Ägyptologie*. Wiesbaden (West
Germany): Harrassowitz, 1972–.
Scholarly, detailed encyclopaedia on Egyptology.

Directory (biographical)

412 Dawson, W. R. and **Uphill, E. P.** *Who was who in Egyptology: a biographical
index of Egyptologists; of travellers, explorers, and excavators in Egypt; of collectors of
and dealers in Egyptian antiquities; of consuls, officials, authors, benefactors, and others
whose names occur in the literature of Egyptology, from the year 1500 to the present day,
but excluding persons now living*. 2nd rev. ed. London: Egypt Exploration Society,
1972. 329 pp.
Some 1,000 entries, including many archaeologists, alphabetically arranged.
Each entry includes a bibliography.

West Africa

(Benin, Cameroon, Cape Verde Islands, Gambia, Ghana, Guinea, Guinea-
Bissau, Ivory Coast, Liberia, Mali, Mauritania, Niger, Nigeria, Senegal, Sierra
Leone, Togo, Upper Volta)

Survey

413 Shaw, T. *Nigeria: its archaeology and early history*. London: Thames and
Hudson, 1978. (Ancient Peoples and Places, 88.) 216 pp. Bibliography: pp.
195–208.
Descriptive account of early Nigeria.

Periodicals

414 *Archaeology in Ghana: Newsletter of Department of Archaeology, University of Ghana.*
Legon (Ghana): Department of Archaeology, University of Ghana, 1978–.
Every two years. En.
Archaeology in Ghana. Includes 'Recent literature'.

415 *West African Journal of Archaeology/Revue Ouest Africaine d'Archéologie.* Ibadan
(Nigeria): (West African Archaeological Association) Ibadan University
Press, 1971–. Annual. En. (occasionally Fr.).
West African archaeology. Book reviews.

Central Africa

(Burundi, Central African Republic, Chad, Congo, Equatorial Guinea, Gabon,
Kenya, Rwanda, Tanzania, Uganda, Zaire)

Survey

416 Van Noten, F. *The archaeology of Central Africa.* Graz (Austria): Akademische
Druck- u. Verlagsanstalt, 1982. 152 pp. Select bibliography: pp. 101–44.
Synthesis of all archaeological work undertaken in Central Africa.

Periodical

417 *Azania: Journal of the British Institute in Eastern Africa.* Nairobi (Kenya):
British Institute in Eastern Africa, 1966–. Annual. En. Cumulative index: vols.
1–3 (1966–68); vols. 9–12 (1974–78).
Archaeology and precolonial history of East and Central Africa. Includes a
summary of research in progress. Book reviews.

Southern Africa

(Angola, Botswana, Lesotho, Madagascar, Malawi, Mauritius, Mozambique,
Namibia, South Africa, Swaziland, Zambia, Zimbabwe)

General bibliographical guides

418 Holm, S. E. *Bibliography of South African pre- and proto-historic archaeology.*
Pretoria (South Africa): Van Schaik, 1966. 169 pp.
Has 1,151 annotated entries, almost all pre-1960, mostly for the Republic of
South Africa. Includes useful abstracts from, or references to, reviews.

419 Phillipson, D. W. *An annotated bibliography of the archaeology of Zambia.*
Lusaka (Zambia): National Monuments Commission, 1968. 29 pp.
Covers all works published up to 1966.
    Continued by R. M. Derricourt: *A supplementary bibliography of the archaeology of
Zambia 1967–1973.* Lusaka (Zambia): National Monuments Commission, 1975.
15 pp.
    The two vols. together list 220 works, with brief annotation.

Periodicals

420 *Archaeologia Zambiana: an Occasional Newsletter of Zambian Archaeology.* Livingstone (Zambia): Commission for the Preservation of Natural and Historical Monuments and Relics, 1971–. Irreg. En.
Zambian archaeology. Notes and news.

421 *South African Archaeological Bulletin/Suid-Afrikaanse Argeologiese Bulletin.* Claremont (South Africa): South African Archaeological Society, 1945–. Twice a year. En.
South African archaeology. Book reviews.

America
(in general)

General bibliographical guides

422 *Abstracts of New World archaeology.* Washington: Society for American Archaeology, 1959–60 (publ. 1960–61).
Abstracts of publications covering New World archaeology (North, South and Mesoamerica, Arctic) including masters' and doctors' theses. The 1959 vol. had 676 abstracts, and the 1960 vol. had 1,124. Arranged geographically after a general section including bibliographical sources, the history, theory, scope and role of archaeology, and methods and techniques. Author index.

423 Wolf, C. E. and **Folk, K. R.** *Indians of North and South America: a bibliography based on the collection at the Willard E. Tager Library-Museum, Hartwich College, Oneonta, NY.* London: Scarecrow Press, 1977. 585 pp.
Unannotated bibliography of 4,387 publications of all kinds on the native inhabitants of the New World. Arranged alphabetically by author. Title index; series index; subject index; list of tribes cited in subject order.

Abstracting, indexing, current awareness services

424 *Bibliographie Américaniste.* Paris: Société des Américanistes, 1967–. Twice a year. Published in two series: *Linguistique Amerindienne; Archéologie et Préhistoire, Anthropologie et Ethnohistoire.*
Unannotated listing of material covering all the Americas, including the Caribbean. The second series has sections: 'Archéologie et préhistoire'; 'Anthropologie physique, physiologie, pathologie'; 'Anthropologie sociale, ethnologie, folklore'; 'Géographie humaine'; 'Ethnohistoire'. Ethnic group index; geographic index; author index.

425 *Index to Literature on the American Indian.* San Francisco: (American Indian Historical Society) Indian Historian Press, 1970–. (publ. 1972–). Annual.
Unannotated listing of American publications dealing with the native Ameri-

cans. Arranged alphabetically by subject and by author within each major subject grouping. Covers over 100 US and Canadian journals.

Survey

426 Willey, G. R. *An introduction to American archaeology.* Englewood Cliffs (New Jersey): Prentice-Hall. Vol. 1: *North and Middle America.* 1966. 540 pp. Bibliography: pp. 485–516. Vol. 2: *South America.* 1971. 573 pp. Bibliography: pp. 513–47. (Prentice-Hall Anthropology series.)
Massive, authoritative work on New World prehistory from man's first appearance to the coming of Europeans. Each vol. concludes with a 'Summary and perspective'.

Periodicals

427 *American Antiquity.* Washington: Society for American Archaeology, 1935–. Quarterly. En. Cumulative index: vols. 1–30 (1935–64).
New World archaeology and related areas. Includes an annual review of Old World archaeology, obituaries, current research, lengthy book reviews and book abstracts.

428 *Journal de la Société des Américanistes.* Paris: Société des Américanistes, 1896–. Annual. En. Fr. De. Es. Pt. Cumulative indexes: 1896–1946; 1947–76.
Covers the aboriginal cultures of North and South America: prehistory, archaeology, ethnography, linguistics, sociology, folklore, geography. Book reviews.

429 *Journal of New World Archaeology.* Los Angeles: University of California, Institute of Archaeology, 1975–. Quarterly. En.
Reports on original research throughout the Americas.

430 *Papers of the Peabody Museum of Archaeology and Ethnology.* Cambridge (Mass.): Peabody Museum of Archaeology and Ethnology, Harvard University, 1891–. Irreg. En.
Worldwide coverage of archaeology, with strong emphasis on North and Mesoamerica.

431 *Smithsonian Contributions to Anthropology.* Washington: Smithsonian Institution, 1965–. Irreg. En.
Major series, each volume covering a particular aspect of anthropology or archaeology, with emphasis on the Americas.

Directory

432 Suárez, I. L. and **Sánchez, M. E. (Comps.).** *Latinoamericanistas en Europa; registro-bio-bibliografico.* Amsterdam: Centro de Estudios y Documentación Latinoamericanos. 1981. 263 pp.
Directory of Latinamericanists based in Europe. Arranged alphabetically by name. Geographical index; subject index (includes twenty-five specialists under 'Archaeology').

North America
(Canada, USA)

General bibliographical guides

433 Beers, H. P. *Bibliographies in American history, 1942–1978: guide to materials for research.* Woodbridge (Connecticut): Research Publications, 1982. 2 vols. 946 pp.
Unannotated list of 11,784 bibliographic listings (including bibliographies in periodicals) on all aspects of US history, including archaeology. Index lists thirty bibliographies under 'Archaeology', including some on individual states.
Preceded by Beers, H. P. *Bibliographies in American history; guide to materials for research.* (Rev. ed. New York: Wilson, 1942 (repr. 1973) 487 pp.), arranged on similar lines, listing 7,806 items published up to 1941. Index lists thirty-three bibliographies under 'Archaeology', including some on individual states.

434 Haas, M. L. A basic guide to reference sources for the study of the North American Indian. *Reference Services Review,* 7:3 (1979), 15–36. Bibliography: pp. 30–5 (110 items).
Lists and describes reference works of all types providing information on the North American Indian. Archaeology is well covered.

435 Heizer, R. F. *Archaeology: a bibliographical guide to the basic literature.* New York and London: Garland, 1980. 445 pp. (see also [9])
Section V, 'Sources of primary data', includes seventy-four bibliographies of archaeology worldwide, but with a strong emphasis on North America.

436 Murdock, G. P. and **O'Leary, T. J.** *Ethnographic bibliography of North America.* 4th ed. New Haven (Connecticut): Human Relations Area Files, 1975. 5 vols. (Behavior Science Bibliographies.)
Lists nearly 40,000 publications of all types on the cultures of the native North American peoples through to 1972. Ethnography is the subject covered most completely, but there is a great deal of archaeology. Arranged by area and within each area by ethnic groups. Each vol. includes an ethnonymy (list of names of ethnic groups) and a general ethnic map of native North America.

437 National Museum of Canada. *Bibliography of Canadian anthropology, 1954–62.* Compiled by T. F. McIlwraith.
Included in *National Bulletin.* no. 142 (1956), no. 147 (1957), no. 162 (1960), no. 167 (1960), no. 173 (1961), no. 190 (1963), no. 194 (1964), no. 204 (1967).
Preceded by 'Recent publications relating to Canada: Ethnology, anthropology and archaeology', an annual bibliography which appeared in *Canadian Historical Review,* 6–35 (1925–54).

Abstracting, indexing, current awareness service

438 *America: History and Life.* Santa Barbara (California): American Bibliographical Center; Clio, 1954– (publ. 1965–).

Detailed guide to publications of all kinds on the history and culture of North America, from prehistory to the present. Includes some archaeology. Some 2,000 journals published worldwide are scanned. In four parts – A: *Article abstracts and citations* (three times a year); basically arranged by region, with subdivisions, with a subject index and author index per issue. B: *Index to book reviews* (twice a year); arranged alphabetically by author, with a title index and reviewer index. C: *American history bibliography* (annual); lists books and articles in Parts A and B, with the addition of dissertations, alphabetically by author. D: *Annual index*; comprises cumulative subject index and author index to Parts A, B and C, book title index and book reviewer index. Cumulative indexes: vols. 1–5 (1964–8); vols. 6–10 (1969–73). Delay: *c.* one to two years. Can be searched online through DIALOG.

Survey

439 Sturtevant, W. C. (ed.). *Handbook of North American Indians.* Washington: Smithsonian Institution, 1978–.
Projected twenty vol. set summarizing the prehistory, history and cultures of North American aboriginal peoples, each vol. including a detailed bibliography. This will remain a standard work for many years.

Periodicals

440 *American Archeology.* (formerly: *Contract Abstracts and CRM Archeology.*) Albuquerque (New Mexico): Atechiston, 1980–. Three times a year. En.
Describes archaeological work done under contract in advance of development; some articles include summaries. Also includes abstracts of work done under contract at other sites, and articles on resources management and current directions in federal, state, commercial and local contract archaeology.

441 *Archaeological Fieldwork and Opportunities Bulletin.* New York: Archaeological Institute of America, 19[?]–. Annual. En.
Lists excavations and courses being conducted in the USA (and a wide range of other countries) which may need staff members, students or volunteers.

442 *Canadian Journal of Archaeology.* Ottawa: Canadian Archaeological Association, 1977–. Annual. En. Fr.
Canadian archaeology. Book reviews.

443 *Historical Archaeology: Journal of the Society for Historical Archaeology.* Washington: Society for Historical Archaeology, 1967–. Annual. En.
Historical archaeology of North America from the 16th to the 20th century. Includes abstracts of articles. Book reviews.

444 *Midcontinental Journal of Archaeology.* Kent (Ohio): Kent State University Press, 1976–. Twice a year. En.
Archaeology of the region between the Appalachian Mountains and the great Plains, from the Boreal Forests to the Gulf of Mexico.

445 *North American Archaeologist.* Farmingdale (New York): Baywood, 1979–. Twice a year. En.
Archaeology of North America from the prehistoric to the modern industrial period, with special emphasis on Indian cultures.

Directories (biographical, organizational)

446 American Anthropological Association. *Guide to departments of anthropology.* Washington: American Anthropological Association. Annual.
Gives information on anthropology departments at US and Canadian universities, museum departments, research departments at some institutions, and recent PhD dissertations in anthropology. Details include degrees offered in anthropology, names of staff with their fields of interest (21st ed. (1982–83) included 5,394 individuals) and details of courses. Index of individuals; sources of degrees held by individuals, etc.

447 Ash, L. *Subject collections: a guide to special book collections and subject emphases as reported by university, college, public, and special libraries and museums in the United States and Canada.* 5th rev. ed. New York and London: Bowker, 1978. 1,194 pp.
Gives information such as address, number of vols., and special collections for nearly 100 major North American archaeological libraries, in addition to those in other subject fields. Arranged alphabetically by subject.

448 *Directory of historical societies and agencies in the United States and Canada*; compiled and ed. by T. L. Craig. 12th ed. Nashville (Tennessee): American Association for State and Local History, 1982. 422 pp.
Gives details of 5,865 US and Canadian societies and agencies in all branches of history. Each entry includes name, address, telephone number, year of foundation, name of director, number of members, etc. Arranged by state, then by place. General index; special interest index (lists forty-eight under 'Archaeology'). List of historical areas administered by the National Park Service. Branch listings of federal archives and records centres.

449 *Directory of special libraries and information centers*; ed. by B. T. Darnay. 8th ed. Detroit (Michigan): Gale, 1983. 3 vols.
Gives information such as address, number of vols. and subjects covered for over 16,000 North American special libraries and information centres. Arranged alphabetically by title. Subject index (over sixty entries under 'Archeology').

450 *Encyclopedia of associations.* 18th ed. Detroit (Michigan): Gale Research, 1984. 3 vols.
Vol. 1 (two parts) lists over 17,500 national organizations of the US arranged in broad subject sections. Alphabetical and keyword index; nearly fifty organizations are listed under 'Archaeology'. Vol. 2 comprises geographic and executive indexes covering the material in Vol. 1, and Vol. 3 *New associations and projects* lists newly formed associations.

451 Herman, K. and **Carstens, P.** *Guide to departments of sociology, anthropology,*

archaeology in universities and museums in Canada. Ottawa: National Museum of Man, National Museums of Canada, 1978. 193 pp. (National Museum of Man. Mercury series. Directorate Paper, 1.)
Lists 1,374 scholars in the subjects covered, including degrees and interests. Complete coverage for Canadian universities but only partial coverage for museums. Alphabetically arranged by university, then alphabetical by museum. Index of names.

452 *The National faculty directory: an alphabetical list, with addresses, of about 597,000 members of teaching faculties at junior colleges, colleges, and universities in the United States and at selected Canadian institutions*. Detroit (Michigan): Gale Research, 1970–. Irreg. 3 vols.
A single alphabetical list of names and addresses.

Central America
(Belize, Costa Rica, El Salvador, Guatemala, Honduras, Mexico, Nicaragua, Panama, Caribbean islands)

General bibliographical guides

453 Bernal, I. *Bibliografía de arqueología y etnografía: Mesoamérica y norte de México, 1514–1960*. Mexico City: Instituto Nacional de Antropología e Historia, 1962. 650 pp.
The fullest bibliography on the archaeology and ethnology of Mesoamerica and northern Mexico. Has 13,990 unannotated entries, listing material published between 1514 and 1960. Arrangement is basically geographical with some general sections. Author index.

454 Kendall, A. *The art and archaeology of pre-Columbian Middle America: an annotated bibliography of works in English*. Boston (Mass.): Hall, 1977. 338 pp. (Reference Publications in Latin American Studies.)
Annotated bibliography of 2,147 publications of all kinds in English on all aspects of the art, architecture and archaeology of Mexico, Guatemala, El Salvador, Honduras, Belize, Costa Rica, Nicaragua and Panama. Arranged alphabetically by author in two sequences: books; periodical articles. Appendix gives a representative listing of doctoral dissertations. Subject index (brief).

455 Magee, S. F. *Mesoamerican archaeology: a guide to the literature and other information sources*. Austin (Texas): Institute of Latin American Studies, University of Texas, 1981. 79 pp. (Guides and Bibliographies series, 12.)
Discusses the various types of literature in all languages available for Mesoamerican archaeology and analyses individual titles.

Abstracting, indexing, current awareness services

456 *Handbook of Latin American Studies*. Austin: University of Texas Press, 1935– (publ. 1936–). Annual.
Extensive annotated bibliography of publications of all kinds relating to Latin America, including excellent coverage of archaeology. Alternate vols. cover the

humanities and social sciences. Humanities vols. contain a small amount of archaeology, mainly under 'ethnohistory', but most archaeological material is in the social sciences vols. where the archaeology section (a sub-section of anthropology) is divided into Mesoamerica, Caribbean area and South America (1979 vol. contained 617 annotated items under 'Archaeology'). An introductory note to each area comments briefly on research and publication trends. Some 600 periodicals are scanned for material. Subject index; author index. Delay: *c.* two to three years. Cumulative author index to vols. 1–28 (1936–66) (Gainesville: University of Florida Press, 1968. 421 pp.).

457 *Hispanic American Periodicals Index.* Los Angeles: UCLA Latin American Center, 1970–. Annual.
Unannotated listing of material on Latin America, including the Caribbean, from nearly 250 journals published worldwide, including some major archaeological and anthropological ones. Subject section; author section. Delay: *c.* three years.

Surveys

458 Adams, R. *Prehistoric Mesoamerica.* Boston (Massachusetts): Little, Brown, 1977. 384 pp.
Synthesis of Mesoamerican prehistory.

459 Wauchope, R. (ed.). *Handbook of Middle American Indians.* Austin: University of Texas Press, 1964–76. 16 vols. + supplements 1– (1981–).
A major series covering the natural environment, early cultures, archaeology, linguistics, social anthropology and ethnology. The archaeological information given, e.g. in vols. 2–3 *Archaeology of Southern Mesoamerica* (1965), vol. 4 *Archaeological frontiers and external connections* (1966), and vols. 10–11 *Archaeology of Northern Mesoamerica* (1971), has been updated by Supplement 1 *Archaeology.* This comprises an introduction, ten chapters on some of the most significant projects of the last twenty years and their implications, and three chapters on particular topics; bibliography (pp. 403–48); index.

460 Weaver, M. P. *The Aztecs, Maya and their predecessors: archaeology of Mesoamerica.* 2nd ed. New York and London: Academic Press, 1981. (Studies in Archaeology.) 620 pp. References: pp. 537–72.
Synthesis of Mesoamerican prehistory.

Periodicals

461 *Anales de Antropología.* Mexico City: Universidad Nacional Autónoma de México, Instituto de Investigaciones Antropológicas, 1964–. Annual. Es. Cumulative index: vols. 1–12 (1964–75).
Mexican archaeology. Book reviews.

462 *Anales del Instituto Nacional de Antropología e Historia.* Córdoba (Mexico): Instituto Nacional de Antropología e Historia, 1939– (publ. 1945–). Irreg. Es.
Central American archaeology, linguistics, ethnology and history.

463 *Boletín del Museo del Hombre Dominicano.* Santo Domingo (Dominican Republic): Museo del Hombre Dominicano, 1972–. Quarterly. Es.
Central American archaeology.

464 *Cuba Arqueológica.* Santiago de Cuba: Editorial Oriente, 1978–. Irreg. Es.
Cuban archaeology.

465 *Journal of the Virgin Islands Archaeological Society.* Frederiksted (Virgin Islands): Virgin Islands Archaeological Society, 1974–. Twice a year. En.
Virgin Islands archaeology.

466 *Memoirs of the Peabody Museum of Archaeology and Ethnology.* Cambridge (Mass.): Peabody Museum of Archaeology and Ethnology, Harvard University, 1896–. Irreg. En.
Coverage is mainly Central America and, in particular, the Maya.

467 *Vínculos: Revista de Antropología del Museo Nacional de Costa Rica.* San Jose (Costa Rica): Museo Nacional de Costa Rica, Departamento de Antropología e Historia, 1975–. Irreg. En. Es. (abstracts in Es. and En.).
New World anthropology, including archaeology, with emphasis on Central America.

468 *Yaxkin.* Tegucigalpa (Honduras): Instituto Hondureño de Antropología e Historia, 1975–. Twice a year. Es.
Archaeology, anthropology and history of Honduras.

South America
(Argentina, Bolivia, Brazil, Chile, Colombia, Ecuador, Guyana, Paraguay, Peru, Suriname, Uruguay, Venezuela)

General bibliographical guide

469 O'Leary, T. J. *Ethnographic bibliography of South America.* New Haven (Connecticut): Human Relations Area Files, 1963. (Behavior Science Bibliographies.) 413 pp.
Comprehensive (*c.* 24,000 items) unannotated bibliography of publications on all ethnographical subjects relating to South America, including archaeology. Arranged by geographical area and by tribal group within each area. Index of tribal names.

Abstracting, indexing, current awareness services

470 *Handbook of Latin American Studies.* (see [456])

471 *Hispanic American Periodicals Index.* (see [457])

Survey

472 Steward, J. H. (ed.). *Handbook of South American Indians.* New York: Cooper

Square Publishers, 1963. (Smithsonian Institution. Bureau of American Ethnology. Bulletin 143.) 7 vols. (Originally publ. 1946–59.)
Still a valuable first source of reference in spite of its age. Comprises narrative accounts of the tribes, with a good deal of archaeology. Vol. 1: *The marginal tribes*; vol. 2: *The Andean civilizations*; vol. 3: *The tropical forest tribes*; vol. 4: *The circum-Caribbean tribes*; vol. 5: *The comparative ethnology of South American Indians*; vol. 6: *Physical anthropology, linguistics, and cultural geography of South American Indians*; vol. 7: index (very detailed; includes tribal names). Vols. 1–6 each include an extensive bibliography.

Periodicals

473 *Anales de Arqueología y Etnología*. Mendoza (Argentina): Universidad Nacional de Cuyo, Instituto de Arqueología y Etnología, 1940–. Irreg. Es.
South American archaeology and anthropology.

474 *Boletim do Museu Nacional Rio de Janeiro: Antropologia*. Rio de Janeiro: Museu Nacional, 1942–. Irreg. Pt.
Brazilian archaeology and anthropology.

475 *Boletín – Museo del Oro*. Bogotá (Colombia): Banco de la República, 1978–. Three times a year. Es.
Colombian archaeology.

476 *Chungara*. Arica (Chile): Universidad de Tarapaca, Depto de Antropología, 1972–. Annual. Es. (summaries in En.).
Andean archaeology, anthropology, ethnohistory.

477 *Cuadernos de Historia y Arqueología*. Guayaquil (Ecuador): Casa de la Cultura Ecuatoriana, Nucleo del Guayas, 1950–. Irreg. Es.
Ecuadorean archaeology. Includes a bibliography on Ecuadorean anthropology.

478 *Dédalo*. São Paulo (Brazil): Universidade de São Paulo, Museu de Arqueologia e Etnologia, 1965–. Twice a year. Es. Pt. (summaries in En. or Fr.).
South American art and archaeology.

479 *Estudios Atacameños*. Antofagasta (Chile): Universidad del Norte, 1973–. Irreg. Es.
Andean archaeology and anthropology.

480 *Ñawpa Pacha*. Berkeley (California): Institute of Andean Studies, 1963–. Annual. En.
Archaeology, art and ethnohistory of the Andean region of South America. Includes 'New publications of interest to our readers'.

481 *Revista Colombiana de Antropología*. Bogotá (Colombia): Instituto Colombiano de Antropología, 1953–. Annual. Es.
Colombian archaeology and anthropology.

482 *Revista del Instituto de Antropología.* Córdoba (Argentina): Universidad Nacional de Córdoba, 1960–. Irreg. Es.
South American archaeology and anthropology.

483 *Revista del Museo Nacional.* Lima (Peru): Museo Nacional de la Cultura Peruana, 1932–. Annual. Es.
Peruvian archaeology and anthropology.

484 *Revista do Museu Paulista.* São Paulo (Brazil): Universidade de São Paulo, 1947–. Annual. Pt. (abstracts in En.)
Brazilian archaeology and anthropology.

485 *Sarance: Revista del Instituto Otavaleño de Antropología.* Otavalo (Ecuador): Instituto Otavaleño de Antropología, 1975–. Three times a year. Es.
Archaeology, anthropology, history, sociology, etc. of Ecuador.

Asia
(in general, including USSR)

Abstracting, indexing, current awareness service

486 *Bibliography of Asian Studies.* Ann Arbor (Michigan): Association for Asian Studies, 1969– (publ. 1971–). Annual.
Very detailed unannotated listing of publications of all kinds, mainly in the humanities and social sciences, in western languages on the Far East, South and South-east Asia. Some 1,000 periodicals are scanned, including many containing archaeological material. Arranged by region, then by topic. Most of the archaeology appears in the 'History' section. Author index. Delay: *c.* three years.
   Cumulative vols.: *Cumulative bibliography of Asian Studies, 1966–70* (Author bibliography. 3 vols. 1973; Subject bibliography. 3 vols. 1972. Hall). *Cumulative bibliography of Asian Studies, 1941–65* (Author bibliography. 4 vols. 1969; Subject bibliography. 4 vols. 1970. Hall).
   Formerly (1957–69) part of the *Journal of Asian Studies*; previously (1941–56) was the 'Far Eastern Bibliography' (part of the *Far Eastern Quarterly*); previously (1936–40) was the *Bulletin of Far Eastern Bibliography.*

Survey

487 **Gupta, S. P.** *Archaeology of Soviet Central Asia and the Indian Borderlands.* Delhi: B.R. Publishing Corporation. Vol. 1: *Prehistory.* 1979. 217 pp. Bibliography: pp. 183–8; vol. 2: *Protohistory.* 1979. 375 pp. Bibliography: pp. 321–30.
Synthesis of the archaeology of Central Asia, northern India, Pakistan and Afghanistan.

USSR

General bibliographical guides

488 **Akademiya Nauk SSSR. Institut Istorii Material'noi Kul'tury.** *Sovets-*

kaya arkheologicheskaya literatura; bibliografiya 1918–72. ed. by N. A. Vinberg and others. Leningrad: Nauka, 1959–80. 4 vols.
Comprehensive classified bibliography of Soviet archaeological publications of all kinds from the Palaeolithic to the 17th century. Arranged geographically, preceded by a general section. Author index; subject index.

489 Field, H. *Bibliography of Soviet archaeology and physical anthropology, 1936–1972.* Miami (Florida): Field Research Projects, 1972. 25 pp.
Unannotated list of 189 selected publications of all kinds on Soviet archaeology and physical anthropology translated from Soviet sources. Arranged numerically. Also includes a list of publications by Field Research Projects, some of which are archaeological studies covering various parts of the world. No index.

Abstracting and indexing services

490 *Arkheologiya SSSR: Svod Arkheologicheskikh Istochnikov.* Moscow: Akademiya Nauk SSSR, 1961–. Irreg.
A corpus of archaeological sources for the USSR. Divided into sub-series on a chronological basis: Palaeolithic; Mesolithic; Neolithic; Bronze Age; Classical antiquities; Iron Age; Medieval antiquities. Within these sub-series, division is often geographical, but some fascicles cover different periods of a particular area. Most fascicles include distribution maps, documented lists of sites keyed to the maps, a bibliography, and indexes; some fascicles have summaries in Fr.

491 *Novaya Sovetskaya Literatura po Istorii, Arkheologii i Etnografii.* Moscow: Izdatel'stvo Akademiya Nauk, 1934–. Monthly.
Lists current Soviet archaeological publications.

Surveys

492 Frumkin, G. *Archaeology in Soviet Central Asia.* Leiden: Brill, 1970. (Handbuch der Orientalistik. Siebente Abteilung III Band, 1 Abschnitt.) 235 pp. Bibliography: pp. 159–98.
Survey of the archaeology of a vast area from the Palaeolithic to the middle ages.

493 Masson, V. M. and **Sarianidi, V. I.** *Central Asia: Turkmenia before the Achaemenids*; transl. [from the Russian MSS] and ed. with a preface by R. Tringham. London: Thames and Hudson, 1972. 219 pp. (Ancient Peoples and Places, 79.) Bibliography: pp. 173–80.
Synthesis of the prehistory of Central Asia.

494 Sulimirski, T. *Prehistoric Russia: an outline.* London: Baker, 1970. 472 pp. Bibliography: pp. 429–35.
Survey of the prehistory of Eastern Europe to the end of the 7th century BC.

Periodical

495 *Sovetskaya Arkheologiya.* Moscow: Akademiya Nauk SSSR, Institut Arkheologii, 1957–. Quarterly. Ru. (contents page and summaries in En.).
Soviet archaeology. Book reviews.

Middle East
(Bahrain, Iran, Iraq, Israel, Jordan, Kuwait, Lebanon, Oman, Qatar, Saudi
Arabia, Syria, Turkey, United Arab Emirates, Yemen)

General bibliographical guides

496 Al-Haik, A. R. *Key lists of archaeological excavations in Iraq, 1842–1965.* Ed. by
H. Field and E. M. Laird. Coconut Grove (USA): Field Research Projects,
1968. 171 pp. *Key lists of archaeological excavations in Iraq: II, 1966–71.* Coconut
Grove (Florida); Field Research Projects, 1971. 133 pp.
Main part of each vol. is chapter 2: 'History of sites', which comprises history
sheets, each relating to a particular site. Other chapters comprise an introduction, indexes (to sites, personal names, sponsors and supporters of explorations
and excavations, expeditions), bibliography, appendices and an Arabic introduction.

497 Battersby, H. R. *Anatolian archaeology: a bibliography.* New Haven (Connecticut): Human Relations Area Files, 1976. 2 vols.
Lists 5,169 publications of all kinds in two author sequences. Index by topic or
excavation site.

498 École Biblique et Archéologique Française, Jerusalem. *Catalogue de la
Bibliothèque de l'École biblique et archéologique française.* Boston (Mass.): Hall, 1975.
13 vols.
Lists over 50,000 books and articles on the Old and New Testament, Judaism,
Christian antiquity, papyrology, linguistics, epigraphy, numismatics, archaeology, Assyriology, Egyptology, Oriental history, etc. Single alphabetical sequence of authors and subjects. No list of subject headings.

499 Ellis, R. S. *A bibliography of Mesopotamian archaeological sites.* Wiesbaden:
Harrassowitz, 1972. 137 pp.
List of books and articles on ancient sites in pre-Islamic Mesopotamia. Alpha-
betically arranged by site.

500 Pearson, J. D. (ed.). *A bibliography of pre-Islamic Persia.* London: Mansell,
1975. (Persian Studies series, 2.) 317 pp.
Unannotated list of 7,311 publications of all kinds from *c.* 450 periodicals and
other collective works. Arranged in four sections; Section D: 'Art and archaeology' has 1,008 items. Author index.

501 Vanden Berghe, L. *Bibliographie analytique de l'archéologie de l'Iran ancien.*
Leiden: Brill, 1979. 354 pp. + Supplément 1: 1978–1980 (Leiden: Brill, 1981.
124 pp.)
The two vols. comprise an unannotated bibliography of 4,714 publications of all
kinds. Each is arranged in three parts: general section; bibliography by regions
and sites; bibliography by periods. Topographic index; author index.

502 Vanden Berghe, L. and **Mussche, H. F.** *Bibliographie analytique de l'Assyrio-*

logie et de l'archéologie du Proche-Orient. Leiden: Brill. Vol. 1, section A: *L'Archéologie 1954–55.* 1956. 146 pp. Vol. 2, section A: *L'Archéologie 1956–57.* 1960. 188 pp.

The combined vols. comprise 1,637 references on Assyriology and Near Eastern archaeology. Each vol. is in three parts: general bibliography; bibliography by regions; notices of publications appearing before 1954 and 1956 respectively. Each section has an author index and geographic index.

Abstracting, indexing, current awareness service

503 *Orientalia.* Rome: Pontificium Institutum Biblicum, 1932–. Quarterly, En. Fr. De. It. (see also [521])

Includes 'Keilschriftbibliographie' (detailed bibliographical listings covering the Middle East).

Surveys

504 Beek, M. A. *Atlas of Mesopotamia: a survey of the history and civilisaticn of Mesopotamia from the Stone Age to the fall of Babylon;* ed. by H. H. Rowley. London: Nelson, 1962. 164 pp. No bibliographies.

Survey of the civilization of Sumeria, Assyria and Babylonia, with illustrations and maps a particular feature.

505 Hawkes, J. *The first great civilizations: life in Mesopotamia, the Indus valley and Egypt.* New York: Knopf, 1973. 508 pp. Selected bibliography: pp. 463–5.

Covers all aspects of the major civilizations of the Near East (the bulk of the book) and the Indus valley.

506 Lloyd, S. *The archaeology of Mesopotamia: from the Old Stone Age to the Persian Conquest.* London: Thames and Hudson, 1978. 252 pp. (The World of Archaeology.) Bibliography: pp. 238–43.

A synthesis of Mesopotamian archaeology.

507 Mellaart, J. *The Neolithic of the Near East.* London: Thames and Hudson, 1975. 300 pp. (The World of Archaeology.) Bibliography: pp. 289–96.

Survey of man's development from *c.* 15,000 BC to *c.* 5,000 BC in the Near East, broadly interpreted, i.e. from the plains of Hungary to Central Asia and the Sahara.

508 Redman, C. L. *The rise of civilization: from early farmers to urban society in the Ancient Near East.* San Francisco: Freeman and Co., 1978. 375 pp. Bibliography: pp. 325–59.

Covers the Ancient Near East, including a brief section on Egypt, with a few key sites described in detail as case studies.

Periodicals

509 *Anatolian Studies: Journal of the British Institute of Archaeology at Ankara.* London: British Institute of Archaeology at Ankara, 1951–. Annual. En. Cumulative indexes: vols. 1–10 (1951–60); vols. 11–20 (1961–70).

Detailed coverage of excavations in Anatolia. Includes reports and summaries of the Institute's work and a survey of recent archaeological research in Turkey.

510 *Annales Archéologiques Arabes Syriennes: Revue d'Archéologie et d'Histoire*. Damascus: Direction Generale des Antiquités et des Musées, 1951–. Annual. En. Fr. Ar. Cumulative index: vols. 1–25.
Syrian archaeology.

511 *Atlal: the Journal of Saudi Arabian Archaeology*. Riyadh: Department of Antiquities and Museums, 1977–. Annual. En. Ar.
Saudi Arabian archaeology. 'News and events' section.

512 *Berytus: Archaeological Studies*. Beirut: American University of Beirut, 1934–. Annual. En. Fr. De.
Historical and archaeological studies on Syria and Lebanon from prehistoric to early Islamic times. Book reviews.

513 *Biblical Archaeologist*. Cambridge (Mass.): American Schools of Oriental Research, 1938–. En. Quarterly. Cumulative index every five years; vols. 1–30 (1938–67).
Semi-popular coverage of archaeological discoveries relating to the Bible. Book reviews, fine illustrations.

514 *Bulletin of the American Schools of Oriental Research*. Cambridge (Mass.): American Schools of Oriental Research, 1919–. Quarterly. En. Cumulative indexes: nos. 1–50 (1919–33); nos. 51–70 (1933–38) in no. 76; nos. 71–100 (1938–45) in no. 105; five-yearly cumulations (1946–).
Scholarly coverage of Near Eastern archaeology. Book reviews.

515 *Dilmun: Journal of the Bahrain Historical and Archaeological Society*. Bahrain: Bahrain Historical and Archaeological Society, 1971–. Annual. En.
History and archaeology of Bahrain.

516 *Iran: Journal of the British Institute of Persian Studies*. London: British Institute of Persian Studies, 1963–. Annual. En. (occasionally Fr. De.).
Persian studies. Includes a survey of excavations of the previous year.

517 *Iraq*. London: British School of Archaeology in Iraq, 1934–. Twice a year. En. Cumulative index: vols. 1–30 (1934–68).
Studies of the history, art, archaeology, religion, economic and social life of Iraq from earliest times to about AD 1700.

518 *Israel Exploration Journal*. Jerusalem: Israel Exploration Society, 1950/51–. Quarterly. En. Cumulative index every ten years.
History and archaeology of Israel and the Near East from Palaeolithic to early medieval times. Notes and news. Book reviews.

519 *Journal of Oman Studies.* Oman: Ministry of National Heritage and Culture, 1975–. Annual. En.
Archaeology of Oman.

520 *Levant: Journal of the British School of Archaeology in Jerusalem and the British Institute at Amman for Archaeology and History.* London: British School of Archaeology in Jerusalem; British Institute at Amman for Archaeology and History, 1969–. Annual. En.
Archaeology of Palestine and neighbouring countries from earliest times to *c.* AD 1800.

521 *Orientalia.* Rome: Pontificium Institutum Biblicum, 1932–. Quarterly. En. Fr. De. It. (see also [503])
Ancient history, archaeology, and philology of the Near East. Includes 'Keilschriftbibliographie' (detailed bibliographical listings).

522 *Palestine Exploration Quarterly.* London: Palestine Exploration Fund, 1869–. Twice a year. En. Cumulative indexes: 1869–92; 1893–1910; 1911–68.
All aspects of archaeology in Israel from earliest times to *c.* AD 1800. Notes and news. Book reviews.

523 *Sumer: a Journal of Archaeology and History in Arab World.* Baghdad: State Organization of Antiquities and Heritage of Iraq, 1945–. Annual. Ar. En.
Mesopotamian archaeology.

524 *Syria: Revue d'Art Oriental et d'Archéologie.* Paris: (Institut Français d'Archéologie du Proche-Orient) Librairie Orientaliste Paul Geuthner, 1920–. Two double issues a year. Fr.
Art and archaeology of the Middle East. Book reviews.

525 *Zeitschrift für Assyriologie und Vorderasiatische Archäologie.* Berlin: de Gruyter, 1884–. Twice a year. De. En.
Archaeology of the Near East, with a bias towards Mesopotamia. Book reviews.

Dictionaries, encyclopaedias, atlases

526 Avi-Yonah, M. (ed.). *Encyclopedia of archaeological excavations in the Holy Land.* London: Oxford University Press; Jerusalem: Massada Press, 1975–78. 4 vols. Bibliography at the end of each entry.
Very detailed, comprehensive summary of excavated sites in Israel from prehistoric times to the Crusader period. Brings together information dispersed in numerous books and articles as well as material previously unpublished. Single alphabetical arrangement by site, by topic (e.g. churches) and by area (e.g. Jordan valley). Some 2000 maps, charts, plans, diagrams, etc. Chronological tables. Vol. IV includes index to names, index to places.

527 Baly, D. and **Tushingham, A. D.** *Atlas of the biblical world.* New York: World Publishing Company, 1971. 221 pp. Bibliography: pp. 180–85.

Explains and describes the biblical environment. Maps and text mainly by a professional geographer. Most material covers the geographical features, but there are chapters on archaeology and ancient environments and the ancient topography of Jerusalem. Index to the text; index to the maps.

528 Negev, A. (ed.). *Archaeological encyclopedia of the Holy Land.* London: Weiden-feld and Nicolson, 1972. 354 pp.
Lists most of the geographical names in the Bible, both in Israel and elsewhere in the Middle East, identifies them as far as possible, describes excavation done at them and analyses importance of finds. Glossary. List of ancient sources used. Chronological tables.

529 *Reallexikon der Assyriologie und vorderasiatischen Archäologie.* Founded by E. Ebeling and B. Meissner; ed. by D. O. Edzard. Berlin: de Gruyter, 1928–. Lengthy bibliographies at the end of articles.
Scholarly encyclopaedia on Assyriology and Near Eastern archaeology.

Directory (organizational)

530 Wiseman, D. J. *European research resources: Assyriology.* Strasbourg: Council of Europe. Council for Cultural Co-operation, 1967. 32 pp.
Based on the results of a questionnaire. Covers the scope of Assyriology, European teaching institutions concerned with Assyriology, research organization and facilities (including libraries), publications, international co-operation, European Institutes in the Near East, with recommendations for improvements. Appendices include details of centres of Assyriological teaching and research in Europe and the Near East, European journals primarily concerned with Assyriology, etc. Needs updating but still useful.

South Asia

(Afghanistan, Bangladesh, Bhutan, Burma, India, Nepal, Pakistan, Sri Lanka)

General bibliographical guides

531 King, D. E. (ed.). *Comprehensive bibliography of Pakistan archeology: paleolithic to historic times.* East Lansing (Michigan): Asian Studies Center, Michigan State University, 1975. (S. Asia Ser. Occ. Paper, 24.) 95 pp.
Comprehensive listing for Pakistan archaeology.

532 Pande, B. M. and **Ramachandran, K. S.** *Bibliography of the Harappan culture.* Coconut Grove (USA): Field Research Projects, 1971. 58 pp. (Field Research Projects.)
Some 1,400 unannotated references on the Indus Valley culture, with special emphasis on Harappa, alphabetically arranged by author. List of reviews of major publications. List of sites. Carbon 14 dates of sites.

533 Patterson, M. L. P. *South Asian civilizations: a bibliographic synthesis.* Chicago and London: University of Chicago Press, 1981. 890 pp.
Detailed, selective, unannotated bibliography of over 28,000 Western-language

publications of all kinds on South Asian civilizations. Includes a good deal of archaeological material; subject index notes 352 items under 'archaeology'. Main arrangement is chronological, then geographic and topical. Author index; subject index.

Abstracting, indexing, current awareness service

534 *Annual Bibliography of Indian Archaeology*. Leiden: (Kern Institute, Leiden) Reidel, 1926– (publ. 1928–). Irreg.
Comprehensive, international annotated bibliography of all kinds of publications on the archaeology of the Indian subcontinent and areas within its cultural influence: Sri Lanka, South-east Asia, Afghanistan, Central Asia, Nepal, Tibet. Arranged geographically. Author index. Delay: many years (vol. 22 for 1967–69 was published in 1982).

Surveys

535 Allchin, B. and **Allchin, F. R.** *The rise of civilization in India and Pakistan.* Cambridge (England): Cambridge University Press, 1982. 393 pp. (Cambridge World Archaeology.) Select bibliography: pp. 362–71.
A well-produced synthesis of the prehistory of India and Pakistan.

536 Allchin, F. R. and **Hammond, N.** (eds.). *The archaeology of Afghanistan from earliest times to the Timurid period.* London: Academic Press, 1978. 474 pp. Bibliography: pp. 415–33.
Synthesis of archaeology in Afghanistan.

537 Hammond, N. (ed.). *South Asian archaeology*: papers from the First International Conference of South Asian Archaeologists held in the University of Cambridge. London: Duckworth, 1973. 320 pp. References at the end of each chapter.
Series of papers covering a very wide range of topics from remote prehistory to the 19th century. The first paper (R. Allchin) outlines the general history of archaeology in South Asia. Further biennial conferences have been held and the papers published.

Periodicals

538 *Afghan Studies*. London: (Society for South Asian Studies) British Institute of Afghan Studies, 1978–. Irreg. En.
History, antiquities, archaeology, ethnography, languages, literature, art, culture, customs and natural history of Afghanistan.

539 *Ancient Ceylon: Journal of the Archaeological Survey Department of Ceylon*. Colombo: Commissioner of Archaeology, Department of Archaeology, 1971–. Irreg. En.
Archaeology of Sri Lanka.

540 *Ancient Nepal*. Kathmandu: Department of Archaeology, 1967–. Every two months. En. Np.
Archaeology, history and art of Nepal.

541 *Indian Archaeology – a Review.* New Delhi: Archaeological Survey of India, 1954–. Annual. En.
Official report on archaeological activities in India.

542 *Pakistan Archaeology.* Karachi: (National Museum of Pakistan) Department of Archaeology and Museums, 1964–. Annual. En.
Reports of Pakistan archaeology.

543 *Puratattva: Bulletin of the Indian Archaeological Society.* New Delhi: Indian Archaeological Society, 1967–. Annual. En.
Archaeology of India and neighbouring countries. Notes and news. Book reviews.

South-East Asia

(Brunei, Indonesia, Kampuchea, Laos, Malaysia, Philippines, Singapore, Thailand, Viet-Nam)

Surveys

544 Bellwood, P. *Man's conquest of the Pacific: the prehistory of South-East Asia and Oceania.* Auckland and London: Collins, 1978. 462 pp. Bibliography: pp. 425–51.
Comprehensive survey of the prehistory of an enormous area.

545 Jocano, F. L. *Philippine prehistory: an anthropological overview of the beginnings of Filipino society and culture.* Quezon City: Philippine Center for Advanced Studies, University of the Philippines, 1975. 298 pp. Bibliography: pp. 251–61.
Synthesis of Filipino prehistory.

546 Loofs, H. H. E. *Archäologie der Philippinen.* Leiden: Brill, 1978. (Handbuch der Orientalistik. Siebente Abteilung: Kunst und Archäologie. Sechster Band – Südostasien; sechster Abschnitt.) 103 pp. Bibliography: pp. 75–92.
An introduction is followed by a history of research and summary of the present state of research.

547 Smith, R. B. and **Watson, W.** (eds.). *Early South East Asia: essays in archaeology, history and historical geography.* Oxford: Oxford University Press, 1979. 575 pp. Bibliography: pp. 531–52.
Papers covering widely differing subjects given at a colloquy on first millennium BC and first millennium AD South-East Asia held at the School of Oriental and African Studies of the University of London in 1973. Some are surveys of particular areas such as Viet-Nam, the Malay peninsula, the Philippines, Indonesia, Sumatra, etc.

Periodicals

548 *Bulletin of Prehistory/Berita Prasejarah.* Jakarta: National Archaeological Institute of Indonesia, 1974–. Irreg. En. In.
Indonesian archaeology.

549 *Journal of the Malaysian Branch of the Royal Asiatic Society.* Selangor (Malaysia): Malaysian Branch of the Royal Asiatic Society, 1878–. Twice a year. En. Cumulative index: 1878–1980.
Malaysian history, archaeology, ethnography, language.

550 *Khảo cô 'học (Archaeology).* Hanoi: Institute of Archaeology, Vietnam Social Sciences Committee, 1969–. Quarterly. Vi. (contents and abstracts in En. and Fr.).
Vietnamese archaeology of all periods. Book reviews.

551 *Muang Boran (Ancient City).* Bangkok: Muang Boran Institute for Thai Art, 1974–. Quarterly. Th. En.
Art, archaeology and history of Thailand.

Far East
(China, Hong Kong, Japan, Korea, Mongolia, Taiwan)

General bibliographical guides

552 Befu, H., Chard, C. S., and **Okada, A.** An annotated bibliography of the preceramic archaeology of Japan. *Arctic Anthropology*, 2:1 (1964), 1–83.
Annotated list of 430 publications on Japanese archaeology, alphabetically arranged by author. List of sources in Western languages. Subject index; index of sites.

553 Chen, C. M. and **Stamps, R. B.** *An index to Chinese archaeological works published in the People's Republic of China, 1949–1965.* East Lansing (Michigan): Asian Studies Center, Michigan State University, 1972. (East Asia Series, 3.) 84 pp.
Unannotated list of books and articles on Chinese archaeology published in China 1949–65. Arranged chronologically, then geographically.

554 Chinese Academy of Social Sciences, Institute of Archaeology, Library (ed.). *Zhongguo Kaoguxue Wenxian Mulu 1949–1966 (Bibliography of Chinese archaeological literature, 1949–1966).* Beijing (China): Wenwu Press, 1978.
First part lists 537 monographs, second part over 7,000 titles of articles in periodicals, newspapers and other collective works, on Chinese archaeology.

555 Editorial Committee of Wenwu (ed.). *Wenwu Kaogu Gongzuo Sanshinian 1949–1979 (Thirty years of cultural relics work and archaeology, 1949–79).* Beijing (China): Wenwu Press, 1979.
Lists the most fundamental publications on Chinese archaeology that appeared during the period covered. Over 1,000 entries, arranged by province.

556 Knez, E. I. and **Swanson, C.-S.** *A selected and annotated bibliography of Korean anthropology.* Washington: National Technical Information Service, US Department of Commerce, 1978.

557 Okada, A., Okada, H. and **Chard, C. S.** An annotated bibliography of the archaeology of Hokkaido. *Arctic Anthropology*, 4:1 (1967), 1–163.
Lists 787 annotated references on Hokkaido archaeology, alphabetically arranged by author. Attempts to be complete up to 1962. Subject index; index of sites.

558 Rudolph, R. C. (ed.). *Chinese archaeological abstracts.* Los Angeles: University of California, Los Angeles, Institute of Archaeology, 1978. (Monumenta Archaeologica, 6.)
Contains 567 abstracts of articles taken from 88 issues of 3 major Chinese archaeological journals (*Kaogu* [572], *Kaogu Xuebao* [573], *Wenwu* [575]) covering the years 1963–66. Coverage is from the Palaeolithic to the 20th century. Arranged chronologically. Index of subjects.

559 Vanderstappen, H. (ed.). *The T. L. Yüan bibliography of Western writings on Chinese art and archaeology.* London: Mansell, 1975. 606 pp.
Over 15,000 items on Chinese art and archaeology written in En., De., Nd., Scandinavian, Slavic and Romance languages published between 1920 and 1965. Arranged by subject, with books and articles in separate sections. Author index.

Abstracting, indexing, current awareness service

560 *Revue Bibliographique de Sinologie.* Paris: Mouton, 1955– (publ. 1957–). Annual. Annotations in Fr. En. or De.
General bibliography on Chinese studies. Each vol. includes section on 'Archéologie, art et épigraphie' with subdivisions. Covers literature in Western and Oriental languages. Index of authors; index of subjects and proper names.

Surveys

561 Aikens, C. M. and **Higuchi, T.** *Prehistory of Japan.* New York and London: Academic Press, 1982. (Studies in Archaeology.) 369 pp. References: pp. 339–47.
Japanese prehistory from the Palaeolithic to AD 700, with a chronological arrangement.

562 Chang, Kwang-chih. *The archaeology of ancient China.* 3rd ed. New Haven (Connecticut): Yale University Press, 1977. 553 pp. Bibliography: pp. 517–20.
Comprehensive survey of Chinese archaeology.

563 Chard, C. S. *Northeast Asia in prehistory.* Madison: University of Wisconsin Press, 1974. 230 pp. Bibliography at the end of each chapter.
Prehistory of Japan, Eastern Siberia, Mongolia and Korea.

564 Ikawa-Smith, F. Current issues in Japanese archaeology. *American Scientist,* 68 (1980), 134–45. Thirty-eight references.
Brief survey of Japanese prehistory.

565 Kim, J.-H. *The prehistory of Korea*; transl. and ed. by R. Pearson and K.

Pearson. Honolulu: University Press of Hawaii, 1978. 272 pp. Bibliography: pp. 189–202.
Synthesis of Korean prehistory.

566 Pearson, R. The contribution of archaeology to Japanese studies. *Journal of Japanese Studies*, 2:2 (1976), 305–27. Sixty-eight references.
Surveys recent developments in Japanese archaeological studies and their potential contributions to other areas of Japanese studies.

567 Rawson, J. *Ancient China: art and archaeology.* London: British Museum, 1980. 240 pp. Bibliography: pp. 221–8.
Summarizes the major cultural characteristics of China from the Neolithic to the Han Dynasty.

Periodicals

568 *Archaeologia Japonica.* Tokyo: Japanese Archaeologists' Association, 1948–. Irreg. Ja. (summaries in En.).
Japanese archaeology.

569 *Archaeology in Korea.* Seoul: Seoul National University, 1973–. Annual. Ko. (summaries in En.).
Korean archaeology.

570 *Bulletin of the Department of Archaeology and Anthropology, National Taiwan University.* Taipei (Taiwan): National Taiwan University, Department of Archaeology and Anthropology, 1953–. Irreg. Ch. En.
Archaeology and anthropology of Taiwan.

571 *Journal of the Hong Kong Archaeological Society.* Hong Kong: Hong Kong Museum of History, 1968–. Annual. En.
Archaeology of Hong Kong, South China and South East Asia. Book reviews.

572 *Kaogu (Archaeology).* Peking: Kexue chubanshe, 1955–. Every two months. Ch.
Chinese archaeology. Includes bibliography of recently published monographs and articles.

573 *Kaogu Xuebao (Chinese Journal of Archaeology).* Peking: Kexue chubanshe, 1936–. Quarterly. Ch. (summaries in En.).
Chinese archaeology.

574 *Kōkogaku Zasshi (Archaeological Review).* Tokyo: Archaeological Society of Japan, 1952–. Quarterly. Ja. (summaries in En.).
Japanese archaeology.

575 *Wenwu (Cultural Relics).* Peking: Wenwu chubanshe, 1950–. Monthly. Ch. (contents page in En.).

Chinese art and archaeology; rapid reports of finds. Includes a bibliography of current monographs and articles.

Atlas

576 Chinese Academy of Sciences, Institute of Vertebrate Paleontology and Paleoanthropology. *Atlas of primitive man in China.* Beijing (China): Science Press, 1980. 176 pp.

Collection of 287 colour photographs of Chinese palaeolithic sites, artefacts, fauna and hominid remains. Each site is briefly introduced. No bibliography or index.

Australasia

(Australia, Melanesia, Micronesia, New Zealand, Papua New Guinea, Polynesia)

Abstracting, indexing, current awareness services

577 *Annual Bibliography of the Australian Institute of Aboriginal Studies.* Canberra: Australian Institute of Aboriginal Studies, 1975–. Annual.

The main source for Australian Aboriginal studies. Lists accessions to the Library of the AIAS. In two sequences: books, pamphlets, and periodical articles (from *c.* 300 periodicals); and manuscripts. Arrangement is basically regional. Delay: only a few months.

578 *Australian Public Affairs Information Service: a Subject Index to Current Literature.* Canberra: National Library of Australia, 1945–. Monthly (except December) with annual cumulations.

Guide to the contents of *c.* 200 Australian scholarly journals and other selected material (e.g., newspaper articles) relating to Australia in the social sciences and humanities, including some archaeology. Arranged alphabetically by subject. Author index. Delay: most items published within last year.

Surveys

579 Bellwood, P. *Man's conquest of the Pacific: the prehistory of South-East Asia and Oceania.* (see [544])

580 Mulvaney, D. J. *The prehistory of Australia.* Rev. ed. Harmondsworth (England): Penguin, 1975. 327 pp. Bibliography: pp. 304–20.

Authoritative survey of Australian prehistory.

581 White J. P. and **O'Connell, J. F.** *A prehistory of Australia, New Guinea and Sahul.* Sydney, New York and London: Academic Press, 1982. 298 pp. Bibliography: pp. 239–68.

Up-to-date synthesis of the area, with a very valuable and extensive bibliography.

Periodicals

582 *Archaeology in Oceania.* (formerly: *Archaeology and Physical Anthropology in Oceania.*) Sydney: University of Sydney, 1966–. Three times a year. Cumulative index: vols. 1–15 (1966–80). En.
Archaeology of the lands of the western Pacific rim and all the islands of the Pacific including Australia. Book reviews.

583 *The Artefact.* South Yarra (Australia): Archaeological and Anthropological Society of Victoria, 1976–. Quarterly. En.
Archaeology of the Pacific and circum-Pacific area. Notes and news. Book reviews.

584 *Australian Aboriginal Studies: Journal of the Australian Institute of Aboriginal Studies.* (formerly: *Newsletter of the Australian Institute of Aboriginal Studies.*) Canberra: Australian Institute of Aboriginal Studies, 1963–. Twice a year. En.
Aboriginal studies. Includes news of the AIAS. Book reviews.

585 *Australian Archaeology.* Canberra: (Australian Archaeological Association) Department of Prehistory, Research School of Pacific Studies, Australian National University, 1974–. Twice a year. En.
Archaeology of all periods of Australia and nearby areas. Book reviews.

586 *Journal of the Polynesian Society: a Study of the Native Peoples of the Pacific Area.* Auckland: Polynesian Society, University of Auckland, 1892–. Quarterly. En. Cumulative index: 1892–1966.
Archaeology and anthropology of the Pacific area.

587 *Mankind.* Sydney: Anthropological Society of New South Wales, 1931–. Three times a year. En.
Presents and interprets data from anthropology and related disciplines particularly concerning Australia and adjacent countries. Books received. Book reviews.

588 *New Zealand Journal of Archaeology.* Dunedin: New Zealand Archaeological Association, 1979–. Annual. En.
Prehistoric and historic archaeology in New Zealand and the Pacific.

589 *Newsletter of the New Zealand Archaeological Association.* Dunedin: New Zealand Archaeological Association, 1957–. Quarterly. En. Cumulative index: 1957–74.
Includes brief reports on current archaeological excavations and activities in New Zealand. Notes and news. Book reviews.

Glossary

590 *A glossary of useful archaeological terms.* [Melbourne]: Victoria Archaeological Survey, 1977. 11 pp. (Technical Series, 3.)
A brief listing of terms with special reference to Australian archaeology.

Arctic

General bibliographical guide

591 Dekin, A. A. *Arctic archaeology: a bibliography and history.* New York: Garland, 1978. 279 pp.

The most complete list of references on arctic and subarctic archaeology. Over 1,200 items from the 19th century to 1977, alphabetically arranged by author.

Indexing service

592 *Recent Polar and Glaciological Literature.* (formerly: *Recent Polar Literature.*) Cambridge (England): Scott Polar Research Institute, 1981–. Three times a year.

Selective coverage of publications of all kinds on the polar regions. Arranged by Universal Decimal Classification (UDC). Section 902/903 (Archaeology and prehistory) contains about ten to twenty items per issue. No indexes. Delay: *c.* one to two years.

Survey

593 Dumond, D. E. *The Eskimos and Aleuts.* London: Thames and Hudson, 1977. 180 pp. (Ancient Peoples and Places, 87.) Select bibliography: pp. 161–8.

Outline of Eskaleut prehistory.

Periodical

594 *Arctic Anthropology.* Madison: University of Wisconsin Press, 1962–. Twice a year. En.

International journal devoted to the study of northern cultures and peoples, past and present, in the Old and New Worlds.

PART III

List of selected organizations

List of selected organizations

Part III of this *Keyguide* is a list of selected archaeological organizations of various kinds. It is arranged alphabetically by country, with one organization for each country; the list of countries is based upon that given in the *Statesman's year-book: statistical and historical annual of the states of the world for the year 1983–1984* (London: Macmillan.Annual). International and multi-regional organizations are listed separately at the beginning of the sequence.

The selected organizations are of various kinds: government bodies, councils, societies, institutes, university bodies, museums, etc. Each one has been selected as a useful contact point for information, but it must not be assumed that it is necessarily the most important archaeological organization for the country concerned. Many other organizations are listed in the *Archaeologists' year book* [160] and other directories described in Chapter 3 of Part I.

The information given for each organization comprises its name, contact point, address, telephone and telex numbers (where known), a brief note of aims and activities, and details of publications (where appropriate). In the case of museums, only the briefest information about holdings can be included; more details will be found in the *Directory of museums* [168], *Museums of the world* [173], and *World of learning* [179].

An asterisk in front of an organization's name indicates that it did not reply to the questionnaire sent.

International and Multi-Regional Organizations

595 Aerial Archaeology Publications
Executive editor: 15, Colin McLean Road, East Dereham, Norfolk NR19 2RY, England.
Will supply information on all aspects of aerial archaeology worldwide.
Publications: *Aerial Archaeology* [94]; *Orbit* (an occasional serial).

596 Comité pour la Sidérurgie Ancienne de l'UISPP
Secretary: Institute of Archaeology, 118 01 Prague 1, Letenská 4, Czechoslovakia (Tel: Prague 53 93 51).
Acts as a forum for the exchange of information concerning the ancient and early iron industry. Currently involves about 140 corresponding members

worldwide. Organizes symposia on selected problems of early iron smelting and making.

Publications: *Communications* (part of some issues of *Archeologické Rozhledy* [360]; includes abstracts of work in progress and an annotated current bibliography).

597 Indo-Pacific Prehistory Association (IPPA)

Secretary: Dept of Prehistory and Anthropology, Australian National University, P.O. Box 4, Canberra, ACT 2600, Australia.

Promotes co-operation in the study of the prehistory of eastern Asia (east of 70° longitude) and the Pacific region; eastern limit is Easter Island, western is Pakistan. Maintains scholarly communication through regular congresses and publications. Upholds ethical standards in prehistorical research and helps countries in the IPPA area to prevent illegal excavation and trade in antiquities.

Publications: *Bulletin* (annual); *Newsletter* (occasional).

598 International Centre for the Study of the Preservation and Restoration of Cultural Property (ICCROM)

The Library: Via di San Michele 13, I-00153 Rome, Italy (Tel: (06) 589–4741/589–2622/580–9021; Telex: 613114 ICCROM I).

Collects, studies and circulates documentation concerned with scientific and technical problems of the preservation and restoration of cultural property. Co-ordinates, stimulates and institutes research in this domain. Gives advice and recommendations on conservation problems. Assists in training research workers and technicians. Library and documentation service covers every aspect of the conservation of cultural property.

Publications: Many fundamental works, published in conjunction with ICOMOS [601], ICOM [600] and IIC [602]; *Technical Notes*; *Newsletter*.

599 International Council for Archaeozoology

General Secretary: Biologisch-Archaeologisch Instituut, Poststraat 6, NL-9712 ER Groningen, The Netherlands (Tel: 050–115661/115666).

Aims: to develop and stimulate archaeozoological research; to strengthen co-operation among archaeozoologists; to foster co-operation with archaeologists and other scientists working in the field of archaeology. Promotes conferences, makes recommendations and disseminates information on the standardization of data recording, nomenclature, measurements, and policies relating to archaeozoology, and patronizes major scientific publications of international importance.

Publications: *Bibliographie zur Archäo-Zoologie und Geschichte der Haustiere* [192]; *Newsletter*; *Ichthyo-osteo-archaeology News*; *Animals and archaeology* (1983); conference proceedings; list of current research projects (annual).

600 International Council of Museums (ICOM)

UNESCO-ICOM Documentation Centre: Maison de l'UNESCO, 1, rue Miollis, F-75732 Paris, Cedex 15, France (Tel: 734–05–00/577–16–10; Cables: ICOM PARIS).

Dedicated to the improvement and advancement of the world's museums. The Documentation Centre, the world's largest repository of information on all aspects of museum management, is not primarily orientated to archaeology but can supply information on archaeological museums or collections and problems relating to them.

Publications: *Basic museum bibliography* (Paris, 1980); *ICOM News* (quarterly); various monographs.

601 International Council on Monuments and Sites (ICOMOS)

UNESCO-ICOMOS Documentation Centre: 75 rue du Temple, F-75003 Paris, France (Tel: 277–35–76; Telex: 240 91 B TRACE Ref 617).
Enhancement of archaeological sites. Conservation and restoration of sites. Urban archaeology, methodology, theory and techniques. The Documentation Centre, part of the UNESCO-ICOM-ICOMOS documentation network, collects relevant information in all these areas, organizes it to make it easily accessible and disseminates it to all interested parties. To achieve these objectives, the Centre was computerized and a specialized data bank (ICOMMOS) created on the protection of the heritage. The collection comprises *c.* 8,000 units in the library, *c.* 300 periodicals regularly received and *c.* 1,000 slides and plans.

Publications: *Newsletter*; *Monumentum* (quarterly); *Bulletin*; Numerous monographs and symposia.

602 International Institute for Conservation of Historic and Artistic Works (IIC)

Secretary-General: 6 Buckingham Street, London WC2N 6BA, England (Tel: 01–839 5975).
Provides a permanent organization for co-ordinating and improving the knowledge, methods and working standards needed to protect and preserve precious materials of all kinds, through its publications, conferences and regional groups.

Publications: *Art and Archaeology Technical Abstracts* [191]; *Studies in Conservation* [211]; *Bulletin* (bi-monthly); various monographs.

603 International Union of Anthropological and Ethnological Sciences (IUAES)

Secretary-General: University of Durham Department of Anthropology, 43, Old Elvet, Durham DH1 3HN, England (Tel: 0385–64466 Ext. 548; Telex: 537–351 DURLIB.G.).
The IUAES, through its world congresses, inter congresses and commissions, periodically brings together large numbers of individuals with interests in anthropology, archaeology and related matters. One section – the Commission on Documentation – is concerned with the computerization of anthropological data, data retrieval, etc. and issues a Newsletter of its own.

Publications: *Newsletter* (three times a year); conference proceedings.

604 Organisation for Museums, Monuments and Sites of Africa (OMMSA)

Secretary-General, OMMSA Secretariat: Box 3343, Accra, Ghana (Tel: 21633).
Co-ordinates major activities in museums and monuments services in African countries. Provides information and puts enquirers in touch with relevant sources of information.

Publications: *OMMSA Bulletin* (annual); [with the UNESCO-ICOM Documentation Centre] *Directory of African Museums*.

605 PACT – European Study Group for the Application of Physical, Chemical, Mathematical, Biological Techniques to Archaeology
Enquiries: 28a av. Léopold, B-1330 Rixensart, Belgium (Tel: 32–2–653.96.91) or, Council of Europe, Commission for Science and Technology, BP 431 R 6 F–67006, Strasbourg Cédex (Tel: 33–88–61.49.61).
Concerned with the links between the natural sciences and archaeology and in particular, isotopes, thermoluminescence, archaeomagnetism and geophysical prospection, analytical methods, mathematics and statistics. Advises special European postgraduate schools and promotes co-operation.
    Publications: *PACT: Journal of the European Study Group on Physical, Chemical and Mathematical Techniques applied to Archaeology* [205]; *Professional Directory of Laboratories; PACT-Education* (teaching modules in the fields of ceramics, metals, paper, etc.); *Newsletter* (irreg.); monographs and conference proceedings.

606 Society for South Asian Studies
Secretary: c/o British Academy, 20–21 Cornwall Terrace, London NW1 4QP, England.
Promotes studies, including fieldwork in various disciplines, with regard to Afghanistan, India, Pakistan and other South Asian countries. Supports and controls the British Institute of Afghan Studies [609].
    Publications: *Afghan Studies* [538].

607 Society of Africanist Archaeologists in America (SAAAM)
Editor of *Nyame Akuma* [397]: Department of Anthropology, University of Alberta, Edmonton, Alberta, Canada T6G 2H4 (Tel: (403) 432–5394; Telex: 037–2979).
Disseminates information on current research on African archaeology.
    Publications: *Nyame Akuma* [397].

608 Union Internationale des Sciences Préhistoriques et Protohistoriques (UISPP)
Secretary-General: Prof. Dr. J. Nenquin, Séminaire d'Archéologie de l'Université 2, Blandijnberg, B-9000 Gent, Belgium (Tel: 91/25.75.71).
Objectives: to promote prehistoric and protohistoric studies by organizing international congresses of prehistoric and protohistoric sciences, by sponsoring scientific publications of an international nature, by organizing large-scale excavations, and in general, by collaborating with scholars worldwide for the promotion of prehistoric and protohistoric sciences.
    Publications: *Inventaria Archaeologica* [231]: other monographs.

Organizations by Country

Afghanistan
609 *British Institute of Afghan Studies
Director: P.O.B. 3052, Kabul, Afghanistan.
Supported and controlled by the Society for South Asian Studies [606]. Afghan archaeology, history, culture, languages, geography (and related subjects).
    Publications: *Annual Report*; *Afghan Studies* [538].

Albania

610 *Qendra e Kërkimeve Arkeologjike (Centre for Archaeological Research)
Director: Tirana, Albania.
Publications: *Iliria* [385].

Algeria

611 *Direction des Musées de l'Archéologie et des Monuments et Sites Historiques
Director: Ministère de l'Information et de la Culture, 119 rue Didouche Mourad, Algiers, Algeria.
Controls museums, restoration, conservation and excavation.
Publications: *Bulletin d'Archéologie Algérienne* [403].

Angola

612 *Departamento Nacional de Museus e Monumentos
Director: Luanda, Angola.
Coverage includes Angolan prehistory, ethnography and anthropology.

Argentina

613 Universidad Nacional de Buenos Aires, Facultad de Filosofía y Letras, Museo Etnográfico
Director: Moreno 350, Buenos Aires, Capital Federal, Argentina (Tel: 34–4970).
Collections include much archaeological, ethnographical and anthropological material, particularly relating to Argentina.
Publications: *Runa* (annual).

Australia

614 Australian Heritage Commission
Information Officer or Librarian: P.O.B. 1567, Canberra City, ACT 2601, Australia (Tel: 062–723966).
A statutory authority established in 1975 as the Australian Federal Government's policy advisory and administrative body responsible for the National Estate. Identifies and enters significant archaeological sites in the Register of the National Estate, and endeavours to conserve them.
Publications: *Annual Report*; *Heritage Newsletter*; (by Macmillan Australia in association with the A.H.C.) *The heritage of Australia: the illustrated Register of the National Estate* (1983).

Austria

615 *Bundesdenkmalamt (Federal Monuments Office)
Secretary: A-1010 Vienna, Hofburg, Austria.

Responsible for protection and restoration of historical, artistic and cultural monuments. Controls excavations and art export.
Publications: various periodicals.

Bahamas

616 *Bahamia Museum
Director: P.O.B. N1510, Nassau, Bahamas.
Coverage includes anthropology.

Bahrain

617 Bahrain Historical and Archaeological Society
Secretary: P.O.B. 5087, Manama, Bahrain (Tel: 714360).
Objectives: to encourage the study of the history and archaeology of Bahrain and to promote research and publication in the field; to encourage the preservation of Bahrain's archaeological heritage; to assist archaeological programmes and to promote such activities by exhibition and the preparation of full photographic records; to develop closer relations and co-operate fully with organizations pursuing similar objectives.
Publications: *Dilmun* [515]; Clarke, A.: *The islands of Bahrain* (1981).

Bangladesh

618 *Dacca Museum
Director: P.O.B. 355, Ramna, Dacca 2, Bangladesh.
Coverage is mainly art and archaeology of Bengal.
Publications: various reports and monographs.

Barbados

619 Barbados Museum and Historical Society
Director: St Ann's Garrison, Barbados, West Indies (Tel: 70201).
Coverage includes prehistory of Barbados.
Publications: *Journal* (annual).

Belgium

620 Centre National de Recherches Archéologiques en Belgique – Natio-naal Centrum voor Oudheidkundige Navorsingen in België
Director: 1, Parc du Cinquantenaire, B-1040 Brussels, Belgium (Tel: 02/735.41.60).
Publications: Repertories of all archaeological publications for Belgium: short descriptions of finds and excavations, per municipality, with full bibliography; descriptions of archaeological collections; repertories on specific fields (e.g. Roman graves); *Archéologie* [303].

Belize

621 Department of Archaeology
Archaeological Commissioner: c/o Ministry of Trade and Industry, Belmopan, Belize (Tel: 08–2106).
The Department is a branch of the Government of Belize with the responsibility of protecting and preserving the cultural resources and heritage of Belize. Carries out salvage excavations, consolidates and maintains sites and artefacts, exercises control over foreign archaeological teams working in Belize, and all else connected with archaeology and anthropology in Belize.

Benin

622 *Musée Ethnographique
Director: BP 6, Porto-Novo, Benin.
Ethnographical material on the country's tribes.

Bermuda

623 *Bermuda Historical Society Museum
Director: Par-la-Ville, Hamilton, Bermuda, West Indies.
Artefacts relating to Bermuda's history.

Bhutan

624 *National Museum of Bhutan
Director: Tag-Dzong, Paro, Bhutan.
History and ethnography of Bhutan.

Bolivia

625 *Sociedad Arqueológica de Bolivia
Secretary: Av. Chacaltaya 500, Casilla 1487, Bolivia.
Publications: *Anales de la Arqueología de Bolivia*.

Botswana

626 National Museum and Art Gallery
The Archaeologist: Private Bag 00114, Gaborone, Botswana (Tel: Gaborone 53792).
Basic surveying of the whole country. Specific examination of key early Iron Age sites around and in Kalahari. Location and examination of monuments. Interpretation of prehistoric materials. Implementation of National Monuments Act.
Publications: (with Botswana Society Museum) *Botswana Notes and Records* (semi-scientific journal which includes archaeological papers); *Settlement in Botswana* (proceedings of a symposium).

Brazil

627 Fundação Nacional Pró-Memória da Sub-Secretaria do Patrimônio Histórico e Artístico Nacional, Setor de Arqueologia.
Secretary: Rua da Imprensa, 16, 8° andar 20.030, Rio de Janeiro, Rj Brazil (Tel: 220–9841; Telex: 02134108 FNPM RJ).
Supervision, inspection and registration of archaeological sites, and control of all excavations undertaken by any organization. These powers derive from the Law (no. 3924 of 26 June 1961) on the protection of archaeological and prehistoric monuments.

Brunei

628 *Brunei Museum
Director: Kota Batu, Brunei.
Coverage includes archaeology and ethnography of Brunei.
Publications: *Brunei Museum Journal* (annual).

Bulgaria

629 *Centre for Research in History, Institute of Archaeology and Museum
Director: Bulgarian Academy of Sciences, Sofia, '7 Noemvri' 1, Bulgaria (Tel: 8–41–41).
Publications: *Arheologija* [381]

Burma

630 *Archaeological Department
Director: Ministry of Culture, 32-D Prome Road, Rangoon, Burma.
Responsible for the maintenance of ancient monuments, epigraphical research, exploration and excavation of historical sites, and maintenance of site museums.

Burundi

631 Musée National de Gitega
Le Conservateur: B.P. 110 Gitega, Burundi.
Coverage includes Burundi's art, history and ethnography.

Cameroon

632 *Office National de la Recherche Scientifique et Technique (ONAREST).
Director: B.P. 1457, Yaoundé, Cameroon.
Archaeological research (amongst other subjects).
Publications: *Cahiers* (quarterly); *Recherches et Études Camerounaises*.

Canada

633 National Museum of Man, Archaeological Survey of Canada
Secretary: Ashton Press Building, 27 Northside Road, Bells Corners, Ontario K1A 0M8, Canada (Tel: 613–996–5250).
Objectives: to conduct staff research, to excavate, analyse and prepare for publication information pertinent to filling the present gaps in Canada's prehistory with particular emphasis upon lands under federal jurisdiction and relative to the requirements of the new Museum; to manage and curate, for present and future generations, the national archaeological collections; to conduct rescue archaeology in co-operation with the territorial governments and pertinent federal departments in order to mitigate the impact of economic development upon the prehistoric heritage; to publish and disseminate scientific information on Canada's prehistory; to provide effective information services relative to the national collections and their associated documentation.
Publications: *Annual Review*; numerous publications in the *Mercury Series*; monographs.

Central African Republic

634 *Mission Sociologique du Haut-Oubangui.
Director: B.P. 68, Bangassou, Central African Republic.
Sociological and archaeological studies.
Publications: *Recherches Oubanguiennes* (occasionally).

Chad

635 *Institut National des Sciences Humaines (INSH)
Director: B.P. 503, N'Djaména, Chad.
Research on pre- and protohistory and anthropology (amongst other subjects).
Publications: *I.N.S.H. – Informations*; *Études et Documents Tchadiens*.

Chile

636 Universidad de Antofagasta, Instituto de Investigaciones Arqueológicas y Restauración Monumental
Director: Casilla 1240, Antofagasta, Chile (Tel: 222248–214).
Studies the processes of human development and change in Chile from man's origins to historical times, through excavations and laboratory studies, applying archaeological and anthropological methodology.
Publications: *Estudios Arqueológicos*; *Documentos de Trabajo*.

China

637 Cultural Relics Publishing House
Director: Cultural Relics Publishing House, 29 Wusi Dajie, Beijing, People's Republic of China (Tel: 441761).
Deals with collections of Chinese museums, albums of key historical sites, scientific reports and theses on major archaeological excavations, ancient

paintings, rubbings from stone inscriptions, duplicates of rare books, teaching materials on cultural relics and archaeology, albums of places of historical interest.

Publications: *Wenwu* [575]; *Wenwu Tiandi* (bimonthly).

Colombia

638 Instituto Colombiano de Antropología
Director: Carrera 7 No. 28–66, Apartado Aéreo 407, Bogotá, Colombia (Tel: 245–48–43; 234–15–29).
Responsible for archaeological investigations in Colombia and the preservation of the archaeological heritage.
Publications: *Revista Colombiana de Antropología* [481].

Congo People's Republic

639 *Musée National
Director: B.P. 459, Brazzaville, Congo People's Republic.
History and ethnography of the Congo.

Costa Rica

640 *Museo Nacional
Director: Apdo. 749, San José, Costa Rica.
Coverage includes archaeology and ethnography of Costa Rica.
Publications: *Brenesia*; *Vínculos* [467].

Cuba

641 *Museo Nacional
Director: Palacio de Bellas Artes, Animas y Zulueta, Havana, Cuba.
Includes works of art from Egypt, Greece and Italy.

Cyprus

642 Department of Antiquities
Archaeological Officer: Ministry of Communications and Works, Nicosia, Cyprus.
Archaeological collections of all periods.
Publications: *Annual Report*.

Czechoslovakia

643 Slovenská Akademia Vied, Archeologicky Ustav
Secretary: 949 21 Nitra-hrad, Czechoslovakia (Tel: 262 40).
Co-ordinates and conducts archaeological investigations; keeps central archives of documentation; evaluates the results obtained by excavation; acts as an education centre.

Publications: *Slovenská Archeológia* [364]; *Archaeologica Slovaca—Fontes*; *Archaeologica Slovaca—Catalogi*; *Archaeologica Slovaca—Monographiae*; various other monographs.

Denmark

644 Forhistorisk Museum
Secretary: Moesgård, DK-8270 Højbjerg, Denmark (Tel: 06–27–24–33).
Covers the prehistoric period up to and including the Viking Age and the early middle ages.
Publications: Results are published mainly through the Jutland Archaeological Society.

Dominican Republic

645 *Museo del Hombre Dominicano
Director: Calle Pedro Henríquez Ureña, Plaza de la Cultura, Santa Domingo, Dominican Republic.
Includes much pre-Columbian archaeological, anthropological and ethnographical material.
Publications: *Boletín* [463].

Ecuador

646 Museo Arqueológico y Galerías de Arte 'Guillermo Perez Chiriboga' del Banco Central del Ecuador
Director: Banco Central, Avenida 10 de Agosto y Briceño, 5to. piso, Quito, Ecuador (Tel: 510–302/519–651; Telex: 2165/2182/2359).
Permanent exhibition of Ecuadorian archaeology and colonial art. Temporary exhibitions of contemporary art, archaeology, etc. Archaeological investigation, restoration and care of monuments.
Publications: Information sheets; catalogues and museum guides.

Egypt

647 Egyptian Museum Library
The Librarian: Mariette Pasha St, Kasr el-Nil, Cairo, Egypt (Tel: 772352).
Special library for the organization of Egyptian antiquities, covering ancient Egypt, ancient Near East, Greece and Rome and ancient civilizations in general.

El Salvador

648 Administración de Patrimonio Cultural, Dirección de Investigaciones, Departamento de Arqueología
Director: Edificio Museo Nacional 'David J. Guzmán', Col. San Benito, Avenida La Revolución, San Salvador, El Salvador (Tel: 23–6246, 23–5428, 24–3679).
Conducts archaeological research of Salvadoran antiquities and sites, undertakes

curatorial duties for the National Museum, and operates a series of archaeological monuments or parks.

Publications: *Anales del Museo Nacional*; *Colección de Antropología e Historia*; *Xipe*.

Equatorial Guinea

649 *Museum of Ethnography
Director: Malabo, Equatorial Guinea.
National prehistory and ethnography.

Ethiopia

650 *Institut d'Archéologie
Director: P.O.B. 1907, Addis Ababa, Ethiopia.
Undertakes excavation and preservation work.
Publications: *Annales d'Éthiopie*.

Fiji

651 Fiji Museum
Director: P.O.B. 2023 Government Buildings, Suva, Fiji.
Includes archaeological and ethnological collections relating to Fiji, the Solomon Islands and other islands of the South-West Pacific.

Publications: *Bulletins of the Fiji Museum*; *Fiji Museum Records* (both contain some archaeological material).

Finland

652 Museovirasto – National Board of Antiquities
Director General: Box 913, SF-00101 Helsinki 10, Finland (Tel: 358–0–40251).
Directs and supervises the administration of Finland's antiquities. Conducts research into the nation's cultural heritage. Promotes and oversees the preservation of culturally and historically important artefacts, buildings and scenery. Maintains museum activities at the National Museum of Finland and other museums under its supervision. Assists in educational work.

Publications: *Fennoscandia Antiqua*.

France

653 Centre National de la Recherche Scientifique, Centre de Recherches Archéologiques
Director: Rue Albert Einstein, Sophia Antipolis, F-06565 Valbonne Cedex, France (Tel: (93)–33–30–30).
Undertakes an extensive research programme on many aspects of archaeological science, e.g. bioarchaeology, geoarchaeology, palynology, petrography, etc.

Publications: Various series and monographs.

Gabon

654 *Musée des Arts et Traditions du Gabon
Director: Avenue du Général de Gaulle, P.O.B. 3115, Libreville, Gabon.
Coverage includes national prehistory and ethnography.

Germany (Democratic Republic)

655 Akademie der Wissenschaften der DDR, Zentralinstitut für Alte Geschichte und Archäologie
Director: DDR-108 Berlin, Leipziger Strasse 3–4, German Democratic Republic (Tel: 22 004 41; Telex: 011 468).
Finances and conducts excavation.
Publications: *Mitteilungen*; *Archäologie. Zeitschrift* [301]; *Ausgrabungen und Funde* [305]; *Schriften zur Ur- und Frühgeschichte*; *Bibliographie zur Archäo-Zoologie und Geschichte der Haustiere* [192]; numerous monographs and other serials.

Germany (Federal Republic)

656 Römisch-Germanisches Zentralmuseum, Forschungsinstitut für Vor- und Frühgeschichte
Director: Ernst-Ludwig-Platz 2, D-6500 Mainz 1, Federal Republic of Germany (Tel: 06131/23–22–31).
A research institute for the pre- and early history of the Ancient World. It has a representative collection of finds on European pre- and early history. Finds from Germany and abroad are examined and restored.
Publications: *Archäologisches Korrespondenzblatt* [302]; *Jahrbuch* [315]; *Arbeitsblätter für Restauratoren*; *Monographien*; *Studien zu der Anfängen der Metallurgie*; *Kataloge vor- und frühgeschichtlicher Altertümer*; *Corpus Signorum Imperii Romani*; various monographs.

Ghana

657 Ghana Museums and Monuments Board
Principal Keeper: P.O.B. 3343, Barnes Road, Accra, Ghana (Tel: Accra 21633; Cable: 'DIRMUSMONS').
Acquisition, restoration, conservation, protection, and renovation of the cultural heritage of Ghana, including monuments.
Publications: various monographs.

Gibraltar

658 *Gibraltar Museum
Director: 18–20 Bomb House Lane, Gibraltar.
Coverage includes archaeology (Palaeolithic to Roman).

Greece

659 *Archaiologiki Hetaireia (Archaeological Association)
Director: Odos Panepistimiou 22, Athens, Greece.
Publications: *Archaiologiki Ephimeris* [379].

Grenada

660 *Grenada National Museum
Director: Young Street, St George's, Grenada.

Guatemala

661 Instituto de Antropología e Historia de Guatemala
Secretaria Ejecutiva: Salón No. 6 La Aurora, zona 13, Guatemala (Tel: 310902–310403).
Aims: to examine, list and catalogue the cultural heritage of Guatemala; to encourage the creation of new museums and ensure their well-being; to use the cultural and natural heritage for the benefit of education; to conserve scientifically and restore the cultural possessions of Guatemala; to encourage scientific investigation of Guatemalan anthropology and history; to train personnel in the various aspects of the cultural heritage; to assess and supervise personnel and institutions, public and private, national and international in the investigation and processes of conservation and restoration of cultural property; to promote knowledge of the cultural worth of Guatemala in order to strengthen Guatemalan identity and nationality within and outside the country.
Publications: *Anuario*; various monographs.

Guinea

662 *Musée National
Curator: B.P. 561, Conakry, Guinea.
Coverage includes national prehistory and ethnography.

Guinea-Bissau

663 *Museum of Guinea-Bissau
Director: Praça do Império, Bissau, Guinea-Bissau.
Coverage includes national ethnography and history.

Guyana

664 Walter Roth Museum of Anthropology
Director: P.O.B. 10187, 61, Main Street, Georgetown, Guyana (Tel: 02–58486).
Anthropological archaeology in northern Amazonia and the Antilles.
Publications: *Archaeology and Anthropology* (twice a year).

Haiti

665 Bureau d'Ethnologie de la République d'Haiti
Director: Avenue Magny 2, Place des Héros de l'Indépendance, Port-au-Prince, Haiti (Tel: 2–5232).
Co-ordinates and supervises all archaeological research within Haiti. Conducts research in the pre-Columbian archaeology of Haiti.
Publications: *Bulletin du Bureau d'Ethnologie*.

Honduras

666 Instituto Hondureño de Antropología e Historia
Librarian: Villa Roy B° Buenos Aires, Tegucigalpa, P.O.B. 1518, Honduras (Tel: 22–34–70/22–14–68/22–25/52).
Conducts anthropological, archaeological and historical investigations.
Publications: *Yaxkin* [468]; *Revista de Estudios Antropológicos e Históricos*.

Hong Kong

667 Hong Kong Museum of History
Information Counter: Blocks 61 and 62, Kowloon Park, Haiphong Road, Tsimshatsui, Kowloon, Hong Kong (Tel: 3–671124; Telex: 38484 USDHK HX).
Public museum, under the auspices of the Urban Council of Hong Kong, devoted to the study, collection and preservation, exhibition, publication and organization of related extended anthropology, and educational services of the archaeology, ethnology, natural history and prehistory of Hong Kong and the neighbouring region.
Publications: *Journal of the Hong Kong Archaeological Society* [571]; monographs.

Hungary

668 *Magyar Régészeti és Müvészettörténeti Társulat (Hungarian Society of Archaeology and History of Fine Arts)
Secretary: Budapest, VIII, Múzeum-krt. 14, Hungary.
Publications: *Archaeológiai Értesítö* [358].

Iceland

669 *Thjódminjasafn (National Museum)
Director: P.O.B. 1439, Sudurgata 41, Reykjavík, Iceland.
Mainly Icelandic antiquities.
Publications: *Árbók hins Íslenzka Fornleifafélags* [283]; various monographs.

India

670 Archaeological Survey of India
Director General: Janpath, New Delhi – 110011, India (Tel: 385451 Ext. 17).
Co-ordinates all archaeological activities in India (field archaeology, structural and chemical preservation of monuments, epigraphy, numismatics, scientific dating, archaeological museums, landscaping around archaeological sites and monuments).
Publications: *Epigraphia Indica*; *Indian Archaeology – a Review* [541].

Indonesia

671 *Direktorat Perlindungan dan Pembinaan Peninggalan Sejarah dan Purbakala (Directorate for the Protection and Development of the Historical and Archaeological Heritage)
Director: Jalan Cilacap 4, P.O.B. 2533, Jakarta, Indonesia.

Iran

672 British Institute of Persian Studies
Assistant Director: P.O.B. 2617, Tehran, Iran (Tel: Tehran 264901).
Cultural research institute covering mainly archaeology but also history, language, literature and religion, with a research library of *c.* 10,000 vols. Can refer problems to other organizations in Iran.
Publications: *Iran: Journal of the British Institute of Persian Studies* [516].

Iraq

673 British Archaeological Expedition to Iraq/British School of Archaeology in Iraq (Gertrude Bell Memorial)
Assistant Director: 2/21/4, Mansour, Baghdad, Iraq (Tel: Baghdad 5519450); or, Secretary: 31–34 Gordon Square, London WC1H 0PY
Conducts research into all aspects of the archaeology, history and literatures of Mesopotamia from prehistoric times to the Islamic period.
Publications: *Iraq* [517]; Curtis, J. (ed.): *Fifty years of Mesopotamian discovery: the work of the British School of Archaeology in Iraq 1932–1982*; other monographs and series.

Ireland

674 Office of Public Works, National Monuments Branch
Director: 51, St Stephen's Green, Dublin 2 (Tel: 01–764071).
Excavation and conservation of national monuments in Ireland.

Israel

675 Ministry of Education and Culture, Department of Antiquities and Museums
Director: P.O.B. 586, Jerusalem 91004, Israel (Tel: 02–285151–3).
Responsible for all aspects of antiquities and museums in Israel.
Publications: *Atiqot, Journal of the Israel Department of Antiquities* (English series, Hebrew series); *Hadashot Arkheologiyot (Archaeological Newsletter)* (Hebrew); monographs.

Italy

676 British School at Rome
Director: Via Gramsci 61, I-00197 Rome, Italy (Tel: Rome 87.34.24).
A major activity of the School is archaeological excavation and survey.
Publications: *Papers* [341]; *Supplementary volumes* [341].

Ivory Coast

677 *Musée de la Côte d'Ivoire et Centre des Sciences Humaines
Director: B.P. 1600, Abidjan, Ivory Coast.
Mainly ethnographic material.

Jamaica

678 Port Royal Project Centre for Archaeological and Conservation Research
Director: Old Naval Hospital, Port Royal, Kingston, Jamaica (Tel: 809–92–87871/809–92–86782).
Responsible for all archaeological research conducted on all prehistoric and historic sites in Jamaica, on land or underwater. Also responsible for all artefactual conservation, preservation and restoration. Part of the Jamaica National Heritage Trust, a Government of Jamaica public sector statutory body established in 1957 for the preservation of the cultural heritage.
Publications: various monographs.

Japan

679 *Nihon Kōkogaku Kyōkai (Japanese Archaeologists' Association)
Secretary: Akamon Building, 3–26–4 Hongo, Bunkyo-ku, Tokyo 113, Japan (Tel: (03)811–2169).
Publications: *Archaeologia Japonica* [568].

Jordan

680 British Institute at Amman for Archaeology and History
Director: P.O.B. 925071, Amman, Jordan (Tel: Amman 841317).
Undertakes, sponsors and publishes studies on the history and archaeology of Jordan and adjacent countries.
Publications: *Levant* [520].

Kampuchea

681 *Musée National
Director: Phnom Penh, Kampuchea.
Coverage includes archaeology, ethnography and Khmer art from the 5th to 13th centuries.

Kenya

682 British Institute in Eastern Africa
Director: P.O.B. 30710, Nairobi, Kenya (Tel: Nairobi 43674/43330)
or, Secretary: c/o Royal Geographical Society, 1 Kensington Gore, London SW7 2AR (Tel: 01–5844653).
Conducts research into the pre-colonial history and archaeology (but not early man studies) of Eastern Africa, which is broadly defined to include, for example, Zambia and Ethiopia. Awards occasional scholarships and *ad hoc* grants to support relevant fieldwork.
Publications: *Azania* [417]; *Memoirs*; *Annual Report*.

Korea (Democratic People's Republic)

683 *Korean Central Historical Museum
Director: Central District, Pyongyang, Korea.
Korean history from prehistory to the 20th century.

Korea (Republic)

684 *National Museum
Director: Kyongbok Palace, Seoul, Korea.
Korean archaeology, culture and folklore.

Kuwait

685 *Department of Antiquities and Museums
Director: Ministry of Information, Kuwait City, Kuwait.

Laos

686 *Ho Phakeo (National Museum)
Director: Setthathiraj Road, Vientiane, Laos.

Lebanon

687 Direction Générale des Antiquités
Chef du Service des Musées: Beirut, Lebanon.
General control and organization of antiquities in Lebanon.
Publications: *Bulletin du Musée de Beyrouth.*

Lesotho

688 Protection and Preservation Commission
Secretary: P.O.B. 1125, Maseru 100, Lesotho (Tel: 0501–24862).
Provides for the preservation and protection of natural and historical monuments, relics, antiques, fauna and flora, and for connected matters.
Publications: *Lesotho's heritage in jeopardy* (1983).

Liberia

689 *National Museum
Director: Capital Hill, Monrovia, Liberia.
National history and ethnography.

Libya

690 Department of Antiquities
Director: Saray al-Hamra, Tripoli, Libya (Tel: Tripoli 40166).
Responsible for all museums and archaeological sites in Libya. Conducts excavations. Controls the national archives.

Luxemburg

691 *Commission des Sites et Monuments Nationales
Director: 21, Route de Diekirch, Walferdange, Luxemburg.

Madagascar

692 Université de Madagascar, Musée d'Art et d'Archéologie
Director: 17, rue Dr Villette, B.P. 564, 101-Antananarivo, Madagascar (Tel: 210–47).
Archaeological excavation; ethnology; social anthropology; exhibition; publication.
Publications: *Série Taloha; Série Travaux et Documents.*

Malawi

693 Department of Antiquities
Principal Conservator of Antiquities: P.O.B. 264, Lilongwe, Malawi (Tel: Lilongwe 721844).
Conducts archaeological, historical and ethnographical research throughout Malawi. Publishes the results of research and generally disseminates knowledge on Malawi's history and antiquities. Investigates, designates, erects and maintains monuments of national interest and, where applicable, sets up small site museums.
Publications: numerous monographs.

Malaysia

694 Museums Department
Curator of Archaeology: Jalan Damansara, Kuala Lumpur 10–06, Malaysia (Tel: 03–280255, 03–280169).
Responsible for controlling and undertaking all archaeological activities (research, excavation, restoration and maintenance of archaeological sites) under the Antiquities Act, 1976.
Publications: *Federation Museums Journal* (annual).

Mali

695 *Musée National du Mali
Director: Rue du Général Leclerc, B.P. 159, Bamako, Mali.
Coverage includes ethnology.

Malta

696 *National Museum of Malta
Director: Kingsway, Valletta, Malta.
Coverage includes archaeology (Palaeolithic to Arab).

Mauritania

697 *Archives Nationales
Director: B.P. 77, Nouakchott, Mauritania.

Mauritius

698 Mauritius Institute
Director: P.O.B. 54, Port Louis, Mauritius.
The Institute, a Department of the Ministry of Education and Cultural Affairs, administers three museums and the Public Library (Port Louis).
Publications: *Bulletin* (contains original papers within the general field of natural sciences, marine archaeology and national heritage – both natural and cultural – of the region West of the Indian Ocean).

Mexico

699 Instituto Nacional de Antropología e Historia
Director: Córdoba 45, Mexico 7, D.F. (Tel: 5–25–07–37).
Responsible for the protection of the archaeological and historical patrimony of Mexico. Carries out most of the archaeological research, publishes the results and uses other means of diffusion (museums, conferences, archaeological exhibits, guided tours, etc.).
Publications: *Anales* [462]; *Boletín*; numerous monographs and series.

Monaco

700 *Musée d'Anthropologie Préhistorique
Curator: Blvd du Jardin Exotique, Monte Carlo, Monaco.
Prehistoric tools, and human and animal remains.
Publications: *Bulletin*.

Mongolian People's Republic

701 *State Central Museum
Director: Ulan Bator, Mongolian People's Republic.
Coverage includes Mongolian archaeology and history.

Morocco

702 *Division de l'Archéologie des Monuments Historiques, des Sites et des Musées
Chief of Archaeological Service: Ministère d'État chargé des Affaires Culturelles, rue Gandhi, Rabat, Morocco.
Publications: *Bulletin d'Archéologie Marocaine* [404]; *Études et Travaux d'Archéologie*.

Mozambique

703 Eduardo Mondlane University, Department of Archaeology and Anthropology

Head of Department: C.P. 257, Maputo, Mozambique (Tel: 743111/741135/ 743828; Telex: 6–374 MICEX-MO).

Sole research body for archaeological studies in Mozambique. Trains archaeological technicians at a basic level (university-level training planned for 1985 onwards). Main research: archaeological survey programme.

Publications: various articles and reports.

Namibia

704 *State Museum

Director: P.O.B. 1203, Windhoek, Namibia.

Coverage includes national archaeology, anthropology and ethnography.

Nepal

705 *National Museum of Nepal

Director: Museum Road, Chhauni, Kathmandu, Nepal.

Coverage includes national history and ethnography.

Netherlands

706 *Rijksdienst voor het Oudheidkundig Bodemonderzoek

Director: Mariënhof, Kleine Haag 2, Amersfoort, Netherlands.

Publications: *Berichten* [306].

New Zealand

707 New Zealand Archaeological Association

Secretary: c/o Anthropology Department, University of Auckland, Private Bag, Auckland, New Zealand (Tel: Auckland 30443).

Objectives are to preserve the rich archaeological heritage of New Zealand and to promote and foster research into the prehistory of New Zealand and related areas in the Pacific. Holds annual conferences, disseminates information, and is building up a national register of archaeological sites.

Publications: *Newsletter* [589]; *New Zealand Journal of Archaeology* [588]; various monographs.

Nicaragua

708 *Museo Nacional de Nicaragua

Director: 4a Avenida No. 606, Managua, Nicaragua.

Coverage includes national archaeology.

Niger

709 *Musée National du Niger
Curator: B.P. 248, Niamey, Niger.
Coverage includes national archaeology and ethnography.

Nigeria

710 National Commission for Museums and Monuments
Director: Nigerian Museum, P.M.B. 12556, Onikan Road, Lagos, Nigeria
(Tel: 01–633890).
Conducts field excavations and researches into Nigerian archaeology. Issues excavation permits.

Norway

711 *Norsk Arkeologisk Selskap (Norwegian Archaeological Society)
Secretary-General: Frederiks gt. 2, Oslo 1, Norway.
Publications: *Viking* [290].

Oman

712 Ministry of National Heritage and Culture, Department of Antiquities
Director: P.O.B. 668, Muscat, Oman (Tel: 602555 Ext. 131; Telex: 3649–OMNHCV MB).
Supervision of antiquities in Oman.
Publications: *Journal of Oman Studies* [519].

Pakistan

713 *National Museum of Pakistan
Director: Burns Garden, Karachi, Pakistan.
Mainly national archaeology and ethnography.
Publications: *Pakistan Archaeology* [542]; *Museum Journal*.

Panama

714 *Directora Nacional del Patrimonio Histórico
Director: Apdo. 662, Panamá 1, Panama.

Papua New Guinea

715 National Museum
Curator of Prehistory: P.O.B. 5560 Boroko, Papua New Guinea (Tel: 252422).
Controls the national archaeological collection. Issues excavation permits and monitors archaeological research in Papua New Guinea, including salvage archaeology. Issues temporary loan permits for archaeological material going

overseas for study. Carries out and promotes research into the prehistory of Papua New Guinea. Educates the public by displays and publications.
Publications: *Museum Records*; monographs.

Paraguay

716 *Instituto de Numismática y Antigüedades del Paraguay
Secretary: Calle 25 de Mayo 802 esquina Tacuarí, Asunción, Paraguay.

Peru

717 *Instituto Nacional de Cultura
Director: Casilla 5247, Lima, Peru.
Controls all fieldwork, local and foreign, in Peru.

Philippines

718 National Museum of the Philippines, Anthropology Division
Curator: P.O.B. 2659, Manila, Philippines (Tel: 49–80–06).
Undertakes research in anthropology (archaeology and ethnology) and publishes the results.
Publications: *Publications on Archaeology*; *Monographs*.

Poland

719 *Instytut Historii Kultury Materialnej (Institute of the History of Material Culture)
Director: 00–140 Warsaw, ul. Świerczewskiego 105, Poland.
Research in archaeology of all periods.
Publications: *Polish Archaeological Abstracts* [353]; *Archeologia Polski* [359]; *Informator Archeologiczny* [361]; *Sprawozdania Archeologiczne* [365]; other periodicals and monographs.

Portugal

720 Associação dos Arqueólogos Portugueses
Secretary: Largo do Carmo, 1200 Lisbon, Portugal.
Holds meetings on the research done by members. Maintains a museum and a library.
Publications: *Arqueologia e História* [332].

Puerto Rico

721 Universidad de Puerto Rico, Centro de Investigaciones Arqueológicas
Director: Apdo. 22603, U.P.R. Station, Rio Piedras, Puerto Rico (Tel: 764–0000).
Directs and organizes all archaeological activities and expeditions.
Publications: various monographs.

Qatar

722 *National Museum
Director: Doha, Qatar.
Coverage includes national archaeology and ethnography.

Romania

723 *Institutul de Arheologie
Director: Bucharest, Str. I.C. Frimu 11, Romania.
Publications: *Studii şi Cercetări de Istorie Veche şi Arheologie* [387]; *Biblioteca de Arheologie* [384]; other periodicals.

Saudi Arabia

724 Department of Antiquities and Museums
Director: P.O.B. 3734, Riyadh, Saudi Arabia (Tel: Riyadh 4355821; Telex: ARCHAEO 202650).
Responsible for administration and organization of museums and ancient monuments and the safeguarding of antiquities and national treasures generally. Conducts research (results published in *Atlal* (see below). As part of the Ministry of Education, it plays a general educational role.
   Publications: *Atlal: the Journal of Saudi Arabian Archaeology* [511]; *Introduction to Saudi Arabian Antiquities*; series of brief guides to principal regions or monuments.

Senegal

725 *Musées de l'Institut Fondamental d'Afrique Noire
Director: B.P. 206, Dakar, Senegal.
Coverage includes national ethnography and prehistory.

Sierra Leone

726 *Sierra Leone National Museum
Curator: Cotton Tree Building, P.O.B. 908, Freetown, Sierra Leone.
Coverage includes national archaeology and ethnography.

Singapore

727 *British Institute in South-East Asia
Director: D1-A 5th storey, International Building, Orchard Road, Singapore 0923.
Promotes South-east Asian Studies, especially history, archaeology and cultural anthropology.
   Publications: *South-East Asian Studies Newsletter* (quarterly).

Solomon Islands

728 *Solomon Islands National Museum and Cultural Centre
Curator: P.O.B. 313, Honiara, Solomon Islands.

Research into all aspects of Solomons culture, including archaeology and ethnography.
Publications: *Journal*; *Custom Stories*.

Somalia

729 *National Museum of Somalia
Director: Corso Republica, Mogadishu, Somalia.
Coverage includes ethnology and history.

South Africa

730 South African Archaeological Society
Secretary: Private Bag X4, 8009 Leeusig, Cape Town, South Africa (Tel: 021–229588).
Aims to promote interest and research into the prehistory of southern Africa; this includes the Stone Age, Iron Age and modern or early historic archaeology.
Publications: *South African Archaeological Bulletin* [421]; *Goodwin Series* (irreg.); *Monograph Series* (occasional); *Newsletter*.

Spain

731 *Instituto Español de Prehistoria
Director: Serrano 13, Madrid 1, Spain.
Publications: *Bibliotheca Praehistorica Hispana* [335].

Sri Lanka

732 Ministry of Cultural Affairs, Central Cultural Fund
Director General: 212, Bauddhaloka Mawatha, Colombo 7, Sri Lanka (Tel: 587912).
Conservation and restoration of the ancient monuments and sites within the cultural triangle of Sri Lanka.
Publications: *UNESCO–Sri Lanka project of the cultural triangle*; various guide books; various excavation reports.

Sudan

733 Sudan Antiquities Service and National Museums
Director: P.O.B. 178, Nile Avenue, Khartoum, Sudan (Tel: 80935).
Supervision of museums and archaeology (display, preservation, study).
Publications: *Kush* [407].

Suriname

734 Archeologische Dienst
Office: Prins Hendrikstraat 31, Paramaribo, Suriname (Tel: 75503).
Systematic excavation of Amerindian prehistoric settlements.

Swaziland

735 *Swaziland National Museum
Director: P.O.B. 100, Lobamba, Swaziland.
Coverage includes national archaeology and ethnology.

Sweden

736 Riksantikvarieämbetet och Statens Historiska Museer
Director: Box 5405, S-114 84 Stockholm, Sweden (Tel: 08–22 89 00).
The Board of National Antiquities is responsible for the care and preservation of Swedish historical and ancient monuments, and carries out most of the excavations done in Sweden. Reports from all excavations in Sweden are kept in the central Antiquarian Topographical Archive in Stockholm.
Publications: *Swedish archaeology today* (Stockholm, 1979).

Switzerland

737 Schweizerische Gesellschaft für Ur- und Frühgeschichte
Secretary: Rheinsprung 20, CH-4001 Basel, Switzerland (Tel: 061/25 30 78).
Objectives: to develop interest in Swiss prehistory and archaeology; to support research in this field; to protect archaeological remains; to collaborate with universities, federal and cantonal authorities, and other specialist organizations both in Switzerland and abroad.
Publications: *Archäologie der Schweiz* [300]; *Jahrbuch* [314]; *Guides archéologiques de la Suisse*; monographs.

Syria

738 Directorate General of Antiquities and Museums
Office: Damascus, Syria (Tel: 228566–114854/55).
Official administration for archaeology and museums.
Publications: *Annales Archéologiques Arabes Syriennes* [510]; various individual monographs.

Taiwan

739 *Institute of History and Philology
Director: Academia Sinica, Nankang, Taipei, Taiwan.

Tanzania

740 National Museum of Tanzania
Director: Box 511, Dar es Salaam, Tanzania (Tel: 31365/6 or 20843 Dar es Salaam).
Houses archaeological and human palaeontological materials dating from the last four million years. Provides research facilities for national and visiting scholars. Conducts occasional archaeological research and excavations of Palaeolithic, Middle Stone Age, Late Stone Age and Rock Art sites in Tanzania.
Publications: *Occasional Papers*; *Annual Report*.

Thailand

741 *National Museum
Director: Na Phra-dhart Road, Bangkok 2, Thailand.
Coverage includes national archaeology and ethnography.

Togo

742 Institut National de la Recherche Scientifique
Director: B.P. 2240, Lomé, Togo (Tel: 21–01–39/21–39–94).
Co-ordinates national scientific research.
Publications: *Études Togolaises*.

Trinidad and Tobago

743 *National Museum and Art Gallery
Director: 117, Frederick St, Port-of-Spain, Trinidad and Tobago.
Coverage includes national archaeology and ethnography.

Tunisia

744 *Institut National d'Archéologie et d'Art
Director: 4, place du Château, Tunis, Tunisia.
Coverage includes archaeology and ethnography.

Turkey

745 British Institute of Archaeology at Ankara
Director: Tahran Caddesi 24, Kavaklidere, Ankara, Turkey (Tel: Ankara 27 54 87).
Carries out major excavation in Turkey and survey/research projects. Provides a centre for British archaeologists working in Turkey. Houses an extensive library and a number of study collections comprising pottery, botanical material, a comparative bone collection and an epigraphic squeeze collection.
Publications: *Anatolian Studies* [509]; *Occasional Publications Series*; *Monograph Series*.

Uganda

746 *Uganda Museum
Curator: 5–7 Kira Road, P.O.B. 365, Kampala, Uganda.
Centre for archaeological research in Uganda.

USSR

747 *Institute of Archaeology (Order of the Red Banner of Labour)
Director: Academy of Sciences of the USSR, Moscow, Ul. Dm. Ulyanova 19, USSR.

United Kingdom

748 Council for British Archaeology

Information Officer: 112 Kennington Road, London SE11 6RE, England (Tel: 01–582 0494).

Represents and co-ordinates archaeological opinion in Britain. Aims: to ensure the safeguarding of all kinds of archaeological material, and to urge the strengthening of existing measures for the care of ancient and historic buildings, monuments, and antiquities; to stimulate an informed interest in the monuments and records of the past; to forward archaeological research and its publication; to promote the interchange of ideas on all aspects of archaeology; to obtain recognition of archaeology in education; to organize the provision of financial assistance to supplement the resources of learned societies concerned with British archaeology. Co-operates with Regional Groups, which are primarily responsible for dealing with local problems.

Publications: *Archaeological bibliography* [241]; *British Archaeological Abstracts* [245]; *Archaeology in Britain* (i.e. annual report) [253]; *Newsletter and Calendar* [256]; *Research reports* [257]; various other monographs and series; record cards.

United States

749 Archaeological Institute of America

Executive Director: 53 Park Place, New York, New York 10007 (Tel: 212–732–6677).

The oldest learned society in the USA devoted to archaeology. Sponsors archaeological research, protects archaeological resources, disseminates the results of research carried out by professional archaeologists. Sponsors various scholarly programmes including an annual professional meeting, regional symposia and research fellowships, maintains official relations with sister organizations worldwide, represents the profession in matters of archaeological policy and legislation.

Publications: *American Journal of Archaeology* [95]; *Archaeology* [103]; *Archaeological Fieldwork and Opportunities Bulletin* [441]; *Annual Bulletin*; Rowe, J. H.: *Archaeology as a career* (1979).

Upper Volta

750 *Direction des Musées, des Sites et Monuments

Director: B.P. 55, Ouagadougou, Upper Volta.

Uruguay

751 *Sociedad de Amigos de Arqueología

Secretary: Buenos Aires 652, Casilla 399, Uruguay.
Publications: *Revista*.

Venezuela

752 Asociación Venezolana de Arqueología

Secretary: Apartado 1827, Caracas, 1010A, Venezuela (Tel: Caracas 747176; Telex: 21338).

Aims: to promote collaboration between individuals and organizations interested in the national archaeological heritage, both at home and abroad; to help the development of archaeology as a discipline; to encourage publication of the results of systematic investigation; to develop a professional ethic; to propose protection for archaeological remains; to promote conferences, congresses, meetings, etc.; to encourage the creation of regional museums of archaeology.

Viet-Nam

753 *Viet-Nam Social Sciences Committee, Institute of Archaeology
Director: 61, Phan Chu Trinh, Hanoi, Viet-Nam.
Publications: *Annual Report*.

Yemen (Arab Republic)

754 *Yemen National Museum
Director: San'a, Yemen Arab Republic.
Coverage includes South Arabian antiquities of the pre-Islamic and Islamic periods.

Yemen (People's Democratic Republic)

755 *Department of Antiquities and Museums
Director: P.O.B. 473, Ministry of Culture and Guidance, Aden, People's Democratic Republic of Yemen.
Protects antiquities and archaeological sites; supervises museums; investigates and surveys sites; applies the Antiquities and Museums Ordinance.
Publications: *Report*; *Bulletin*.

Yugoslavia

756 *Jugoslovenski Institut za Zaštitu Spomenika Kulture (Yugoslav Institute for the Preservation of Historical Monuments)
Director: Belgrade, Božidara Adžije 11, Yugoslavia.
Concerned with research into and preservation of cultural possessions.
Publications: *Zbornik Zašite Spomenika Kulture*.

Zaire

757 Institut des Musées Nationaux du Zaire
Director: B.P. 4249, Kinshasa 2, Zaire (Tel: 59.356).
One of the five sections is concerned with archaeology. Excavations have so far mainly related to the Iron Age.

Zambia

758 National Monuments Commission
Director: P.O.B. 60124, Livingstone, Zambia (Tel: 2711).
Objectives are to preserve and protect Zambia's immovable natural and cultural

heritage, to promote the preservation and protection of national monuments/ heritage, to carry out archaeological and palaeontological research into Zambia's past, to disseminate results of such research, to control site investigations and the movement and export of heritage objects, and to co-ordinate all activities in connection with monuments and relics.

Publications: *Annual Report*; *Archaeologia Zambiana* [420]; Phillipson, D. W.: *An annotated bibliography of the archaeology of Zambia* (Lusaka, 1968) [419]; Derricourt, R. M.: *A supplementary bibliography of the archaeology of Zambia 1967–73* (Lusaka, 1975) [419]; other monographs.

Zimbabwe

759 Prehistory Society of Zimbabwe

Secretary: P.O.B. 876, Harare, Zimbabwe (Tel: Harare 35519).

Aims to promote the study of the early history, prehistory and archaeology of Africa, with particular reference to Zimbabwe; to foster and maintain interest in such studies through publications, exhibitions, lectures, meetings, field visits or any other means; and to assist, co-operate in or conduct research work in these fields.

Publications: *Zimbabwe Prehistory* (annual); newsletters.

Index

The Index is a single alphabetical sequence of authors, titles, subjects and organizations. All publications and organizations listed in Parts II and III are included, with the exception of publications such as *Bulletins* and *Annual Reports*, and also monographs, in Part III, which can be traced through the names of organizations. Also included are important topics and sources of information discussed in Part I. Users should bear in mind that material on any given area (e.g. Spain) or aspect of archaeology (e.g. iron industry) may also be found in the 'General archaeology' and 'Archaeological science' sections.

Works entered under editor or compiler are also listed under title; title entries are also included for dictionaries, encyclopaedias, atlases and a few other works well known by their titles.

The arrangement is word by word with abbreviations and acronyms treated as single words.

Numbers without brackets refer to page numbers in Part I; numbers within brackets refer to item numbers in Parts II and III.